MW00523182

Purchased by: *Mary Lee Farrington*

CONSUMERISM AND AMERICAN GIRLS' LITERATURE, 1860–1940

Why did the figure of the girl come to dominate the American imagination from the middle of the nineteenth century into the twentieth? In *Consumerism and American Girls' Literature*, Peter Stoneley looks at how women fictionalized for the girl reader ways of achieving a powerful social and cultural presence. He explores why and how a scenario of "buying into womanhood" became, between 1860 and 1940, one of the nation's central allegories, one of its favorite means of negotiating social change. From Jo March to Nancy Drew, girls' fiction operated in dynamic relation to consumerism, performing a series of otherwise awkward maneuvers: between country and metropolis, uncouth and unspoilt, modern and anti-modern. Covering a wide range of works and writers, this book will be of interest to cultural and literary scholars alike.

PETER STONELEY is Lecturer in the School of English at Queen's University, Belfast. He is the author of *Mark Twain and the Feminine Aesthetic* (Cambridge, 1992).

CAMBRIDGE STUDIES IN AMERICAN LITERATURE AND CULTURE

CONSUMERISM AND AMERICAN GIRLS' LITERATURE, 1860–1940

PETER STONELEY

Queen's University, Belfast

CAMBRIDGE UNIVERSITY PRESS

PUBLISHED BY THE PRESS SYNDICATE OF THE UNIVERSITY OF CAMBRIDGE
The Pitt Building, Trumpington Street, Cambridge CB2 IRP, United Kingdom

CAMBRIDGE UNIVERSITY PRESS
The Edinburgh Building, Cambridge, CB2 2RU, UK
40 West 20th Street, New York, NY 10011-4211, USA
477 Williamstown Road, Port Melbourne, VIC 3207, Australia
Ruiz de Alarcón 13, 28014 Madrid, Spain
Dock House, The Waterfront, Cape Town 8001, South Africa

http://www.cambridge.org

© Peter Stoneley 2003

First published 2003

Printed in the United Kingdom at the University Press, Cambridge

Typeface Adobe Garamond 11/12.5 pt   *System* LaTeX 2ε   [TB]

A catalogue record for this book is available from the British Library

Library of Congress Cataloguing in Publication data

ISBN 0 521 82187 8 hardback

To Clare and Ginevra

Contents

Illustrations

Acknowledgments

For granting access to their collections, I am grateful to the Houghton Library, the British Library, the Library at Trinity College, Dublin, the John Johnson Collection at the Bodleian Library, the New York Historical Society, and Vassar College; for giving me help from a distance, I am grateful to Donald Glassman at Barnard College, Lorett Treese at Bryn Mawr College, and Nancy Young at Smith College. For access and also for guidance, I am grateful to Leslie Perrin Wilson at the Concord Free Public Library, and Heather Wager at Orchard House. For help with photographic reproduction, I thank Dean M. Rogers at the Special Collections, Vassar College, and the Perry-Castañeda Library at the University of Texas. I acknowledge that parts of chapter 1 are based on an article that was published in *Studies in American Fiction*, and that parts of the conclusion are based on an article that was published in *American Literature*. Karín Lesnik-Oberstein invited me to try out this topic in the form of a research paper at the Center for International Research into Children's Literature at the University of Reading, and I am grateful for comments received on that occasion. I thank Gretchen Sharlow and the Center for Mark Twain Studies at Elmira College, New York, for a Spring Research Fellowship, and for the friendship and encouragement I get on visits to Elmira. This book benefitted greatly from the shrewd and detailed critiques of Caroline Levander and Cindy Weinstein; all remaining deficiencies are entirely my responsibility. I am grateful to Ray Ryan at Cambridge University Press, whose dealings with me have been patient and thoughtful. My academic colleagues, the support staff, and the students at the School of English, Queen's University, Belfast, have provided many kinds of help. In spite of various pressures, the School remains a friendly and interesting place in which to work. Queen's Academic Council has provided me with essential research funds. I have been aided by the congenial staff at Queen's Library, and especially by Michael Smallman and Florence Gray. My personal thanks are due to Carmen

Brun for her friendship and hospitality on visits to the United States; to Jennifer FitzGerald for many years of indispensable advice and encouragement; to Robert and Shirley Stoneley for their characteristic parental mix of sympathy and impatience; and to the dedicatees, my sisters, for inspiration.

Introduction: "Buying into womanhood"

Why did the girl – the girl at the "awkward age" – come to dominate the American imagination from the nineteenth century into the twentieth? By way of answer, this book looks at the way in which women fictionalized the process of "buying into womanhood"; at how, during the rise of consumerism, they envisaged for the girl reader and others the ways of achieving a powerful social and cultural presence. I explore why and how this scenario of buying into womanhood became, between 1860 and 1940, one of the nation's central allegories, one of its favourite means of negotiating social change. The exemplary novelistic scenario here is that of the "backwoods" girl-heroine who achieves a love-match with a successful but disillusioned middle-aged businessman. In managing this, the girl also manages, in concentrated symbolic form, to enact the progress of fifty years. She moves from a modest, rural background to urban, monied display. The girl allows fiction – and the culture generally – to perform a series of otherwise awkward maneuvers: between country and metropolis, "uncouth" and "unspoilt," modern and anti-modern. While her gender identifies her as malleable, her youth symbolizes the vitality of an earlier America. She serves to mitigate the perception that the modern age is, to adopt the terms of the period, "artificial." Her "breathless audacity" stands in contrast to the "weightlessness" and "blandness" of a systematized and incorporated nation. As William Dean Howells observed from his "Editor's Study," the "real" child was required to improve the "spoiled child" that the American adult had become.[1]

The girl – and above all, the middle-class girl – could serve as the vehicle for both nostalgia and optimism. In doing so, she became pivotal. Henry James noted that she was the key figure in a newly consumerized world. Such was her importance, such was her "exposure" indeed, that James ventriloquized her consequent fears and resentments:

How can I do *all* the grace, *all* the interest, as I'm expected to? . . . By what combination of other presences ever am I disburdened, ever relegated and reduced, ever
restored, in a word, to my right relation to the whole?[2]

The girl provides a centeredness within the chaos of modern abundance.
She, as James puts it, provides "*all* the grace." Center-stage and larger than
life, she is not to be restored to some more modest "right relation to the
whole." This is a tricky position, and hence her fear. She must provide a
liberatory "audacity," while also assuring the presence of "grace." That is to
say, she must move between the possibilities of disruption and containment.
The very mobility that makes her so useful for negotiating change is also
what makes her dangerous. Again one thinks of James here, of Daisy Miller
and the comment that Daisy "was composed of charming little parts that
didn't match and that made no *ensemble*." The girl represents both the
possibility of coherence (of "ensemble") and the threat of incoherence.
She shifts between childhood and adulthood, and this instability seems to
activate anxieties over the transmission of values from one generation to
another. As Lynn Wardley notes, the incoherence of Daisy Miller's "flirting
with anyone she can pick up" raises the possibility of "affiliation across the
constructed borders of race, ethnicity, gender, and class."[3] If the middle-
class girl cannot be made to perform the rites of social continuity, she may
become the representative of a variety of dangerous new coalitions. Her
volatility becomes a metaphor of class, racial, and ethnic uncertainty; the
possibility of "fixing" her coalesces with the possibility of resolving such
social uncertainties. Daisy Miller is one example of the girl's important
function, and of the price that must be paid for getting it wrong.

   The girl, then, is instrumental to articulating and assuaging the fear of
social change. Her growing up can naturalize change and make it seem more
manageable. But what, precisely, were the changes that she was deployed to
manage, and why did juvenile fiction become the means of this deployment?
I want now to introduce some key terms and contextual reference points,
namely those of consumerism, class, agency, race, and gender, and then
to place the girl in relation to the emergent social-sexological discourse of
adolescence. I subsequently offer a chapter-by-chapter outline of how these
issues are developed in relation to the fiction.

   To begin with the rise of consumerism, the historicist perspective is that
advanced capitalism destabilized traditional markers and values of class.
The centralizing of production drew people away from static, rural hierarchies, and a newer, more fluid social currency evolved. In an otherwise
confused and unregulated social arena, the urban bourgeoisie used their

money to locate themselves in "communities of taste." Social demarcation came to depend on what Jean-Christophe Agnew has referred to as "cognitive appetite," as the newly enriched white collar and business classes asserted themselves via a showcasing of self and home. This was an upward spiral: growth in production and consumption enabled the rise of the middle class, who in turn confirmed their rise through consumption.[4]

The middle class, then, is understood to have emerged from amongst the relatively low "middling sorts," who emulated the gentry. Clearly, though, actual change was more various and uneven than this would suggest. Among many complicating factors, the emergence of a middle class occurred in the larger towns and cities in an age when most people still lived in small towns and in the country. As a result, the interchange between country and city comes to be experienced as a class dynamic, as the dominant caste of a static rural society encounters the values of an ascendant and more mobile urban stratum.[5] Fiction became a crucial tool for representing and accommodating this interchange. Indeed, Richard Brodhead has argued that it was this growing inequity that caused regionalist writing to become a dominant genre after 1865. Small, local cultures and economies were challenged by the rise of "translocal agglomerations." Regionalist fiction served a "memorial function": it defended older, rural and small-town values whilst also integrating these same values into the emergent order.[6] While I find Brodhead's argument persuasive, I think his regionalist material is quite narrowly class-ed. His key example, Sarah Orne Jewett, was taken up by highly selective "literary" journals and publishers, and was not a bestseller on the scale of the writers I discuss. I would argue that girls' fiction was much more important to the management of such temporal disjunctions. Girls' fiction was often preoccupied with the same "adult" social anxieties as much "adult" fiction, and it was girls' fiction that became the key exhibit in the debate as to what fiction should and should not attempt to represent. Given its immense popularity, and its careful but insistent engagement with class-formation and social change, girls' fiction became the most significant instantiation of realism in fiction. Likewise, it served as "antidote" to the less acceptable, naturalistic forms produced by Dreiser, Norris, Crane, and Sinclair.

But if much adult fiction – by men and by women – mediates consumerism and social change, why is women's fiction for girls of particular interest? The clue lies in the relation between gender and consumerism. Mary P. Ryan and subsequent social historians have explored the ways in which the emergence of the middle class depended on a domestic economy and its ideological bases. The "middling sorts" could secure their newer and higher status by marrying later and investing their economic and emotional resources in fewer children. The simultaneous narrowing and intensification of family life was instrumental in enabling and reproducing middle-class identity.[7] The greater wealth of the smaller, delayed family meant that wives and mothers were increasingly recast as non-productive, domestic beings. In the culture of "conspicuous consumption" of the latter part of the nineteenth century, the middle-class woman's role was to put in evidence her husband's earning capacity, to serve to manifest consumerized class values. As Charlotte Gilman Perkins put it in *Women and Economics* (1898), woman became "the priestess of the temple of consumption." Or, in the words of a more recent cultural historian, the middle-class woman became a "consuming angel."[8] This is the context within which the scenario of "buying into womanhood" achieves its pre-eminence, as the girl's development comes to include – and even to be centered around – the acquisition and management of spending power. I want to develop this further, but first let's introduce one final complicating social factor. Girls' fiction came to prominence during successive waves of immigration, of Irish, Chinese, Germans, and Japanese. Its inception as a dominant form was also contemporaneous with African–American emancipation. At times the fiction manifests a strong sense that the right to wealth was under threat, in that it was to be contested by ever more new arrivals. The fiction often tries to work out an accommodation of relations between a preponderantly white Anglo-Saxon Protestant middle class and an anomalously "foreign" other or others. Sometimes this takes a relatively benign form, as the girl extends sympathy and guidance to the foreign other (one thinks of the aid that the March girls provide to the Hummels in *Little Women*). At other times there is a much more aggressive fictional projection of white fears and wishes, as with the anti-Japanese girls' fiction by Gene Stratton-Porter. But whether the interaction is benign or aggressive, there is always a deeply engrained racial and ethnic aspect to the fiction's articulation of social and financial power.

We are left with a complex layering of elements – social, economic, gendered, generic, racial – all of which should inform and give nuance to the analysis. Given these various and contending factors, the formation of class ideologies under advanced capitalism comes to seem improvisatory, and for this reason numerous theorists have warned against using overly fixed or epochal terms. Raymond Williams, in his classic essay, questions labels such as "feudal," "bourgeois," and "socialist," because they suggest too static a historical sense. He urges "residual," "dominant," and "emergent" as terms that suggest "the internal dynamic relations of any actual process."

He reminds us that hegemonic definitions are always in negotiation with alternative perceptions, both residual and emergent.[9] Certainly this study will bear out the need for a fluid and microcosmic understanding of class-ed experience. But a related and equally difficult question here is that of how to relate our class-ed and consumerized concepts to subjective experience. Or in other words, how does the historical emergence of consumerism relate to the agency not of a class, but to the idea of the individual girl? It is often assumed that consumerism is necessarily bound up with deception. Advanced industrial capitalism generates a crisis of overproduction that can only be alleviated by an endless growth in demand. The subject must orient his or her subjectivity in relation to the commodity spectacle, to the extent that he or she identifies happiness with a purchasable range of goods and services. As Baudrillard points out, the subject's desires are at least as important as his or her labour power.[10] There is then a process of "ideological blinding" at work, whereby the subject's "own" desires become hopelessly tied into the requirements of supply and demand. The girl's perceived innocence and her perceived need of instruction meant that the issue of agency appeared in a particularly sharp and interesting form. Through her we see that consumerism was and is an especially effective means of discipline and control precisely because it seems to liberate and empower. The world of consumerism can create a misleading aura of female agency, in which the girl's powers are ambiguous. This is especially the case because the girl is being prepared for the marriage "market" that will initiate her into adult life: in her the boundary between consumer and commodity becomes blurred. The process of buying into womanhood not only provides the ideological foundation for the girl's identity, but it also transforms her into something to be bought. Her education in consumerism, in other words, produces her as a commodity to be consumed.

In relation to the characters and the readers of girls' fiction, we need to keep in mind the question, is the girl buying, or is she sold? The argument that I have outlined here is strongly Foucaldian. The perceived incoherence of the adolescent girl is initially managed by figures of authority (parents, authors), but that authority is internalized as the girl learns to manage this incoherence via acts of consumption – ultimately the consumption of a notionally coherent white, middle-class identity. This argument, though, might be opposed by the many instances in girls' fiction in which buying into womanhood is represented as an opportunity for individual expression, and for a performative self-awareness. Rather than seeing consumerism as "ideological blinding," it might be viewed positively as a means for creativity and self-expression, and also for containing within itself the possibility of critique. The "progressive obsolescence" of consumerism can serve to de-essentialize the forms and meanings of desire and pleasure, leading to a "loosened" or "decentered" subjectivity. I want to pursue this possibility that a performative concept of self can emerge, and otherness and expressiveness can thrive alongside – even because of – one's immersion within the capitalist infrastructures of modern subjectivity.[11]

A further key concern here must be to understand what the perceived nature of girlhood was in this period, that it could be seen as instrumental to managing social change. Why was the girl significant? We return at this point to Daisy Miller, and to the girl's perceived volatility. The fiction focuses on the "awkward age" of girlhood, which is seen to extend between the ages of fourteen and twenty-four. This awkwardness and its importance is explicitly described in another new "genre" of the period, the social-sexological discourse. The "awkward" girl became known as the "adolescent" girl, and she was discussed in a growing number of treatises from the 1870s onward. G. Stanley Hall would draw on these many studies in his own magisterial two-volume work, *Adolescence: Its Psychology and its Relations to Physiology, Anthropology, Sex, Crime, Religion and Education* (1904). For Hall as for many others, adolescence was the key to social stability, and to the maintenance of white, middle-class authority. He perceived adolescence as a period of immense physiological change and consequent psychological disturbance, a period that he describes – tellingly in an economic metaphor – as one in which "loss exceed[s] profit in the chemical bookkeeping of the metabolism."[12] As the body develops and as motor power and functions change, the child's psychic traits are thrown into disarray. Hall's adolescent, like Jo March and a host of subsequent fictional heroines, is unstable, absorbed by reverie, and moves swiftly between various contradictory attitudes. He or she is intensely self-conscious, and tries out a variety of social possibilities in the assumption of different roles, poses, affectations, and mannerisms: adolescence is a "dramatic" period, and one that seems a physiological instantiation of Williams's dynamic of dominant, residual, and emergent. But Hall argues that while these changes and instabilities may always have occurred, they had been intensified by the middle-class behaviour patterns of the mid to late nineteenth century. As we have noted, the emergent bourgeoisie tended to marry later and have fewer children as a means of managing expenditure and enhancing their power and status. Hall drew attention to this, and argued that it led to the over-nurture of children and consequently to an extreme adolescent precocity. Further, Hall identifies the new intensity of adolescence with other aspects of modernity. Metropolitan life, with its "early emancipation," its many stimuli and its absence of rural exercise, produced a more marked adolescent phase, with its "dangers of both perversion and arrest" (1, p. xv). The "tumult" of modern adolescence, as represented by Hall, could lead to a dangerous social promiscuity, in that during adolescence "the critical faculties are often hardly able to supply reductives of extravagant impulses," and there is a consequent tendency to "idealize unfit persons" (1, pp. 269, 270).

All this takes us back to Daisy Miller's "extravagance," her wandering outside the confines of her class and gender. But we might ask, why the girl and not the boy? The phase of adolescence was seen to affect boys as well as girls. Indeed, to some extent adolescence takes the form of a conflict of genders within each boy and girl:

Not only in the body, but in the psyche of childhood, there are well-marked stages in which male and female traits, sensations, and instincts struggle for prepotency... The fact that both sexes have in them the germ of the other's quality, makes it incumbent upon each to play its sex symphony with no great error, lest the other be more or less desexed in soul... It is one important office of convention, custom, and etiquette to preside over this balance between the relation of the sexes at large.

Hall acknowledges an instability and even arbitrariness in the assignment of gender, in that arrival at one's "correct" gender depends to some extent upon social influences. But we should be careful not to overstate this. Hall and nearly all of his sources see gender as preponderantly determined by biological sex. Indeed, Hall takes to task a "Miss Thompson" for "ascribing sexual differences... to the differences of influences that surround the sexes in early years" (11, p. 565).[13] According to Hall, only Thompson's "feministic" tendencies could have led her to such a false conclusion.

Above all, Hall attaches significance to the adolescence of girls. He thinks it is especially worthwhile to monitor girls, because he thinks their education an important contributory factor to modern social ills, and because, more generally, change manifests itself first and foremost in women. He cites Beard's famous treatise, *American Nervousness* (1881) to this effect, that "the first signs of ascension or of declension are seen in women" in the same way that "the foliage of the delicate plants first shows the early warmth of spring, and the earliest frosts of autumn." In girls and women, Beard, Hall, and others argued, one could see the first "manifestation of national progress or decay" (11, p. 571). Although adolescence is a similarly "tumultuous" experience for boys and girls, Hall parallels fiction in developing a special focus on girlhood. Much as it is Daisy who threatens the established order with her extravagant affiliations, Hall notes that it is girls that are "most prone" to "idealize unfit persons." This is because in them the "affective overtops the intellectual life," a notion that Hall attributes to his sense that in girls and women the "[s]ex organs are larger and more dominant." The girl's and ultimately the woman's physiological sex causes her to be more incoherent, to experience "psychic reverberations" that are "dim, less localized, more all-pervasive" (I, p. 270; II, p. 562). This leads Hall to stress the importance of the girl to the maintenance of white, middle-class authority. He does this particularly in relation to the widely perceived problem of "race suicide." Drawing on a variety of sources, Hall describes a situation in which the birth-rate is decreasing among white middle-class women, due to a "voluntary avoidance of child-bearing" (II, p. 579). These women have been led astray by "excessive intellectualism," overindulgence, and "excessive devotion to society." They have developed an aversion to "brute maternity" (II, p. 609). It is only the "constant influx of foreigners" that has prevented a "steady decadence of birth-rates," as when "the best abstain from child-bearing, then the population is kept up by the lowest." Not only does Hall raise the fear of falling white middle-class birth-rates and the effect on white middle-class predominance. He also raises the fear of cross-racial affiliations, which will intensify problems yet further. A mingling of races will, he suggests, increase the "ferment" and "instability" of adolescence by "multiplying the factors of heredity" (I, p. 322; II, p. 574). As for achieving a higher birth-rate among the "best," Hall advocates the delay and attenuation of girls' education. If, however, women "do not improve" in their attitudes to child-bearing, it may be that there will have to be a "new rape of the Sabines" (II, p. 579).[14]

Hall is one example of a variety of discourses – scientific, educational, religious, and fictional – that betray an anxiety over white middle-class authority, and he is characteristic in that his anxiety comes to center on the adolescent girl. But Hall is also useful because he gives us the clue as to the importance of girls' fiction. From within his own relatively new "genre," he hails the equally recent arrival of girls' fiction. He stresses the point that by the turn of the century "ephebic literature" had developed to the extent that it should be "recognized as a class by itself, and have a place of its own in the history of letters and in criticism." Adolescence had "what might be called a school of its own" (I, p. 589). In other words, modernity has precipitated adolescence in ever more extreme forms, and a literature has emerged to recognize and deal with this fact. For this reason, Hall advocates that adolescent literature should be "prescribed" as a "true stimulus and corrective" (I, p. 550). Literature is aware of and responding to the contemporary problems delineated by Hall. But Hall also makes important discriminations between the sexes here. He believes that women write better about adolescence than men. This is partly because women, given Hall's perception of their unlocalized and pervasive sexual biology, never entirely escape from adolescence (Hall hypothesizes that women "depart less from this totalizing period" and so "dwell in more subjective states" [1, p. 546]). This in turn enables them to recapture the adolescent subject in their writing. Men write less vividly about adolescence, and their efforts are less "confessional," less "personal." Rather, men's writing on and for adolescents is more oriented to "reconstructing the political, industrial, or social world" (1, p. 563). Hall also observes that this axis of gender is reflected in the reading tastes of boys and girls. Citing several reports on children's reading, he notes that "boys read twice as much history and travel as girls and only two-thirds as much poetry and stories." This demonstrates to him that "the emotional and intellectual wants of boys and girls are essentially different before sexual maturity" (11, p. 476). Both boys and girls go through a "craze for reading," and this "greatest greed" occurs between fifteen and twenty-two (11, pp. 477–8). However, girls read more fiction – they have a "special interest" in fiction that begins with adolescence – and while girls will read boys' stories, women writers appeal more to girls, and male writers to boys. Indeed, "the authors named by each sex are almost entirely different" (11, p. 477).[15]

Publishers, writers, and readers as well as social scientists assumed a natural and inevitable division of readerships, in which the idea of the woman writer was conflated with that of the female character, and in turn with the girl reader. It might seem that, in proposing a study of women writing fiction about girls for girls, I am making – or at least acquiescing in – the same essentialist assumptions. Whilst it is a matter of fact that the majority of fiction for and about girls was indeed written by women, it is crucial to question the tidily "natural" appearance of this fact. For instance, many of the novels that I analyze were not simply the bestsellers of girls' fiction, nor the bestselling of children's fiction, but the bestselling of all fiction and all literary forms. The barely disguised truth is that men and women were avid readers of what was conveniently called girls' fiction, and fiction that was ostensibly for girls was more broadly used to debate and to come to terms with economic and social change. Equally, we should not accept too readily that this fiction is "about" girls in any reliable, authentic way. In keeping with Jacqueline Rose's discussion of "the impossibility of children's literature," there is always a distinction to be made between the actual child – whoever and whatever she may be – and the ideological child,

the child as embodiment or projection of adult needs and desires. One of
the main motives ascribed to the production of girls' fiction was that it
could help to create the very girl that it was ostensibly about. While this
attempt at influence seems to have met with some degree of success, there
are also numerous instances of girls as "resisting readers": there was often a
gulf between the prescriptions of girls' fiction and the actual meanings that
girls took from their reading. Also, it would be a mistake to assume that
girls' fiction is an essentialist and uniformly prescriptive genre in the first
place. Although women writers did acquiesce in the supposed naturalness
of their writing for and about girls – and their motives are of interest –
we will find that within this assumed naturalness they offer all kinds of
hesitations, deviations, and choices. Even as women undertook through
their fiction the role of ensuring that girls did indeed buy into womanhood,
they also gestured toward the performative aspect of girls' lives, and toward
the alternative expression that girls and others might find within and to
one side of their consumerized empowerment.

It might yet be asked, though, that if gender is ideological and performative, and if that recognition is embedded in the fiction, is it not
counter-intuitive to isolate a genre that was heavily associated with one
gender alone? Does it not seem to re-naturalize both gender and genre?
Also, it is already apparent that I resist my own logic, with references to
male writers such as James, and to non-fictional discourses such as Hall's.
I do not want to isolate girls' fiction in such a way as to re-naturalize it,
but I do think its qualities and its place are sufficiently important to merit
a sustained analysis. More particularly, girls' fiction performed a function
that other genres and discourses could not. It constitutes a very cohesive
canon, manifesting recurrent concerns and strategies. The goal is not only
to explain the function of girls' fiction, but also to explain why girls' fiction
performed this function and not, say, James's fiction. To offer some initial
thoughts here, a major aspect of this ideological utility lies in popularity.
Girls' fiction is written in an accessible, everyday language rather than in
the "special language" of poetry or in the demanding syntactical structures
of James. The everyday aspect is carried through into the material, in that
girls' fiction is seldom exotic, but invites a close and sustained identification
between reader and character. Yet fiction is also an escape from the reader's
immediate circumstances, and in girls' fiction especially it is a prolonged
escape, with numerous sequels and serials. Fiction, then, is a supremely
useful tool because it is accessible, and it grants repeated and lengthy access
to the reader. Furthermore, like consumerism itself, fiction both empowers
and constrains: it empowers because it permits the reader to assume other

guises; it constrains in the sense that to read is always to engage in an act of "directed invention." The reader spends time physically or mentally apart from others, in the pursuit of pleasure. But this invitation to pleasure is taken to permit a counterbalancing imposition of regulation and responsibility. Reading fiction sets up a "disciplinary intimacy" between author and reader: in granting and structuring the reader's pleasures, the author acquires a quasi-parental authority. The reader is subtly and discreetly made available to the author's didactic intentions. But a further and particularly relevant point here is that the "directed invention" of reading can also apply to the reader's age and gender. That is to say, girls' fiction can interpellate the adult as a girl: he or she is invited to experience life from the girl's point of view. The intense adult enthusiasm for girls' fiction is complex and various, but the possibility for the adult of inhabiting the role ascribed to the girl is always present.[16]

The decision to focus on a relatively neglected popular genre is perhaps inevitably to invoke the debate over the canon. One might try to sidestep this by arguing that we need to look at girls' fiction independently of a writer like James, because girls' fiction does different "cultural work." Certainly it did much more cultural work in that girls' fiction outsold James many times over, and in this rudimentary sense girls' fiction participated more fully in a consumerist culture. But these issues inevitably relate to our sense of the value of respective types of fiction. It would be easy to assume that girls' fiction was more popular because it is not as "good": it has basic and transparent didactic and emotional goals, whereas James probes the equivocations of his characters and the ambiguities of their environment. I do not want to argue that girls' fiction is as "good" as James's, and nor would I deny that the didactic intentions of girls' fiction may at times be tiresome and heavy-handed. Girls' fiction offers a relatively transparent view of class formation, whereas a writer like James offers a subtle and inconclusive critique. But this in itself makes girls' fiction useful, in that it exemplifies particularly well the issues that many other writers were drawn to. I return to this in the conclusion, but leaving aside for now the exemplary power of girls' fiction in relation to other genres, I think it will become clear that the personal and behavioral lessons of girls' fiction are by no means as fixed and simplistic as has traditionally been supposed. This sense, that both the instrumentality of the genre and the true complexities of the genre have not been recognized, is the strongest motive for the present study. But alongside this critical–historical impulse, there is the fact that many of the writers that I analyze – from Louisa May Alcott to Laura Ingalls Wilder – have remained popular to this day. My students here in Belfast always like to discuss whether or not a book such as *Little Women* is "suitable for children," and they do so in the knowledge that this novel from 1868 is still available in every standard bookshop in the city, and indeed that many of them read the book as children. Although my study is periodized, it is implicitly a continuation of these seminar discussions.

In constructing a canon of girls' fiction, I have pursued the principles mentioned in passing above: the texts were bestsellers in their day, were almost without exception written by women, and were "for" and "about" girls. There is an element of survey in that while the treatment is selective, I cover what seem to me to have been the significant variations within the genre across the period. The first section, "Emergence," traces the development of the genre from 1865 to 1890. The three chapters in this first section all demonstrate that, with what I call the "first generation" of writers, the impulse was to resist as much as to accommodate the rise of consumerism. I begin in chapter 1 with Louisa May Alcott, because she allows us to locate all the key issues at the beginning of the period, issues that later writers will reproduce and modify. In her fiction Alcott explored the so-called democratization of wealth, and the effect that this had on social values. She wrote about the increasing significance of consumption and display, focusing especially on the impact of this cultural shift on middle-class girls preparing for womanhood. The issue is more or less present in all of Alcott's fiction for girls, but it appears in particularly clear and insistent form in two of her most popular novels, *Little Women* (1868) and *An Old-Fashioned Girl* (1870). These two works also betray many of the other concerns that we have noted as contingent to buying into womanhood. They deal with the growing importance of regional disparities: one of Alcott's favorite fictional gambits is to take a country-bred girl to the city, and *vice versa*, as a way of drawing attention to the social and cultural implications of metropolitan development. In this way Alcott gives us a sense of class as a regionalized phenomenon. Although race and ethnicity are seldom more than passing issues with Alcott, they do nonetheless feature in *Little Women* and *An Old-Fashioned Girl*, signaling that they are almost necessary presences in any elaboration of class-ed and gendered subjectivity. And although parts of this chapter make Alcott seem a conservative writer, we also find that she uses the "dramatic" phase of adolescence not simply in a way that anticipates Hall's "tumultuousness," but also to explore the de-essentialized, performative quality of social identity. The move toward a spend-and-display culture gives her cause for concern, but the fact of social change is also what drives her fiction and creates chances for her protagonists. Finally, Alcott allows us to develop a sense of the role of the woman writer in relation to her characters and her readers, in that Alcott had a very awkward – one might say, adolescent – relation to her readership, and to her own professional success. She was effectively wrong-footed by fame, in that she became wealthy by praising humble virtues. She set herself against emergent hierarchies of display, but found that she herself had ever more powers and choices within this same culture. In terms of her subject matter, her professional positioning, and her responsibilities to her readers, Alcott was constantly forced to reassess her position. Could she urge modesty from her own position of celebrity and influence? How could such modesty be combined with Alcott's own growing interest in women's independence and professionalization?

In the second chapter I build on some of the issues discussed in chapter 1, but within the context of the most rapidly evolving marketplace for girls' fiction, the magazines. Although the children's magazines were usually established on a conventional, gentrified footing by recognized, "quality" publishers, this market would be transformed by changes in the economics of magazine publishing in the decades after the Civil War. Profits came to depend not on sales as such, but on advertizing revenue. Publishers set out with high notions of instructive literature for youth, but they found that, in order to survive, they had to lower the cover price, increase circulation, promote themselves aggressively, and be less fastidious about the advertizements they would carry. Otherwise economically and socially conservative authors and editors for girls found themselves ambiguously placed, in that they were producing reactionary fiction in the context of new consumerist techniques and values. As with Alcott, magazine writers sought in their fiction to mitigate the very forces that had led to their own enrichment. But this awkwardness would prove productive, in that a series of new and interesting balances emerges in the fiction. Women writers begin in their magazine stories to explore scenarios that allow girls to arrive at independent financial power, even if the same stories are also designed to preserve the class-ed power of the "lady." Girls' fiction for the magazines took different forms, and it would be wrong to suppose that it was always oriented so as to negotiate its own immersion in a consumerist economy. However, as representative samples demonstrate, this was a recurrent feature of the stories, as the girl is used to reconfigure the boundary between public and private, productive and non-productive.

With Alcott and much of the magazine fiction, there is usually a constructive compromise with regard to a changing social economy. There is the sense that the old-fashioned female virtue of "faculty" will enable the girl to work out a satisfactory and valid relation to consumerist modernity, even if the same fiction alerts the reader to the troubling tendencies of the age. This fiction, then, balances its own reactionary tendencies by allowing and developing the girl's agency. She is sufficiently mobile and inventive to assuage contradictions between residual and emergent. But chapter 3 takes into account the elements of girls' fiction that were more fearful. Bestsellers such as *Hans Brinker* (1865) and *Five Little Peppers and How They Grew* (1881) exhibit a social paranoia that the girl-heroine is not able to dispel. The authors of these novels explore what might be called "dramas of exclusion," in that they use their narratives to confront the class endangerment that was implicit in a changing social environment. These texts are written out of a recognition that the economic booms of the postbellum era were punctuated by a series of "panics" and "collapses," and that loss of caste was as much an aspect of the age as was upward mobility. These narratives are more fearful, in that there is a stronger sense of the fortuitousness of both failure and success. They wonder if there is to be any sense of class interest or cohesion between the rising and the falling. At their most stark, these narratives ask, how poor may one become and still be "respectable"?

Having explored the ideological uses of girls' fiction in the period of its growth, the second section looks at "Fulfillment" from the turn of the century onward. The chapters in this section focus on a second generation of authors, and show that with this generation there was a much fuller acquiescence in and celebration of the culture of consumption, and a more marked integration of the girl into the forms and processes of advanced capitalism. We also find that the values of girls' fiction were increasingly construed in comparison with adult fiction. In chapter 4, for instance, I look at how Kate Douglas Wiggin, author of *Rebecca of Sunnybrook Farm* (1903), constructs a relation between Romanticism and consumerism, and how this relates to the "realism wars" of the 1880s and after. In combining Romantic and consumerist ideologies, Wiggin and other notable writers for girls used their fiction to oppose the realist and naturalist tendencies of adult fiction. Above all, *Rebecca of Sunnybrook Farm* is the supreme example of how the girl manages the transition between old, rural economies and expanding corporate practices. Her Romantic power stimulates her speculative adventures, and this in turn enables her to broker an accommodation between the land-wealth of Sunnybrook Farm and the entrepreneurialism of "Mr. Aladdin," her prospective husband. Equally, Romantic power is perilously close to the incoherence of adolescence. In sending Rebecca to an upscale girls' school, the businessman "settles" Rebecca. She is the perfect instance of how Hall's adolescent becomes the Foucaldian subject: she elicits and is elicited by an authority that she then internalizes. This narrative trajectory also relates to Wiggin's commentary on the state of fiction at the turn of the century. The girl of girls' fiction has become the "good" character, and so for Wiggin and others she serves as "antidote" to social problems and to the so-called "dirty fiction" that explored social problems.

The fifth chapter looks at a variant of the Rebecca narrative, in that Jean Webster's *Daddy-Long-Legs* (1912) places the heroine's social and financial ascent in relation to higher education for women. Jerusha Abbot is an orphan who is sent from her children's home to Vassar by a wealthy benefactor. Going to Vassar will enable her to rise, in that it will give her the "finish" that will suit her to being her benefactor's wife. *Daddy-Long-Legs* might then be read as an allegory on the rise of new money, in that a person with no antecedents manages to assimilate herself within an established ruling class. But the college aspect allows Webster to invoke other, more troubling themes. Higher education for women had been an awkward topic, in that it held out the possibility of female professionalization, and suggested the much-demonized figure of the New Woman. To some extent Webster raises this threat in order to contain it. She shows that college, especially at the more exclusive end, had become more "civilizing" than empowering. Vassar does not turn Jerusha into a lawyer or a doctor, so much as make her more marriageable. The novel exemplifies the Veblenian idea that the ruling class must always authenticate its power with non-pecuniary forms of identification: it must be seen to be "above" the money that has enabled its predominance. But Webster is also interested in setting up an axis of reference between the urban poor, Progressive social observers, and the rich and powerful. This realist desire to move between "low life" scenes and privileged habitats forced Webster to engage in the generic debate that had preoccupied Wiggin. Webster too became embroiled in the argument over the relation of girls' fiction to the more "dirty" forms of realism. For Webster and for others, it seemed that the popularity of girls' fiction depended on the inclusion of a realist problematic, but also on the assurance that the girl would mitigate the same problematic. On her path toward an enviable financial position, the girl will serve as the mobile figure that can bring diverse interests into constructive association. She must again be the means of resolving contending forces, both in terms of social issues and in terms of their novelistic representation.

The early and middle chapters of the book investigate fairly conventional models of authorship, in that they focus on women who worked independently, and who could claim a proprietary right over their stories and characters. They work in relation to a realist tradition, in that they are influenced by the domestic realism of mid century, and they explore the ideological possibilities of the girl in relation to the further evolutions of realism and naturalism towards the end of the century. Chapter 6 still represents the fulfillment of the girl's fictional utility, but it also traces a radical departure from the conventional model of authorship. It includes discussion of syndicated, serial fiction. Syndicated fiction is interesting for the way in which its production was so thoroughly informed by advanced capitalism, in that the "literary machine" of the children's fiction syndicates mimicked the "scientific management" of other industries. The ultimate determinant of production was no longer an individual female author, but a syndicate manager who would co-ordinate teams of writers under spuriously individualized identities such as "Carolyn Keene" and "Laura Lee Hope." Entrepreneurs in other fields had constantly sought efficiency, and when this led to a crisis of overproduction, they made efforts to engineer greater consumption. Stratemeyer, the most important syndicate owner, had also rationalized everything, from plotting and writing through to pricing and packaging, and his redesign of literary production and marketing was effectively in keeping with industrial models. Furthermore, the thematics of syndicate fiction reflects the new professional–managerial ethos, in that these novels can be read as allegories of the "upscale emulation" that modernization offered as its ultimate reward. In chapter 6 I look at Stratemeyer's methods and at some representative samples of syndicate fiction, showing how both methods and product were closely oriented toward the imperatives of a consumerist economy.

The final section, "Revision," investigates the less confident and even defensive fictions that emerged in the twentieth century. In chapter 7 this defensiveness takes a peculiarly distasteful form, in that I look at Gene Stratton-Porter, some of whose work has an overtly racist theme. Though now largely forgotten, Stratton-Porter was the most highly paid writer of her day. I focus on two of her works, *A Girl of the Limberlost* (1909) and *Her Father's Daughter* (1921). Stratton-Porter's work becomes most aggressive when she uses the figure of the girl to explore contemporary fears over "race suicide" (the same fears that we noted in Hall's *Adolescence*). Writing in the context of the "Yellow Peril," she seeks to assert the white girl's right to American wealth, which, she suggests, is constantly under threat from racial and ethnic others. As with Wiggin and Webster, Stratton-Porter's fiction demonstrates the extent to which girls' fiction was written with reference to adult genres, in that Stratton-Porter too locates herself and her work in relation to the furore over realism and naturalism. There is the same consumerized pastoralism that we find in *Rebecca of Sunnybrook Farm* and other novels, in that once again the girl serves as the figure through whom country values and the power of new money may be combined. In Stratton-Porter's work, as in Wiggin's, the girl enables the spectacle of the "natural" for the city-dweller, and in return she acquires wealth and social mobility. As Stratton-Porter herself put it, through her and her girl-protagonists, "tired clerks" and others could reclaim "their natural inheritance of field and sky," while at the same time the girl is empowered by and internalizes metropolitan knowledge and values.[17] But Stratton-Porter's sense of this natural was more troubled than was that of Wiggin, and bore the marks of naturalist influence. Although her early novel, *A Girl of the Limberlost*, tries to maintain an affiliation with Romantic ideologies of nature, it also begins to explore a more deterministic and Darwinian natural world. In this novel and in *Her Father's Daughter*, the girl's acquisition of money and status is recast as a barely disguised predatory struggle, in which the strongest and the purest will prevail. In *Her Father's Daughter* this is developed from an explicitly racist point of view, in that the white girl's "natural inheritance" of American wealth also serves to confirm the evolutionary superiority of her breeding. Given the unpleasantness of Stratton-Porter's work, I also use this chapter to reflect again on the motives and principles that might be used in constructing a canon of girls' fiction. That is to say, I discuss the reasons for resuscitating Stratton-Porter alongside the reasons for leaving her in obscurity.

Stratton-Porter's fiction constitutes a revision in that it lacks the consumerist confidence of earlier texts, and seeks to assure the white girl's authority within a primitive, naturalist thematic. The final chapter analyses the defensive revisionism that was to be found in girls' fiction after the crash of 1929. I look at two different forms of Depression writing, with the Nancy Drew series and the Little House books. In the Stratemeyer-produced Nancy Drew Mysteries, it is as though the Depression is not happening. Nancy still has her "snappy little roadster" and her charge accounts at all the downtown stores. She can still unhesitatingly suggest to a friend that they go on a "shopping orgy." But her role as a detective in search of lost fortunes might be read as an oblique recognition that vast sums of money had disappeared after 1929. More importantly, the Nancy Drew series exhibits a social paranoia similar to that of the mid to late nineteenth century, in that once again established classes are seen to be under threat from interlopers. Nancy, who will always find lost or misappropriated treasures, is another example of how fiction makes the girl central to the very processes she stands outside of: control of goods and money. And yet, I argue that the series still keeps the girl at home, bound by patriarchal structures and bought off by the pleasures of modernity. The other series that I read as Depression writing is Laura Ingalls Wilder's Little House series. These novels were written in part as a critique of Roosevelt's welfare policies, in that Wilder lamented the passing of the hardihood and self-reliance of the pioneers. Much as she herself was a traditional author rather than part of a syndicated team, her fiction too sets itself against and reverses the process of modernity by taking her reader back to the 1870s and 1880s. Her fiction describes in close and fascinating detail all the different processes of making and doing, from sewing to making bullets to butchering. There is a tremendous sense of power to be derived from this practical erudition, and Wilder sets this beside the uselessness of the modern subject, who has come to depend on wages, shopping, and labor-saving devices. The irony is, however, that although Wilder takes the reader back, she also brings her forward again. There is a tension between the naive pleasures of the past and the thrills of an emergent consumerism. The lure that takes us on through the series is that the vigilant and hard-working characters will finally be able to let down their guard and surrender to abundance. But the constant lesson is to mistrust the progress that is being worked for. It is never safe to give up one's power, and the old, hard ways are safer. Unable to resolve this tension, the narrative hunger is always for a space in between: brief moments of excess, which can be enjoyed without consequences. In an era of financial disaster, the girl is again a key means of representing and assuaging social and economic disquiet. The stock market crash and subsequent Depression may have caused the dream of consumerist abundance to be postponed, but through the girl such misfortunes could be moralized, and through her also the dream could be kept alive.

In the conclusion I formulate once more the very particular role of girls' fiction, and I do this by comparing this canon with treatments of consumerism and girlhood in the writing of established canonical authors, namely Henry James and Emily Dickinson. Dickinson is especially interesting here because she is invoked as a possible exemplar from within the pages of girls' fiction. When, in *Daddy Long-Legs*, the girl characters attempt to come to terms with a Dickinson poem about shopping, the scene gives very clear expression to the changing ideological context of the girl. More importantly, it suggests the possibility of formulating alternative identities from within that context. The conclusion, then, seeks to assert once more the cultural function of the girl and of "her" fiction, and also to provide a sense of how this function was – or could be – subverted or transcended.

PART I

Emergence

I

The fate of modesty

Girls' fiction came to prominence in the newly invigorated, post-War publishing market, most obviously as a compromise between "preachy" children's fiction and the often sensational domestic novel. Girls' fiction was less heavily didactic than pre-War children's stories, but it did seek to moderate the sentimental and melodramatic "excess" of the domestic narrative: it offered lively but stable and small-scaled narrative trajectories that would be suitable for young, impressionable readers. The leading exemplar of this first generation of girls' fiction, Louisa May Alcott, was typical. In her the realist disapproval of sensational excess was combined with a moralized disapproval of personal immodesty. But her moralized realism was at odds with the consumerizing, gilded age culture within which it emerged. A writer such as Alcott was placed in a false position in that her success, and that of the consumerist economy, were both fuelled by a desire for more. Writers might set themselves against what they perceived as selfish and immodest impulses towards gratification, but their sales depended on the resilience of these same impulses. This first stage of girls' fiction seems to bear out Walter Benn Michaels's analysis of realism more generally, in that realism is both opposed to and complicit with the unlikely and immoral gains of an expanding, speculative economy. The intense pleasures of sensational and material excess must be present as a possibility, even in the realist novel; but the logic and the morality of realism dictates that pleasure be segmented into acceptably modest moments. A complete and overwhelming pleasure is repeatedly deferred in favour of small gains, as the reader-consumer is both rewarded and led on. For all its implicit modesty, realism is ultimately bound up with an acquisitive model of subjectivity, and can no more tolerate stasis than can a capitalist economy.[1]

Alcott is the perfect means for us to explore this complex intersection of genre, pleasure, and capitalism, because we have full access not only to her work but – through journals, letters and ledgers – to her handling of her role as a successful woman writer. The irony is that in spite of her own diffidence,

Alcott achieved enormous renown in a culture that turned increasingly on publicity and display. Similarly, the sudden wealth that she won from her writing would bring into question her insistence on a realist type of narrative in which such stunning things did not happen. These issues were encapsulated in an incident of 1875, in which Alcott, firmly established as the leading writer for girls, became involved in a public debate over money. Her novel, *Eight Cousins*, had been appearing in installments in the *St. Nicholas* magazine, and she took this as an opportunity to criticize popular "sensation" fiction for boys. As one of her fictional mothers complains, the motto of such fiction is not "Be honest, and you will be happy," but "Be smart, and you will be rich." The same mother also objects to the slang, the unpleasant locales, and to the focus on "heroes of the barroom and gutter." When an enthusiastic boy-reader points out that it would be unnatural for a boot-black or a newsboy to use good grammar and no swear-words, she replies:

But my sons are neither boot-blacks nor newsboys, and I object to hearing them use such words as "screamer," "bully," and "buster." In fact, I fail to see the advantage of writing books about such people unless it is done in a very different way. I cannot think they will help to refine the ragamuffins, if they read them, and I'm sure they can do no good to the better class of boys, who through these books are introduced to the police courts, counterfeiters' dens, gambling houses, drinking saloons, and all sorts of low life.

The mother goes on to complain that the hero of this type of fiction is not permitted to gain his living "in a natural way, by hard work and years of patient effort, but is suddenly adopted by a millionaire whose pocketbook he has returned." Alcott identifies her chief target when the mother refers to "these *optical* delusions." With this reference, she marks out William T. Adams, who had achieved great success under the pen-name of "Oliver Optic."[2]

As a scholar of children's book-reviewing has noted, Alcott's criticism "unleashed a storm." Adams struck back in his own *Oliver Optic's Magazine*. Aside from claiming that Alcott had misrepresented his work, he made a stunning personal comment:

Ah, Louise, you are very smart, and you have become rich. Your success mocks that of the juvenile heroes you despise. Even the author of "Dick Dauntless" and "Sam Soaker," whoever he may be, would not dare to write up a heroine who rose so rapidly from poverty and obscurity to riches and fame as you did; but in view of the wholesale perversion of the truth we have pointed out, we must ask you to adopt the motto you recommend for others – "Be honest and you will be happy," instead of the one you seem to have chosen: "Be smart and you will be rich."[3]

Adams's defence would have been even more powerful had he known – or had he chosen to reveal – that Alcott herself had written a series of sensation fictions, largely out of a desire to make money. Alcott and Adams alike were making very good profits from the increase in the market for sensation fiction and especially children's fiction. Prior to the Civil War, children had tended to read "adult" fiction, such as Dickens, Bunyan, and the gothic romances. Children's fiction had been largely didactic, and undifferentiated between stories for girls and stories for boys. Within the newly extended and specialized market, Alcott occupied middle ground. Her work was not as relentlessly moralistic and shoddy as the Sunday School books, but nor was it as low and worldly as Optic and others. Alcott was thought to have introduced new elements of realism and humour into children's fiction, alongside male counterparts such as Mark Twain and Thomas Bailey Aldrich. She was thought to be successful because her stories were genuine, humane, and truly to be enjoyed by girls, and even on occasion by boys.

What does one make, then, of Adams's attack, and of the social innuendo it deals in? Aside from attempting to shame Alcott by exposing her earlier "poverty and obscurity," his priority is to reveal the contradictions of her position. She resented the lack of realism, with the sudden fortunes gained at the hands of benevolent millionaires. Yet she also resented the excess of realism, with the reporting of the slangy speech of the streets. Through her character, Alcott voices the opinion that fiction should seek to improve "ragamuffins," rather than representing the facts of their lives or offering a fantastical escape from those facts. Money, good fortune, it would seem, should be under the governance of a traditional middle-class morality of steady work, thrift, and correctness of behaviour. The author, in this sense, becomes a sort of cultural "gatekeeper," ensuring that access to privilege is achieved on condition of subservience to a somewhat dated *status quo*. But as Adams points out, Alcott herself had been placed under no such constraints. In his view, her rise was sudden and fortuitous, not to say sensational. He implies that Alcott is trying to impose an undemocratic hierarchy, in which only the "deserving" may succeed. Adams would prefer it if Alcott would celebrate the heterogeneity of modern American life, instead of pressing for exclusivity and for the established forms of moralized gentility.

Adams was not alone in his criticism of Alcott's management of her authorial persona. Much as she was loved and revered as the author of *Little Women*, a bad atmosphere hovered over her celebrity. She was reluctant to respond to the adoration of her admirers, and resented the increasing number of day-trippers who journeyed from Boston to Concord in the hope of catching a glimpse of her. She had even dared to satirize the public's reverence for her own person in a fictional episode in which a slavish admirer pilfers from Jo's home. And Alcott, rather than living up to the motherly good nature of Marmee or Jo, was very blunt about not being "giving" to her public. When Louise Chandler Moulton was writing a sketch of her for *Our Famous Women* (1885), Alcott wrote:

Dont forget to mention that L. M. A. doesn't like lion hunters, doesn't send autographs, photographs & autobiographical sketches to the hundreds of boys & girls who ask [for] them . . .[4]

The truth was that Alcott was both giving and not giving. She donated money to various causes, and especially to those concerned with the rights, health, and opportunities of women. In a more immediately personal context, she brought up her niece, and funded her family throughout her career. Yet she remained unhappy about the culture of display that she saw developing around her, and she found herself awkwardly placed in relation to consumerist publicity. From a background of making and doing, she became caught up in the world of the aspirational purchase. I want now to place Alcott within the context of her social background, and then trace her career, both in terms of her writing, and in terms of her negotiation of her success. Time and again, she confronts the question of fashionable appearance, of what money does for girls and young women, and what it ought to do for them. Alcott analyzes the fate of modesty in an urbanizing and increasingly consumerist world. This in turn produces a fiction for girls that is more widely concerned with the relation of wealth to social stability.

In her journal for 1 September 1843, the ten-year-old Alcott recorded that she had risen at five, taken a bath ("I love cold water") and spent the rest of the day in lessons, chores, and exercise. She also mentions being read a story called "The Judicious Father," which she then summarizes:

How a rich girl told a poor girl not to look over the fence at the flowers, and was cross to her because she was unhappy. The father heard her do it, and made the girls change clothes. The poor one was glad to do it, and he told her to keep them. But the rich one was very sad; for she had to wear the old ones a week, and after that she was good to shabby girls. I liked it very much, and I shall be kind to poor people.[5]

This story matches neatly with Anne Scott MacLeod's characterization of children's fiction of the period, which she describes as "clumsy literature, conceptually impoverished and preachy."[6] Alcott, though, was more subject than most to a moralized discourse on fashion and pride. She was at that point living in a community that had a dress code. The family was at Fruitlands, the experimental farm established by Bronson Alcott and Charles Lane. The Fruitlands ethos incorporated a belief in the wearing of simple, practical clothes, which had been manufactured in ways that did not exploit others. To Bronson and Lane, this meant not wearing cotton as it was a product of slavery, and not wearing silk as the silk worm was cruelly destroyed in the production of silk.[7] Alcott was also exposed to a discourse on the morality of fashion in the form of her parents' literary endeavours. Both Bronson and Abba sought to publish texts which offered a commentary on self-display. Bronson compiled an anthology of emblematic texts to be called "Pictures of Thought," intended "principally to aid the Young in Self-Inspection & Self-Culture," many of which evince a concern with the need to see beyond an attractive surface.[8] Similarly, Alcott's mother sought to warn the modern age against the lures of vanity. She produced a new edition of John Owen's *The Fashionable World Displayed*, which she hoped would "be the humble means of restraining folly, or checking extravagance."[9] A further and more light-hearted example of the Alcott parents' interest in wealth, display and morality is to be found in a satirical poem, *Nothing to Wear: An Episode of City Life*, which was owned and cherished by Abba Alcott, by her daughter Abby, and by subsequent family members. The poem recounts the adventures of Miss Flora M'Flimsey of Madison Square, who, in spite of three exhaustive shopping expeditions to Paris, is still left with "nothing to wear."[10] This poem would eventually find its way into *Little Women*: in Chapter XI, the vain Amy is likened to Flora, as she too declares that she has "nothing to wear."

Here and elsewhere, fashion is the sign of new money and secularizing culture. Taken together, they indicate a lack of moral feeling and social responsibility. Like neighbours and contemporaries such as Emerson and Thoreau, the Alcotts were deeply concerned with the ethics of dress. They were troubled by the idea that fashion was a means of enforcing and celebrating social inequity – of "flaunting it." This also relates to much earlier writers and moralists, and to established and emergent methods of production: slavery, the weary dressmaker, the factory system. The Alcotts look back to a simpler age, when materialist and showy attitudes were thought not to be so much in evidence. As a recent historian has observed, "[a]mbivalence about luxury is a national tradition," and such mixed feelings may be traced to the Bible, which tells us of divine splendour alongside warnings against devilish extravagance.[11] But there is a more immediate biographical factor at work in the Alcotts' distrust of new money, and its expression in fashion. Abba herself had connections to old money. She was the daughter of Colonel Joseph May, the niece of Dorothy Quincy

Hancock, and a descendant on her mother's side of Judge Samuel Sewall. Her background incorporated some of the most notable legal and business figures of the seventeenth and eighteenth centuries. But in marrying the improvident Bronson, her financial and class status had been brought into question. As Lydia Maria Child observed and subsequent historians have agreed, class distinctions became more pronounced in the course of the nineteenth century, and the crucial determining factor was the distinction between non-manual and manual labor. As "middling sorts" ascended to a relatively new white collar gentility, the baseline of class status required not working with the hands. Only fully aware of the risk she had taken after it was too late, Abba Alcott expressed her desperation to her father in telling terms: "Would you have me take in washing?"[12]

The Alcotts' social humiliation had consequences for all members of the family. For Louisa May, it resulted in a kind of social disappearance. She wrote in her journal for December 1860 that she had been asked to a "John Brown meeting, but had no 'good gown,' so didn't go" (p. 101). Even in radical reform circles, Alcott's poverty made her feel a loss of social mobility. She also records her disturbance at seeing other, more expensively dressed women in Boston: "In the street I try not to covet fine things" (p. 61). But the most sustained and complex register of this class endangerment is to be found in her fiction. It is here that the intersections of money, gender, display, and class manifest themselves most fully.

Reviewers often saw Alcott's fiction as fit for children because, in style and content, it lacked dressiness or over-sophistication. *Little Women* (1868) was "a simple, natural picture of home life," with "talk" that was "natural and child-like." Her work was "made up of such plain material."[13] To put it another way, *Little Women* does not disguise its puritanical strain. The novel contains many explicit references to *Pilgrim's Progress*, and is structured around this precursor. But it is not directly religious or spiritual in its bent. Its moral values are more frequently conflated with those of class than with those of Christianity. Whilst it is true that the girls are encouraged to be "little women" because it is Christian to be modest, gentle, and self-sacrificing, their discretion and their modesty are also their only remaining guarantees of their middle-class status. The narrative makes specific claims on the girls' behalf to a social position which is in danger of being lost. We are permitted to overhear a conversation in a fine drawing-room, during which the Marches are described as "one of our first families, but reverses of fortune, you know."[14] The novel constantly rescues the social standing of the characters, and by implication, of their real-life counterparts. In compensation for his increasingly fragile claims to middle-class respectability, Bronson's fictional alter ego is given high military rank: Mr. March is a colonel. The patronage of Mr. Lawrence is another means of making frequent allusion to the March family's grander past. Rather than judging on current appearances, Mr. Lawrence respects the status implied by their background and behaviour. And however far they may have fallen, the family is never confused with the lower classes. There is always a broad conceptual gulf between the Marches and their servant, Hannah Mullet, or the poor immigrants to whom the family extends its benevolence. Indeed, the introduction of the destitute, anomalously "foreign" Hummel family makes explicit the ethnicized dimension of class values at this time: the middle class is not made up of recent arrivals, but of white, Anglo-Saxon Protestants. The rescuing of the Hummel family assures the Marches of their residual powers, and it initiates the process of assimilation, of recreating the Hummels in the March image. At this stage, however, the Hummels remain "dangerous," in that it is from them that Beth catches scarlet fever. Alcott explores the drama of poverty from the point of view of an educated, non-laboring, white middle class. But in the process, she uses her fiction to redelineate the social boundaries that her real family was in danger of blurring. Notwithstanding the fact that, in her poverty, Alcott herself had had to work as a servant and as a seamstress, in the fiction she reinstates a sense of social superiority. She insists on the same identification she made when, as a ten-year-old, she heard the story of the rich girl and the poor girl: "I shall be kind to poor people."

Alcott uses *Little Women* to investigate class in explicit relation to femininity and display. The precise nature of Marmee's claims to being a lady are stated with her introduction to the narrative:

"Glad to find you so merry, my girls," said a cheery voice at the door, and actors and audience turned to welcome a tall, motherly lady, with a "can-I-help-you" look about her which was truly delightful. She was not elegantly dressed, but a noble-looking woman, and the girls thought the grey cloak and unfashionable bonnet covered the most splendid mother in the world. (p. 8)

Alcott is very much on the attack here, with her characterization of someone who is both a "lady" and "unfashionable," who is "tall" and "noble," but who seeks to help rather than to command. Marmee is presented as someone who is liable to confuse modern, superficial perceptions of class. This politics of display versus helpful industry is equally present in the March girls' sewing. They are encouraged to sew for reasons beyond the merely practical. Sewing serves to inculcate a genteel feminine virtue, in that it is a quiet accomplishment, far removed from the brutish pleasures of "romping." It is no accident that the most virtuous sister, Beth, is also the most accomplished needlewoman. Through her, Alcott offers a moralized vaunting of old-fashioned womanly skills. But as we saw with Marmee, Alcott's approval of neatness of dress does not preclude a strong mistrust of fashion. Sewing as a subservient, familial activity is set against a more worldly femininity in the chapter in which "Meg Goes to Vanity Fair." Meg allows herself to be dressed up and ornamented for the Moffats' *soirée*: Belle Moffat and Hortense, the French maid, turn her into "a fine lady" (p. 81) and "a fashion-plate" (p. 86). In Alcott's fiction, one thing always leads to another, and soon Meg is drinking champagne, flirting, chattering, and giggling. She becomes, as one man describes her, "a doll." But once the effects of the champagne have worn off, Meg will reproach herself, and her good sense will prevail once more. This mistrust of fashionable pleasures is also conflated, in a semi-humorous way, with dangerously speculative business practices. Amy buys into the fashion of exchanging pickled limes at school, even to the point of taking advantage of "credit" in order to enhance her status and her enjoyments. Of course, this showy, entrepreneurial behavior will lead Amy into her "Valley of Humiliation." She is forced to throw her entire investment of limes out of the school window, where they are gathered up by the "little Irish children" who, like the Hummels, subsist opportunistically at the text's margins.

If Meg's and Amy's narratives align Alcott firmly with a reformist post-Puritan culture, other parts of the novel suggest a different reading. When the relatively well-off Mrs. Gardiner invites Meg and Jo to a New Year's Eve ball, they rush around with humorous desperation, trying to gather together enough of the right clothes to make themselves presentable. With repairs and borrowing, they just about manage. The serious point that lies behind the humour here is that although Alcott disapproves of the vain and foolish shows of *arrivistes*, she also recognizes that to lack the right clothes is to lose social presence altogether. The suggestion is that it is not enough to have genteel manners. To be unable to dress appropriately is to be disqualified from polite society. In her idealistic moments, Alcott harks back to a morally and behaviorally determined social hierarchy, in which fashionable display was a liability as much as anything. But even if such a society had ever existed, *Little Women* testifies to an increasing pressure to live up to more showy forms and codes. Alcott was uncertainly located in this ferment. She had affiliations with the grand old mercantile class of Boston, but these had been weakened, and her immediate family had not participated in the rise to prosperity of the "middling sorts." Her fictional response was to question the egotistical pleasures of new money, while the same narratives are haunted by fears of being left behind.

Alcott remained divided, however, on the defining issue of fashion. This was because her disapproval of the shows of the world was counterbalanced by a Romantic love of exotic, aggrandized personae. In her fiction, she managed these tensions by finding safe, semi-private ways to celebrate display. This is most obvious in the way that the sisters love to dress up for their various theatricals. Within an earnest and moralized ethos, there is also a pleasure in sumptuary splendour. This also introduces a valuable performative element to her characters' lives. In their writing and their dramatic productions, the March sisters create a series of alternative imaginative spaces. Their playfulness deals in an untrammelled possibility that is at odds with the rigid codes that they must follow in their daily lives. The often tempestuous, performative aspect remains present even after the girls have given up their plays. Although Jo may try to carry out the bidding of various more sensible elders – Marmee, Father, Professor Bhaer – the reader knows that Jo is still a character who may do anything, who has an exciting talent for improvisation and reinvention. This potential for alternative creativity within apparently stifling systems is vital to *Little Women* and, indeed, to the entire canon of girls' fiction. The theatrical element of *Little Women* also conforms to the emergent fictional recognition of adolescence, in that it reveals the girls' social incoherence, their unformed and essayistic selves which contain radical possibilities. It is also telling that the girls' performances incorporate a suggestion of the gothic, and especially of violent ruptures of established social relations. Their stories and dramas stage coercive passions, attempted abductions, and shadowy figures, with "The Masked Marriage. A Tale of Venice" and a play with "Dons," witches, arsenic, and fainting fits. While it would be easy to overstate the importance of these literary performances to the novel, their presence confirms the sense of the adolescent girl's insurrectionary potential. In their plays and stories, the girls indicate a reluctance to accept the constraints of the symbolic order, a reluctance which will then manifest itself in subsequent crises.[15]

Perhaps the liberatory potential of performance is circumvented, in that Jo tries to conform – she tries to perform correctness. But how complete is this resolve on the part of author and character? Certainly the novel maintains some level of ambivalence with regard to the possibility of a transformed and pleasured self, and this is clear in the different fates of the sisters. Alcott extolls the earnest virtues of domestic economy in the story of Meg. Having married the impecunious John, Meg must learn to tailor her desires to her budget. But Alcott and her readers may also travel to Europe with another sister. Through Amy, we are permitted the modern, monied pleasure of a continental excursion, and may vicariously enjoy the experience of being courted by a rich and handsome suitor on the lake at Vevey. For all that true worth is to be discerned behind appearances, the novel also grants a romance that consists of wealth, leisure, and "Paris finery." There is, after all, to be "dressing up" and pleasure without repercussions. As Richard Brodhead has so persuasively suggested, "at the same time that it is erecting an ethic of poor but honest virtue against the temptations of affluence, *Little Women* opens an unobtrusive commerce between old-style virtuous domesticity and a new-style lavishness."[16] But finally it is old money that brings the world to rights: the new-style lavishness is made possible by the long-established Lawrence fortune, and when Jo's virtue is finally rewarded, it is with her inheritance of Plumfield from her Aunt March.

Although one could use a number of Alcott's novels and stories to develop the intersections between money, gendered display, and class, I want to focus on *An Old-Fashioned Girl* (1870). I do this because the novel has received very little critical attention, because it deals with the issues of display and class stratification insistently and explicitly, and because it represents a neat structural reversal of its celebrated predecessor, *Little Women*.[17] Its reversal of *Little Women* lies in the fact that, whereas Meg is placed momentarily in Vanity Fair before a return to the comfortable and moralized locale of home, *An Old-Fashioned Girl* is set almost entirely in Boston, as the heroine, Polly Milton, must make her way among various social and economic dangers. This in itself shows that, whatever her views on the relative virtues of town and country, the metropolis of Boston was coming to occupy an increasingly important place in Alcott's life and work. And in exploring a country-city dynamic, this novel brings into view the regionalized divisions that were such an important feature of post-War adult fiction.

An Old-Fashioned Girl has a simple, dichotomous structure, in that it brings together two different types of girl. Polly is presented as natural, sensible and charming. The novel opens with her visit to Boston to stay with her cousin, Fanny Shaw. Although the girls are the same age, Polly's "countrified" Concordian background puts her at odds with Fanny. She wears a "simple blue merino frock, stout boots, and short hair," and is still a girl. Her citified cousin has more advanced notions, both in terms of manner and of dress:

"You are fourteen, and *we* consider ourselves young ladies at that age," continued Fanny, surveying with complacency the pile of hair on the top of her head, with a fringe of fuzz around her forehead and a wavy lock streaming down her back;

likewise, her scarlet and black suit, with its big sash, little *pannier*, bright buttons, points, rosettes – and heaven knows what. There was a locket on her neck, earrings tinkling in her ears, watch and chain at her belt, and several rings on a pair of hands that would have been improved by soap and water.[18]

Alcott is directing her critical attention at the "Girl of the Period" here. Indeed, elsewhere in the novel she refers specifically to this legendary figure. The "Girl of the Period" was an English version of Flora M'Flimsey, designed by Eliza Lynn Linton to typify the sense that young women were increasingly overdressed and frivolous. The points of comparison between Linton's "Girl" and Fanny Shaw and her upper-class friends are clear. Linton suggested that the "Girl" had adopted the extravagant dress of the prostitute, and that in doing so, she too had turned herself into a commodity. Fanny and her friends have secret trysts with fast young men, and seek to marry on mercenary terms. Like Linton's "Girl," Fanny is defined by the immodesty of her appearance. She too is "a creature who dyes her hair and paints her face, as the first articles of her personal religion; whose sole idea of life is plenty of fun and luxury; and whose dress is the object of such thoughts and intellect as she possesses."[19]

Fanny and Polly provide a contrast between old and new. Polly belongs to an unchanging rural class. The daughter of a poor country minister, she does not belong to the mercantile elite, but at the same time she is removed from the prosaic connotations of trade and manual labor. Her surname of Milton suggests both her reformist background and her cultural expertise. The contrast between Polly and Fanny conforms to the model of the static, dominant caste of a declining rural society encountering a more mobile and self-enriching urban bourgeoisie. This contrast is developed in the course of the novel, as Polly is placed beside a variety of other female characters, and as Alcott sets out to explore the roles and possibilities for the women of the age. Fanny's mother, Mrs. Shaw, corresponds to the popular fictional type of the fashionable and ailing mother. When her youngest daughter runs towards her, she pushes her away because the daughter's hands are dirty and will mark her clothes. Polly is on hand to make the silent observation that "the velvet cloak didn't cover a right motherly heart, that the fretful face under the nodding purple plumes was not a tender motherly face." Polly then remembers her own mother, "whose dress was never too fine for little wet cheeks to lie against or loving little arms to press" (p. 114). Mrs. Shaw and her daughter Fanny are caught up in exhibiting new wealth and aping European aristocratic notions. But Alcott suggests that if one pushes back a generation, one will discover true worth. To go back in time is much the same as returning from the city to the country, for Grandma Shaw represents all the stalwart American Revolutionary virtues that are still alive in Polly. As Grandma Shaw comments:

In my day, children of fourteen and fifteen didn't dress in the height of fashion, go to parties, as nearly like those of grown people as it's possible to make them, lead idle, giddy, unhealthy lives, and get *blasé* at twenty. We were little folks till eighteen or so, worked and studied, dressed and played like children, honored our parents, and our days were much longer in the land than now, it seems to me. (p. 12)

She remembers how "we all learned to make bread, and cook, and wore little chintz gowns, and were as gay and hearty as kittens."[20] She compares the benefit of this model of childhood with that of her daughter-in-law, remarking of her siblings that "[a]ll lived to be grandmothers and fathers, and I'm the last - seventy, next birthday, my dear, and not worn out yet, though daughter Shaw is an invalid at forty" (p. 13). "Daughter Shaw" is more vain and self-indulgent than ill, and her weakness is symptomatic of the moral failures of modernity: she is an "in-valid" woman indeed.[21] Grandma Shaw has lived upstairs, neglected by the new generation, until Polly arrives and tries to establish a relationship with her. Grandma Shaw disregards Polly's lack of fashionable clothes, and recognizes her as a true gentlewomanly type, telling her: "you have lived in the country, and haven't learned that modesty has gone out of fashion" (p. 16). But Polly's presence renews the other children's interest in the old accomplishments of cooking and sewing, and they learn to appreciate their grandmother's stories of the old days. Grandma Shaw tells of the old Beacon Hill families of Hancock, Joy, Quincy and May. Of course, Alcott has given Grandma Shaw precisely her own mother's relations. In a moment which has an undisguised biographical resonance, the narrative privileges the modesty of the past, even as it makes an assertion of class status.

Eventually, after Grandma's death, the Shaw family loses its fortune, and must move back into Grandma's house. Alcott uses Grandma's property to surround the characters with a reassuring sense of their background: "The old-fashioned things... now seemed almost like a gift from Grandma, doubly precious in these troublous times" (p. 285).[22] Polly helps the family to manage under reduced circumstances, and all become more humane and independent as a result. Polly marries the previously unreliable Tom Shaw, while the newly chastened Fanny marries a gentleman of the old school. Although Alcott chooses to "save" Fanny and give her a promising future, the novel is much more strident in what it has to say about girlhood and modernity than is *Little Women*. In the earlier novel, Jo March suffers adolescent torments, in spite of her country life and her judicious parents. In *An Old-Fashioned Girl*, on the other hand, Polly remains an untroubled and obedient child, even as she becomes an adult. She has no dramatic or otherwise "gothic" impulses, and she manages to by-pass the tumults that afflict other girl-characters. Fanny is the adolescent in *An Old-Fashioned Girl*, and through the Polly–Fanny dichotomy, Alcott seems to imply that the troubled and incoherent phase of growing up was produced by a modern, metropolitan upbringing. Also, although the regionalist dimension is apparent, there is none of the rich ambivalence that we associate with good regionalist fiction (and that we will find in other girls' fiction). Far from fulfilling the emotionally complex "memorial function" of regionalist writing, Alcott's "region" has a flatly moralized significance, and she engineers her narrative so that, rather than achieving an interesting interplay between past and present, the past returns with a vengeance.

Although *An Old-Fashioned Girl* demonstrates Alcott's affiliation with older models of class and virtue, it would be wrong to suppose that she wishes entirely to ignore the facts of modernity, or that she is completely opposed to the possibilities of the modern. She includes New Woman characters, and the themes of fashion and feminism come together in the story of Jenny, the impoverished seamstress. Jenny attempts suicide rather than starve or become a prostitute. Polly learns of her life, and resolves to talk to a party of rich girls about their duty to such struggling women. The rich young women have come together to make garments for charity, but their skills are so poor that they put sleeves on upside-down, and make jackets inside-out. When the conversation turns to poor seamstresses, a paranoia over fashion and status comes to the fore. As one young woman says of the servant class: "If they spent their wages properly, I shouldn't mind so much, but they think they must be as fine as anybody and dress so well that it is hard to tell the mistress from the maid." Another adds: "Servants ought to be made to dress like servants, as they do abroad, then we should have no more trouble" (p. 199). Alcott uses Jenny to extend the social range of her fiction, and to alert the reader to the difficulties encountered by women in a society that places such severe restrictions on women and work. But Alcott also reveals here the great uncertainty that underlies the increasing emphasis on display as a system of class definition. For if class is what one wears as much as how one thinks and acts, then the lower classes will find it only too easy to mimic their "betters." The problem with gilded age sophistication, then, is not simply that it is immoral, but that it is insecure. Alcott believes in a sympathetic and moral middle class, doubtless because she was thoughtful and compassionate. But she was also an "old-fashioned girl" in her time, and she uses the novel to clarify her sense of her own class pretensions. In pressing the claims of her Beacon Hill background over those of fashionable self-display, she was retrieving what had been lost. This reactionary gesture is ultimately rather troubling. Alcott was attempting to consolidate the basis of class definition, suggesting that it should be as obvious and immovable as Grandma Shaw's old, heavy furniture. We might have inferred this from the story of Jenny, the distressed seamstress. Although Alcott exhibits through Jenny a concern with working women's lives, she has created a very safely "deserving" figure. As Christine Stansell has observed of such stock characters, they were "the kind of working-class woman, housebound, deferential and meek, that genteel people liked." The factory girl, on the other hand, was better off, anti-domestic, and generally "more venturesome and disturbing."[23] Alcott's work seems an uncertain and incomplete effort to address shifts in class-definition. Even as she seeks a radical redress of social inequity, she longs to reunite with the well-modulated conservatism of Beacon Hill.[24] In this sense, Alcott's moral investment in realism was always subservient to her own more personal fears of class endangerment, and to the reactionary tendencies that those fears stimulated.

Surveying Alcott's work, fashion is seen to become increasingly important as a marker of social power, but one that commodifies girls and women. Alcott argues that dress should not be important, and seeks to retrench the forms of class definition that she believes obtained before the rise of the culture of display. Given the poverty and ignominy of so much of her own life, at times she resembles no one so much as Verena Tarrant's mother in that novel full of Alcottian echoes, James's *The Bostonians*: "What she clung to was 'society,' and a position in the world which a secret whisper told her she had never had and a more audible voice told her she was in danger of losing."[25] Alcott's characters' redemption lies in their well-mannered adjustment to reversal of fortune, although she betrays herself somewhat with her characters who "marry well." Alcott did not marry, but she lived long enough and became sufficiently successful to "buy into" the newly consumerized middle class. All her young adult life, she managed with gifts and handed-down, re-made clothes. After her great success with *Little Women*, she was to be diffident about fame, resenting intrusion, but enjoying the delights that had been denied her by youthful poverty. In her middle age she left the old-fashioned girl behind, and began to enjoy some of the pleasures of the "Girl of the Period." She continued to sew throughout her life, but she also began to spend considerable amounts on her wardrobe. She never became a compulsive clothes-buyer, and she certainly never came

close to exceeding her income. She remained financially conservative, and
even as a wealthy woman, would keep a record of bills in cents as well as
dollars. But she did acquiesce in a culture in which status was signified by
expensive self-presentation. She spent more on clothes in a year than her
cook earnt in a year.[26] She also began to make big lump-sum payments
for elaborate, professionally made dresses.[27] She used her wealth to display
her wealth, to "dress the part" of an extremely successful writer. But she
was also caught up in a more pervasive shift. Fashion became so accessible,
so universally inclusive, that the base-level of sartorial respectability went
up. She, along with every one else, had to do more to stay in the same
position. But display may also have had another meaning for Alcott. It was
confirmation that she had finally achieved all the things she had longed for
when a girl. Modish display may have been "vain," but it was also proof of
her professional success, an expression of her self-made security.[28]

Alcott's various decisions in relation to her life and work exhibit a keen
disapproval of gilded age forms and practices. She could never accept her
own accommodation to the order of conspicuous consumption. She tried
to disguise her unmistakable desire for money as a family obligation – to pay
off her father's debts, to save for her nephews and niece. In the face of this
increasingly delusory sense of economic need, she did make decisions as to
what she would and would not do for money. However, this in turn might
be related to non-pecuniary forms of status. For instance, she continued
to write "moral pap for the young," but discontinued her cheap sensation
fiction. Brodhead puts the question that, in an age in which divisions
in literary taste corresponded increasingly to divisions of class, "what is
Alcott's rejection of story-paper writing but a repudiation of a form she
fears will declass her?" (p. 104). In her negotiation of the related categories
of fashion, class, and authority, she disapproves of the showy vulgarity of
cheap romance in the same way that she disapproves of extravagant dress.
Her moderating impulse defines her as more securely-rooted in the middle
class than would a display of "nouveau luxe." Her retreat from fame could
be interpreted in a similar way. As we noted, she became notorious for
her reluctance to appear before her public, scorning to show herself to
the day-trippers who peered up at the windows of Orchard House. By the
late nineteenth century, such demonstrations of middle-class modesty were
irretrievably compromised by financial considerations. One thinks again
of James, and his notion that, in the age of display, "the highest luxury
of all, the supremely expensive thing, is constituted privacy."[29] Alcott's
refusal to display herself to the common public might once have been
seen as virtuous feminine reclusiveness. But in the context of her later life,

it could be construed as "the highest luxury," as a prideful assertion of independent means. As her argument with "Oliver Optic" suggested, there was the perception that she was "classing off." In her various and somewhat ambiguous negotiations of fashion and fiction, she enables us to trace the fate of modesty. It is differently prized as its context evolves. It begins as the discreet expression of genteel womanhood, and ends as the premium choice of the consumer.

2

Magazines and money

Although most studies of children's fiction tend to focus almost exclusively on novels, a significant part of the market for both authors and readers was that of children's magazines. Many novels were serialized in the magazines, and often the short magazine story does what the novel does. But there are also some differences, and these can be related to the specific nature and position of the magazines. There are three closely interconnected issues here: the evolving publishing context of the magazines; the effect this context had on authors' sense of their social role; and the impact these two issues had on stories that were written and published. In the years directly after the Civil War, magazine revenue was largely determined by the cover-price, multiplied by the number of subscribers. However, the magazines' rise to popularity soon made them a favorite target for advertizers. Publishers recognized that the way to future profit was by cutting the cover-price, increasing circulation, and so increasing the value of advertizing space. Although authors and editors were keen to work in such a lucrative market, they were less keen to present themselves in such a conspicuously commercial setting. Their desire to profit placed them at odds with the disinterested values that they wished to urge on children. These paradoxes of production carry through into the stories themselves, in that women writers used their fiction to dramatize the tension between unworldliness and entrepreneurialism, between modernization and tradition. Before turning to the stories, though, let's look at magazines both as an industry and as a social phenomenon.

It has been estimated that there was a growth in the children's periodical product as a whole of over 400 percent in the twenty years from 1865 to 1885, from 700 titles to 3300. This huge expansion after the Civil War was largely due to improvements in printing technology, and in transportation, though the improved literacy rates that came with increased school enrolments were also significant. The most popular periodical for children was *Youth's Companion* (1827–1929), which had a circulation of 500,000 in 1885.

Many others, though, had a readership of over 100,000, and even the most select, the *St. Nicholas* (1873–1940), had over 75,000 subscribers.[1] There was a mirroring of social hierarchies in that there were cheaper magazines which favored sensational stories, and which embraced working-class characters and scenes. There was also a gendered hierarchy, in that the violent, underworld excitements of the cheaper magazines were assumed to be designed for, and enjoyed by, boys rather than girls. Girls had higher cultural destinies and obligations than boys, and so were expected to find themselves more at home in the approved literature. In the cheaper category were *Oliver Optic's Magazine* (1867–1875), *Frank Leslie's Boys' and Girls' Weekly* (1866–1884), *Boys of New York* (1875–1894), and many others. These were set up in competition to the products of the literary élites of Boston and New York. But most of the key magazines in terms of sales and prestige were under the sway of the Boston literati. Fighting against the "moral incoherence" of Oliver Optic and Frank Leslie, the owners, editors, and writers of the culturally approved periodicals assumed that their roles carried a moral responsibility. Kelly observes that "[t]he tradition of the publishing industry reflected [the magazines'] origins in the antebellum period when literature was identified more with gentility, scholarship, and instruction, and less with popular entertainment."[2] Yet one has to be careful not to oversimplify the economic and social hierarchies of magazine-publishing. It was cheaper to subscribe to *Youth's Companion* ($1–50) than to *Frank Leslie's* or *Boys of New York* ($2–50). And not only could none compete with *Youth's Companion* in terms of popularity, but the sensational magazines were not always as successful as the controversies over them might suggest: at the height of its success, *Oliver Optic's* only managed a circulation of 11,000. Equally, when children's magazines disappeared from view, it was often due to the bankruptcy of a holding company, rather than to the failure of the magazine itself.

In terms of content, the "sensational" editors deliberately sought to blur divisions between genteel and popular. *Frank Leslie's* promised to provide "Healthy Fiction," "Science Made Easy," "Natural History," and "Anecdotes illustrating character, selected especially for youth." But as Kelly notes, its "brutality and violence" still exceeded that of any other publication.[3] On the other hand, the genteel editors may have eschewed sensation, but they were keen to offer an advance on the relentless didacticism of earlier, more religiose publications. Mary Mapes Dodge, a leading editor, wanted morality to be present, but incidental. She wanted the lessons to be provided in the form of:

... a few brisk, hearty statements of the difference between right and wrong; a sharp, clean thrust at falsehood, a sunny recognition of truth, a gracious application of politeness, an unwilling glimpse of the odious doings of the uncharitable and base.[4]

The prevailing values were to be those of disinterestedness and self-discipline, but a robust enjoyment must also run through the text.

The genteel magazines had, by their very nature, to obscure their connection to the world of commerce, even though their newly extended readerships were produced by the rise of the white-collar class. Their mode of operation is interesting in this respect, in that in some ways they operated more as a club than as a business. As is in the nature of élites, many of the producers of the magazines already knew each other socially: they were exchanging commissions and stories with members of their own set. In this way "business" was also something of a "personal" transaction. Based in and around Boston, many of the writers and editors were drawn from or connected to the so-called Brahmins: they were highly educated, and associated with the professions and the higher reaches of the mercantile class. The magazines allowed impoverished women at the fringes of this elite to make a living. Writing for children had feminized overtones, in that it was a "motherly" activity, and so allowed women to be in business without losing their status as ladies. This would change as the literary profession itself, and especially the magazines, became more business-like. Increasingly, the genteel aspect of a "profession" would lose ground to the aggressive strategies of an "industry." But at the same time, the market value of the magazines depended on their value as icons of gentility. Owners had to take advantage of the new commercial environment while also maintaining a reputation for seeing beyond the profit motive. Incorporating women into the process was one way for the magazines to keep up an aura of disinterested, cultured benevolence. The cluster of writers surrounding Annie Fields has been stressed as a case in point. Fields was the wife of the publisher and editor, James T. Fields. She was friendly with many of the important writers for girls, including Sarah Orne Jewett, Susan Coolidge, Louise Chandler Moulton, Harriet Lothrop, Rose Cooke, and Mary Wilkins Freeman. Even those who were not particular friends were part of her social purview, including Alcott. This meant that a great many women writers could earn money through their business with James T. Fields, while the whole enterprise seemed like an extension of their association with Annie Fields. This was made to seem more the case by the fact that Fields preferred oral agreements to written contracts, and presented himself in the light of "taking good care" of his "friends," the writers whom he published.[5] Equally, editing a children's magazine could take the guise of maternal responsibility, and so lose its mercenary implications. For this reason, it was one of the few directorial positions available and acceptable to educated women. Many proved their abilities in this way: Mary Mapes Dodge at the *St. Nicholas*, Lucy Larcom and Gail Hamilton at *Our Young Folks*, Alice M. Kellogg at *Treasure Trove*, Louisa May Alcott at *Merry's Museum*, Ella Farman Pratt at *Wide Awake*, and Emily Huntington Miller at the *Little Corporal*. When an editor sought a piece from a writer, this was often a case of a woman doing business with another woman. The correspondence on such occasions reflects the confusion of the personal, the moral, and the mercenary. When Stowe wrote to Alcott asking for a story, she stressed that the youth of America stood in need of Alcott's kind of fiction. Alcott saw through such social and moral colourings, though, and refused to write for the *Christian Union* until it offered her a much higher fee. The *Christian Union* subsequently found itself in a bidding war in which, of course, Alcott was the only real winner. Gail Hamilton, on the other hand, was slower to disentangle personal and business interests. An intimate of Annie Fields's social circle, she trusted James T. Fields to treat her fairly as her publisher and as the publisher of the children's journal with which she was associated. Eventually, though, she came to believe that Annie Fields's friendship was a mask to her husband's sharp practice.[6]

There was a further ostensible parenting aspect to the venture of the magazines beyond that of the mother-editor. The leading children's magazines tended to be side-products of adult publications, and were expected to represent in juvenile form the values of the parent-publication. This was the case with the *St. Nicholas*. Its parent, *Scribner's Monthly*, had been started in the hope of competing with "quality" publications such as the *Atlantic* and *Harper's*. In keeping with these high aspirations, its offspring was "not merely a miscellany," but was "founded on conviction, open-mindedness, ambition for leadership, and a determination to be of public service."[7] Open-mindedness and public service could take strange forms, though, when combined with ambition. The *St. Nicholas* bought up a series of rivals, taking over *Our Young Folks* and *The Children's Hour* in 1874, *The Schoolday Magazine* and *The Little Corporal* in 1875, and *Wide Awake* in 1893. The magazine boosted its own circulation and its roster of authors by cannibalistically removing competitors from the field. Similarly, *Youth's Companion* subsumed *Merry's Museum* in 1872. Parental benevolence and disinterestedness were also brought into question when market forces caused a shift in the attitude towards advertizing. The sensation magazines had always taken as much advertizing as they could get, and had not been fastidious about the products they would publicize. Genteel owners and editors were reluctant to accept advertizing at all, and only did so as the economics of publishing changed. But the increasingly frenzied chase after advertizing revenue meant that the magazines became one of the key features of the consumerist economy that they had set themselves against, and aside from advertizing other products within their pages, they had to market themselves more vigorously.[8] There was a submerged but quite obvious antagonism between the social decorum of the leading magazines, and their actual immersion in a competitive economy. Gradually, and in a variety of ways, a more or less transparent opportunism manifested itself. The journals did not print many reviews, but many of those that did appear were to "puff" books by the magazine's own contributors, and often books that had already been serialized in the magazine. Similarly, letters columns tended to reprint letters from girls who wrote to praise an author or story from a previous issue. Even more ignominiously, the magazines actively sought to commercialize the very children they had pretended to protect, in that they made sales people out of their subscribers. They offered prizes and free subscriptions to those who could bring in new readers. An example of this incitement of the readers' sales potential is the note in *Riverside Magazine*, "A Word to Our Young Folks," which offered a rising scale of success, from "premiums," through "special premiums," to "grand premiums." There was nearly always a certain awkwardness or conflict of tone in this kind of promotion. In 1865, *Our Young Folks* printed a letter sending love from the editors to their "little friends," and reminding them that this magazine's premiums were "the most generous which ever were offered for subscribers." The appeal became more naked in subsequent years. In 1867 the same little friends were told that the editors had "given authors and artists the highest prices to work," and that the next volume – for which they had "already expended many thousands of dollars" – would be even better. But the editors expected a pay-off in kind from their readers: "So now for your share." The reader is more or less blackmailed into finding new subscribers. And year by year, the same editors claim to "offer much larger prizes . . . and more of them." A final instance of this ironic tension between gentility and the desire to turn a profit is to be found in an 1871 issue of *Our Young Folks*, which announced an essay competition on the question, "What are the characteristics of a gentleman?" As an inducement to take part, it announced that cash prizes were to be won: the best boy's essay would get $20, as would the best by a girl.[9]

We have, then, what Kelly calls an "institutional matrix" which seeks to preserve gentry values, even though the means of doing so is that of capitalizing on a developing market. This matrix was more uniformly effective in relation to middle-class girls, whose connection to the economic order was more intensely resisted. They were important consumers-in-waiting, who had nevertheless to remain aloof from trade. The fiction for and about these girls offers a variety of perspectives on the values and uses of both new and old money, and the concern itself – with spending and becoming a woman – seldom goes away. I only analyze a small selection from the vast store of magazine stories, but each of my chosen stories manifests the much more widely apparent thematic of spending and becoming a woman. The stories here are intended to be representative, but each is chosen because it offers a slightly different point of view from within the continuum of responses to money and social identity, from accommodation and to resistance.

Elizabeth Stuart Phelps Ward's "More Ways than One" was first published in *Our Young Folks* in April 1871. It turns on eighteen-year-old Beeb Burden, a girl whose mother is ill, and whose father can only afford one hired girl. Beeb must help with the housework, and with looking after the baby. Wanting less drudgery and more time for study, Beeb calculates how much she would need to earn for her mother to hire a nursery-maid. Her mother assents to the idea that Beeb work outside the home to pay for a nursery-maid, assuring Beeb that she will not think her "ugly nor selfish nor undutiful nor undaughterly nor anything." Beeb sets out to find business opportunities, but these are few and far between in her hometown of Northampton, Massachusetts. A characteristic New England air of meagreness and genteel decline besets Beeb's life. She decides to leave this behind and get involved with modern, technologically driven commerce: she will become an agent for a silver-plating electrotyper she has seen advertized in a magazine. From the beginning, then, magazines are important in that they connect a girl from the country with an inventive, metropolitan elsewhere with its new business opportunities. Discovering that the "Elegant Electrotyper" actually works, Beeb raises capital for her venture by selling her best sash and gloves to a friend for four dollars. She then goes to stay with a cousin in another town to start her business. Clearly she is doubtful about the class implications of her actions, though the cousin tells her that she can "sell silver-plating and be a lady too" (76). In spite of assurances, Beeb feels like a "pedlar" rather than a lady, and this sense is confirmed by her first attempt to make a sale. Going to a big house, she states her business to a servant, and is "briskly" told to go round to the back door. Then the cook tells her they have no need of plating as only solid silver is kept in the house. Beeb subsequently goes to a very modest house, at which a lower-class woman shows interest in the product, but cannot afford to buy. Beeb's commercial interactions are an exploration of the boundaries of wealth and class. She makes her first sale when she encounters a former seminary class-mate. Not only does this friend buy, but she takes Beeb to a neighbor to make further sales. The narrative brings Beeb into contact with both extremes of the socio-economic scale, in that she encounters wealth and poverty. Crucially, however, the story then renegotiates the more elusive intermediate divisions of class. Beeb herself is the member of a declining rural gentry, and she senses very keenly the contradiction between being a lady and being seen to work in public. However, the story permits Beeb to acquire the skills and earning power of the rising white-collar work force, while still remaining acceptable to her seminary-educated peers. There is a constructive compromise between rising and falling groups, and the girl is the winner. Beeb goes on to make the necessary one hundred dollars in four weeks, and so escapes a year of child-minding.

What one notices about this brief and simple story is that it allows a middle-class girl who is not in immediate need to be speculative and commercial rather than home-loving. But Beeb knows she must continue her education and not become a drudge. To preserve her gentility, she must also put it at risk. It is only by working as an agent for silver-plating that she is able to become once more a "lady of leisure" (p. 79). Her narrative encapsulates the girl's need to negotiate between tradition and change, between an increasingly unproductive genteel residuum and an exciting but potentially *déclassé* commercialism. Above all, enterprise is seen as a means to power and mobility: Beeb makes money, gets to travel, and effectively becomes an employer in her own right as her earnings pay for the nursery-maid. But there is nevertheless a reactionary spirit at work. Beeb will return to her sequestered Northampton home to pursue refinement. More insidiously, at no point does the story concern itself with the status, desires, or futures of the hired girls. In this respect the focus is class-ed in an automatic, unspoken way. We are implicitly assumed to be interested in Beeb's fate alone, as someone who is already well-placed to become an agent not just of electrotyping but of social change.

Ward and others carried out such renegotiations in many stories. To show her in a slightly more adventurous light, there is "The Girl Who Could Not Write a Composition," published in *Our Young Folks* in August, 1871. In this instance, the heroine, Jemima "Jem" Jasper, is a western girl who has been sent from her Illinois home to New England to be instructed in high culture. She attends an "awful Massachusetts boarding-school," at which she manages very well in practical and outdoors subjects such as mathematics, natural history, and gymnastics. But she is poor at Latin, Greek, and composition. Her success in modern and useful subjects does not outweigh her failure in the ancient and more culturally esteemed ones: Jem is asked to leave the school. She returns to Illinois, where her carpenter-father resolves to make a place for her in which she will feel useful and clever. She begins to assist him in his work, and when he dies, she carries on the business. Relatives suggest that this "won't do," and that she had better "take in plain sewing" or "teach a few little children at home" (p. 24). But Jem makes a success of her venture and, in an admittedly contrived ending, her boarding-school principal, travelling through the west, stops in at the store and discovers that "that stupid Miss Jasper" is now worth fifty thousand dollars.

Again Ward depicts a brave, energetic girl, who has taken command of her own destiny. As with "More Ways than One," "The Girl Who Could Not Write a Composition" suggests that women of the rising class should not hamper themselves with established notions of a housebound "true womanhood." There is a further liberating element in "The Girl Who Could Not Write a Composition," in that it abandons New England as the place where things happen, and at the same time it undermines New England canons of worth. In both stories, an active, interesting future depends upon a willingness to step outside the realm of the traditional lady, and this means entering the world of buying and selling. This was often the case for the authors themselves. Ward's own escape from an impoverished domesticity was achieved via her career as a writer – a career in which she was promoted by Annie Fields. She chose not to marry until she was in her forties, and by then her financial independence was assured. She and many other women writers were both of the establishment and to one side of it. Often unmarried, widowed, or divorced, they had a range of personal and professional experiences which caused them to question as much as to affirm genteel womanhood. Obliged to enter the commercial world themselves, they were on occasion willing that their heroines should do likewise. It would be easy to overstate this adventurous element, however. More often than not, the magazine fiction betrays unease over the culture of money, and much of this reactionary fiction is for and about girls. Louise Chandler Moulton's "The Cousin from Boston" is a classic example, and it displays its diffidence towards change, as many other stories do, via an exploration of the exchange between country and city. Published in *Youth's Companion* in December 1872, Moulton's story tells of two close friends, Sophie and Nelly, whose relationship is disturbed when Nelly's cousin Lill comes to visit. Previously the two girls had enjoyed an unself-conscious happiness in the beauty of nature, but Lill introduces a different kind of beauty:

> If you are a country girl, who read, and have ever been suddenly confronted with a city young lady in the height of fashion, to whom you were expected to make yourself agreeable, you can, perhaps, understand what I felt... [Lill] was a beauty. She was a little taller than Nelly or I – a slender, graceful creature, with a high-bred air. It was years before they had begun to crimp little girls' hair, but I think Lill's must have been crimped. It was a perfect golden cloud about her face and shoulders, and all full of little shining waves and ripples. Then what eyes she had – star-bright and deep blue, with lashes so long that when they drooped they cast a shadow on the pale pink of her cheeks. Her features were all delicate and pure; her hands were white, with one or two glittering rings upon them; and her clothes! My own gowns had not seemed ill-made before; but now I thought Nelly and I both looked as if we had come out of the ark. (p. 89)

Sophie is plunged into a covetous gloom by Lill's apparent wealth and sophistication. Jealous, and feeling that she cannot compete, she decides to avoid "Miss Fine-Airs" from the city. Things become worse when Sophie learns that Nelly is to return to Boston with Lill, and to spend a year at the same school. Nelly is even to go to the same superior dressmaker. After a miserable year's absence, Nelly returns, but Lill has fallen and damaged her hip over the winter, and is now an invalid. She is still a beauty, but failing fast. Lill confesses to Sophie that she too had been jealous, but is now pleased that Nelly will have her best friend to comfort her after Lill herself has died. Surely enough, Lill dies, and Sophie and Nelly's friendship proves to be the "inalienable riches of a whole life" (p. 93). Although Moulton is more admiring of city sophistication than is Alcott, there is a similar thematics at work as in *Little Women* and *An Old-Fashioned Girl*. Lill is never seen to be wrong or bad, but nonetheless her premature glory is ominously shadowed. Whereas Alcott insists that her characters reform, Moulton lets hers escape into death. For both, the important lesson is that buying into an expensively elegant womanhood will cost more than dollars. It will exact a price of the body or soul. Good girls everywhere are encouraged to be content with their lot. All readers are reminded that the "riches" of friendship are worth more in their "inalienable" permanence than the passing beauties of fashion. At the same time, however, even the country girls in Moulton's world are well-bred. They do not work; they read Dickens and Scott; their dresses are not handed down, but made specifically for them. And even though metropolitan life is brought into question, the girls' connectedness with the centre is established. In spite of the mistrust of citified glory, this story, like that of Beeb in "More Ways Than

One" and of Polly in *An Old-Fashioned Girl*, makes the attempt to rescue the rural middle-class figure, to bring her into constructive relation with the rising metropolitan class.

There is a complex nostalgia at work in this story and in many others like it. The longing is for more simple, country ways, but the story's power is derived from a jealous fear of being left behind. Nelly's year of Boston schools and fashions makes Sophie's rural pleasures seem empty and commonplace. The story thrives on the lure of worldly pleasures and accomplishments, even as it questions their value. Moulton herself became a leading Boston socialite, but she believed that certain lessons and rules are appropriate to certain times of life. In childhood, naturalness and innocence must be preserved, even if adulthood will require a highly developed social awareness. This is the trick of much of the magazine fiction. It reveals to children the importance of their remaining innocent, which in itself acknowledges that childhood innocence is already endangered. The fiction effectively invites children to stave off the knowingness that is also presented to them as their fate. They are encouraged to feel nostalgia over their own childhoods, even as they are living them.[10] They are urged to live up to innocence, to perform it, in a curiously worldly way. There is an air of belatedness about much of this fiction. The old ways are not valued as they once were, and the point of view is often retrospective and "lost." Even the more resistant fiction encodes its own hopelessness, as with the repeated lessons on the relative unimportance of wealth, which admit by their endless denials that money is very important. There is a reluctant awareness that older, "country" values, however worthy, cannot remove the peril of being left behind.

Sarah Orne Jewett is one of the most admired of American writers precisely because she insisted on the detail of the country scene, or indeed of the "backwater." In her work, the regionalist element that was suggested in the country–city scenario takes on a much more developed and interesting form. Certainly there is more at stake in Jewett's work than the moralized pre-consumerist/consumerist binary that we find in much other girls' fiction. She does not offer the "backwater" as a rather uniform, pre-modern ideal, but pays close attention to a variety of idiosyncrasies both admirable and tragic. A recent commentator has described Jewett's as an "intimist art," in that as with the French painter Vuillard, there is a "microcosmic frame" which creates "a shared atmosphere of heightened contemplation."[11] In this respect, Jewett also bears out Brodhead's observation that regionalism marks a distance from the pre-War sentimental novel, in that regionalism offers a complex literary rendering that is freed from "discourses of piety and domestic instruction" (p. 133). But while Jewett brings a characteristically regionalist subtlety to girls' fiction, her sympathy and her interests still have class-ed limitations. One of the Jewett stories that Bernardete and Moe choose to reprint is a particularly fine example of regionalist girls' fiction, but even so, it affirms – in admittedly agonized form – the class-ed aspect of the post-War tradition. "The Girl with the Cannon Dresses" was first published in *Riverside Magazine* in August, 1870. It is narrated by Alice Channing, an eighteen-year-old young lady who is recovering from an unspecified illness. Her well-to-do family plans to "go to the beach or mountains with her as soon as the hotels open." But the doctor, after a private consultation with Alice, suggests something more basic, and less fashionable. Alice is to be sent to the family's former housekeeper, who has married and moved up into the hills of New Hampshire. The house is a mile from its nearest neighbors, and two miles from a small village called the Corners. While in the hills, Alice meets "the queerest folks" (p. 164), namely the Bunt family. Ten-year-old Dulcidora Bunt surprises her in the woods. Initially Alice doesn't know quite what connection she has or wishes for with this strange girl: "I want to ask you some questions, but I don't know what they are" (p. 165). One of the queerest things about Dulcy is her dress. The calico had been bought by her father from a pedlar who was selling it cheaply. It features a pattern of inch-long cannons, each of which is being fired by a man in a red shirt, under the word "Union." Mr. Bunt bought so much of it that Dulcy has three identical gowns. Dulcy has heard a great deal about "Miss Alice" from the housekeeper, and has already fallen in love with her from afar at church. She worries that Alice is too old to be her friend, but decides that she is "a little girl in [her] face" (p. 169). Alice assures Dulcy that she enjoys not wearing the "grown-up clothes" of her city life, and she wants to "make believe" that she is the same age as Dulcy. She decides that they will meet a lot, and as Dulcy lives too far from school to get an education, Alice will give her some lessons. Meanwhile, Alice receives packages of books and shop-bought delicacies from home – canned fruit, candy, olives, tinned biscuits – all of which she shares with Dulcy. These signs of consumerist modernity underscore the fact that Alice's sphere is different to the time-bound eccentricities of Dulcy's family, even if, for a while, the two girls can become friends.

At the end of her story, Jewett brings the reader up to date. Dulcy is now at a country academy twenty miles from home, and Alice hopes that Dulcy "will blossom into a district-school teacher" (p. 172). She thinks back to when she left the Corners. She remembers that when she turned and looked back, Dulcy had "thrown herself on the grass" and "was crying very hard." Back in her own home after her period of rustication, Alice contemplates two photographs. One is of herself in her striped cambric jacket and large straw hat. One is of Dulcy, and is in its very technology a sign of backwardness: it is introduced condescendingly as a "large square tintype" which had been "taken by a traveling artist of renown in those parts." By Alice's "particular request," it shows Dulcy in one of her cannon dresses. These two images, with which Jewett ends her story, encapsulate the gulf between the two girls. Alice's stylish walking outfit marks her as a summer visitor. Dulcy's cannon dress suggests at best a haphazard relation to feminine style. Why does Jewett make Dulcy's dresses the defining image of the story? The hard-wearing calico was obviously intended as some kind of wrap or upholstery, and not for dressmaking. Its Union cannons place the wearer in the period of the Civil War, and not in the "now" of Alice's gilded age fashion. There is also the explosiveness of the image: the cannons are perpetually in the process of being fired. This suggests Dulcy's adolescent incoherence: she has emotional explosions, and cries passionate tears, and gives intense expression to her sense of loss. The fact that she is from "the Corners" also signals a certain as yet unassimilated awkwardness. But this adolescent quality is itself the symbol of a difficult transition between other categories. Dulcy is emergent in that she wants what the "young lady" has, but she is residual in that she belongs to the "past" of rural living. Small wonder that Dulcy cries to see her friend leave. Alice is moving toward a world of progressive styles and accomplishments, a journey for which Dulcy has neither the money nor the "class" to follow. Jewett's narrator looks back fondly, but does not return. The exchange is regretful, but it is not resisted. The possibility of "Union" that is written all over Dulcy's dresses proves to be partial and temporary.[12] Again, the narrative point of view is middle class: it is mobile, and conscious of its own assurance with regard to the gradations of cultural expertise. The story is told by "Miss Alice," not by the housekeeper or the lonely child. And though this story is so much more intricately and stylishly realized than the Moulton story, the invigorating naturalness of the country is reaffirmed in comparison to the smothering deadliness of the town or resort. But the moral is less severe than with Moulton or Alcott: the country has become a charming excursion rather than the secure base of correct feeling. And perhaps here we start to press against the limitations of this story and of Jewett's regionalist point of view. Although this is girls' fiction, it bears the "touristic" marks of regionalism. Brodhead again provides a clue here, in that this story, with its advance into and retreat from the country, supports his comment that regionalism is a kind of "experiential imperialism," and as such it confirms the "mental habit of acquisitiveness" that was implicit in adult, regionalist fiction (p. 133).[13]

I want to conclude this discussion of short fiction with a story that, in a very different way, suggests a mood of compromise between women writers and worldly consumption. Mary Terhune's "Miss Butterfly" does not concern itself with a country–city binary at all, but somewhat unusually with a binary of youth and age. Terhune became famous for romance novels published under the name of Marion Harland, and she also wrote the tremendously successful *Common Sense in the Household* (1871), as well as writing stories and articles for children's magazines. "Miss Butterfly" was published in *Wide Awake* in March 1893. It features Miss Betty Fry, only daughter of the richest widow in town. Miss Fry has gained her sobriquet from a child who, dazzled by her youthful beauty, called her "Miss Butterfly" by mistake. At the start, the narrator invites us to take a dim view of Miss Fry. She has no "staying power." Having attended a "fashionable seminary" where she learns virtually nothing, her mother takes her abroad. But in the real time of the story, Miss Fry has lost her pretty dimples, and her beauty has faded. Almost embarrassingly, she has kept the mannerisms and affectations that had made her so charming as a girl. Her mother has died, and she lives, with servants, in "the fine old homestead upon the hill." Neighbors comment on the fact that she has not married, and that she has "had it easy," but they do not begrudge her. The narrator introduces herself to the story as "an intolerant chit of fifteen, who had lived in Book-land and Dream-world until [she] was clothed in self-conceit as with a garment" (pp. 119–20). This girl, Miss Dowling, has called at Miss Fry's to ask on her mother's behalf if she will take an interest in "a poor family in the lower part of the town" (p. 123). Miss Dowling is surprised to find Miss Fry amusing a group of children with songs and games. As a final treat, Miss Fry shows the children her butterfly as it feeds from a drop of honey on a pearl paper-knife. This is in the middle of winter, and when one of the children's mothers comments that "naturalists tell us that the butterfly is an ephemeron," the reader detects that Miss Fry too has survived beyond her proper era and will soon be destroyed. Miss Dowling continues to suppose her hostess to be "trite, vapid, and, I was sure, heartless." She cannot enjoy the exquisite china and gold spoons, or any aspect of the comfort that surrounds the wealthy spinster:

The whole world was padded, and warmed, and scented for this useless little insect. What mattered it that winter, and poverty, and illness, and sorrow were in other homes, so long as she still sat in the rose's heart? (p. 124)

This prejudice is shaken when Miss Fry gives her a cheque for one hundred dollars, to go to the family in need. So shocked is Miss Dowling by the older woman's generosity, that she calls Miss Fry by her nickname:

"O, Miss Butterfly! Oh! – I beg your pardon." I stopped there, red as fire and longing to sink clean out of sight. (p. 124)

Miss Fry tells her not to worry, and then, as if she had read Miss Dowling's mind, comments on her own nature: "I admire energy, and thrift, and all that, immensely, but, as my slangy nephews say, I wasn't built that way" (p. 124). The following March the old homestead is destroyed by fire. Miss Fry is discovered in the grounds, wrapped in an ermine opera-cloak. She soon falls into a stupor and dies.

Terhune's story is full of moderating impulses. Miss Fry is indeed vapid and trite, but she is also kind-hearted, and a willing benefactor. There is the familiar concern with money and morality. Miss Fry's whimsical personal generosity is out of season and soon to disappear. The future would seem to belong to the "intolerant chit" of the middle class, but there is the crucial hesitation of judgement over the question of femininity and money. The young narrator is forced to rethink. Without entirely surrendering her own bourgeois sense of responsibility, she does learn to appreciate a different type of womanhood. Miss Fry is childish, but this is a part of her impressible goodness. She also has the power to revive innocence in the later generation. Miss Dowling suddenly reverts from the false childhood of the "intolerant chit" to an unselfconscious childhood in which Miss Fry's name is still "Miss Butterfly," and in which she cannot control her blushes. Miss Fry plunges the girl back into a recognition of her own incoherent and emergent state. And the implication is that some fluidity between the stages of womanhood, and between the classes of society – some measure of incoherence – is valuable.

To enter into the protected warmth of the Fry homestead is akin to Alice's journey into the New Hampshire hills in "The Girl in the Cannon Dresses." It is to enter into a different economic realm, and to take warning from it. For all girl-protagonists, money and womanhood must be accommodated to each other: to grow up is to acquire the right attitude toward money. But this process is not simple, and is only achieved at a cost. Lill has to die so that Nelly and Sophie revalue their friendship; Miss Dowling learns tolerance in relation to a "dying breed." There is a punitive element at work: the subliminal cause of death with Lill and Miss Butterfly is luxury and sophistication, whereas the others survive because they have a moderated relation to wealth. But with Miss Dowling, Alice, Sophie, and Beeb, there is the unspoken assumption that they will have the power of money. The womanhood at issue, that is worth investigating and resolving and growing into, is always middle class, even though it is not specified as such. It is the middle-class girls around whom the drama will pivot. Other girls and women may be charming, but they are more easily expendable. The narrative may leave them in the country; it may hire them and then let them go. The focal point is always the girl of the class that can and must adjust. Much like the women who wrote them, the girl-protagonists of these stories must locate a sense of social possibility that acknowledges disinterested gentry values, but alongside the modern forms that will allow them to command and maintain power. In this respect, the stories allegorize the institutional pressures that their authors and editors were under in a rapidly changing publishing industry. The fictional girl must confront girlish problems, but at the same time, she must assuage the fears and give voice to the concerns of an uncertainly placed social and cultural elite.

3

Dramas of exclusion

This chapter explores two bestselling novels that offer an interesting variant fear on the part of a previously dominant class that new money and upward mobility would leave them stranded. Newly conspicuous markers of class may have given pleasure to those on the rise, but they threatened others with exclusion. I focus on *Hans Brinker, or The Silver Skates* (1865) and *Five Little Peppers and How They Grew* (1881), because both stage the spectacle of a sudden and apparently irrecoverable loss of status. In the urbanizing social flux of mid-century, people had to ask once more, of themselves and others, where and how did they fit in? How were you to be known and assessed if you were not part of a pre-existent and stable community? Karen Halttunen suggests that this situation produced a culture of performance, whereby people displayed their social values via deportment, speech, fashion, and accomplishments. People were placed by their ability to style themselves. This was a fragile system, for a person might well perform an identity to which he or she had no authentic claim. There was a consequent preoccupation with "confidence men" and "painted ladies," people who were both more and less than they appeared to be. From another perspective, however, there were those who were losing out in this social and financial flux. What were to be the consequences for those whose fortunes had tumbled? Could you still count as a lady if you were not fashionably dressed? More crucially, could you still count as a lady if, of a sudden, you had to go out to work? As the upwardly mobile sought to make discriminations, the downwardly mobile wondered if they were to be excluded. These issues have already featured to some extent, especially in relation to *Little Women*. But Alcott and other writers provide a robust reassurance for readers, in that the girl-heroine's moral independence and hard work will enable her to reassert her worth. This is why the drama of *Little Women* is primarily that of the heroine's improvement. In the narratives that I designate "dramas of exclusion," the heroine is still good and resourceful, but this is no longer enough to counteract the social paranoia generated by economic uncertainty. Although *Hans Brinker* and *Five Little Peppers* do offer happy endings, these are not achieved through the agency of the heroine. Rather, the rescue of the main characters is as fortuitous as was their initial fall. This points to a contemporary awareness, implicitly denied by much girls' fiction, that in a radically unstable financial environment, the fact of either success or failure has little to do with being "deserving." Both *Hans Brinker* and *Five Little Peppers* are interested in the girl's "goodness," but their dramas are intensified by the fear that morality and social power are not securely wedded.

Mary Mapes Dodge, one of the most famous and influential figures in nineteenth-century children's writing, is a perfect case in point. She was from a well-to-do and educated background, but her family's fortunes took a series of sudden and severe blows. This financial collapse was compounded when Dodge's husband committed suicide, leaving her a widow at a young age. Although she was to recoup her position via her work as an author and editor, *Hans Brinker* comes early in her career, and reveals an obsessive fear of exclusion.[1] The novel is something of a misfit here, in that it concerns Hans at least as much as his sister, Gretel, and generally it is as much populated by boys as by girls. It was typical of the most esteemed children's fiction, in that it was thought to transcend its category. *Hans Brinker* was especially popular with girls, but the *Atlantic Monthly* noted that although the novel "is addressed, indeed, to young people, [it] may be read with pleasure and profit by their elders."[2] It is especially useful to me for the clarity with which it exemplifies the drama of exclusion. *Hans Brinker* is set in Holland, and much of it takes the form of a thinly disguised travelogue. There are frequent and prolonged descriptions of Dutch systems of government, architecture, cultural traditions, and domestic interiors. The interiors are of particular interest, in that they are characterized by a profusion of old and valuable objects. Floors and furniture are "waxed and polished to the utmost." Rich colours and textures of fabrics are lovingly noted, and sometimes even priced: "It was a Japanese spread, marvelous in texture as well as in its variety of brilliant coloring, and worth, as Ben afterward learned, not less than three hundred dollars" (p. 139). The narrative gaze makes these private, wealthy homes accessible, in that the reader is unhesitatingly taken inside and invited to share in the pleasures of looking. The shine on every polished surface indicates a love of property that the narrator then mimics in the writing of her story. There also seems to be a deliberate contrast with the mass-produced objects of modern America, the value of which might fluctuate with the fashions. There is nothing transient or pinchbeck about these Dutch goods. Also, unlike the modern wealth of stocks and shares, there seems little chance that this type of accumulated value will vanish into thin air. The very size of the objects – "massive" chairs and cases, a bell-rope of glass beads "as thick as your wrist" – reassures the reader that this property is literally, emphatically solid. And these authentic and laboriously cared-for domestic spaces also assure us that there is nothing disingenuous or merely performed about the owners' position.

Dodge, who had not been to Holland when she wrote the novel, uses that country as a symbol of security and permanence. The wealth is old bourgeois, in a country in which everyone works to maintain what they have. Dodge even gives us explicit reassurance that in Holland one cannot be ruined by a financial panic. She recounts an incident that makes the point that speculation itself has been discredited. After a bout of feverish speculation in tulip bulbs in which the whole country became involved, the Dutch state made it clear that such risky obligations need not and should not be honoured:

Creditors went to law, and the law turned its back upon them; debts made in gambling were not binding, it said. Then there was a time! Thousands of rich speculators reduced to beggary in an hour. As old Beckman [the historian] says, "the bubble burst." (p. 57)

Dodge finds Holland particularly attractive because the sudden downward mobility that threatened the American entrepreneurial class has, she believes, been effectively outlawed.

Her use of Holland to redress her own social and financial anxieties is also construed with the key myth of Dutch identity – that of the boy who put his finger in the dike. It is tempting to read this as a metaphor for the dangers of adolescent incoherence, and that may be one of the implications. Hans and Gretel are good, simple characters who never become adolescent. The waters are, as it were kept out. As we will see, however, other characters are more troubled by an ingress of questionable thoughts: the narrative must reward Hans and Gretel, while judging the more passionate and interiorized child-characters. But whatever the psychological significance of the dike, its explicit meaning is more narrowly moral and social. The boy's act is not self-interested, but saves the commonwealth of the whole nation. As a result, the notion of leakage serves as a metaphor of community spirit in the face of individual weakness: "Not a leak can show itself anywhere, either, in its politics, honor, or public safety, that a million fingers are not ready to stop it at any cost" (p. 92). This communal inclusiveness is seen to mitigate and even to counteract divisions of class.[3] Hans Brinker's family has been impoverished by an accident that has left the father in a more or less comatose state. Their fortunes have plummeted to such an extent that they now live in a "low cottage," wearing coarse and ragged clothing, and surviving by "drudgery." But even though they now labor with their hands, they are not beneath the notice of the more fortunate. As Peter, who is from a comfortable family, reflects of Hans: "I like that boy, rich or poor" (p. 69). But the point of Dodge's novel, and its main drama, lies in the "leaks" that have begun to appear in this model of social inclusion. This is dramatized in the form of a race on the Zuider Zee. The prize for the winner is a pair of silver skates, but more generally the race functions as a test of social legitimacy. Hilda, a good-natured, wealthy girl, assures Hans and Gretel that "[a]nyone may enter for the prize" (p. 18). But this is questioned by others. A mean-spirited boy named Carl puts the case to the other well-to-do children:

I say, boys, let's put a stop to those young rag-pickers from the idiot's cottage joining the race. Hilda must be crazy to think of it. Katrinka Flack and Rychie Korbes are furious at the very idea of racing with the girl; as for my part, I don't blame them. As for the boy, if we've a spark of manhood in us we will scorn the very idea of –

At this point Carl is brought up short by a more egalitarian youth: "No fellow with a spark of manhood in him would refuse to let in two good skaters just because they were poor" (p. 35). But the growing desire to discriminate bursts through the narrative at other points, too. Of the beautiful and fortunate Rychie, we are told:

To her mind, the poor peasant girl Gretel was not a human being, a God-created creature like herself – she was only something that meant poverty, rags, and dirt. Such as Gretel had no right to feel, to hope; above all, they should never cross the paths of their betters – that is, not in a disagreeable way. They could toil and labor for them at a respectful distance, even admire them, if they would do it humbly, but nothing more. If they rebel, put them down – if they suffer, don't trouble me about it, was Rychie's secret motto. (p. 73)

The fact that Rychie's motto is secret suggests that this exclusiveness, this desire to abject the poor, is still a dissident point of view. The narrative invites us to judge Carl and Rychie. They wish to use their social preeminence to mark out impermeable class boundaries, thus securing their own position. The symbolic event of the race works against them. All may enter, and the spectators are drawn from all classes and creeds, with masters and servants, "girls from the Roman Catholic orphan house," those "dressed like Parisians" alongside "[s]hy young rustics in brazen buckles," and so on. The racers themselves are heterogeneous: Hans is one of four peasants to take part, and Gretel takes part in and wins the girl's event. Hans is in a good position to win in the boy's race, as is the amiable Peter. Carl does his best, but the victory will go to one of the good, equitable boys. In the general spirit of non-discrimination, the narrator refuses to have a favorite between the rich good boy and the poor good boy:

Carl soon breaks the ranks, rushing through with a whiff! Fly Hans, fly Peter, don't let Carl beat [you] again. Carl the bitter, Carl the insolent. [He] is flagging, but you are as strong as ever. Hans and Peter, Peter and Hans; which is foremost? We love them both. We scarcely care which is the fleeter. (p. 223)

In a nation in which community spirit is bound up with the need to preserve the dikes against the incursions of the sea, Carl's "breaking ranks" is a personal failing, but it also has connotations of national treachery. Meanwhile, when one of Peter's skate-straps breaks, Hans insists on giving him his: "You have called me your friend" (p. 224). Peter wins the race, and our sense of the right-mindedness of the people and their systems is affirmed once more. As a slyly humorous reviewer for the *Galaxy* noted of this morally favorable turn of events, "We see that there is, in the long run, little to regret in the possession of Holland by such a people as the Dutch."[4] The happy ending is completed when Mr. Brinker emerges from his illness and reveals where he had hid the family's money. The Brinkers' social status is secure once more. But throughout, Dodge has used her novel to pose the question, how poor may one become and still be respectable? The narrative is driven by the fear that poverty removes any claim to social rights and social value. Even in the idealized state of an imagined Holland, being poor can push one beyond the margins of what it is to be "a human being, a God-created creature."

In *Hans Brinker*, a characteristically contemporary fear over social fragmentation is overcome with the vision of the race, in which all may succeed, and around which all are merged into one joyful crowd. Dodge as narrator can guard against all the disasters that beset her and her family in real life, and in addition she can award victory to her favourite characters. This combination of a fear of an irrecoverable loss of status with a final, willful optimism, is equally apparent in one of the other great popular successes of the period, Harriet Lothrop's *Five Little Peppers and How They Grew* (1881). This novel and its sequels are more openly hungry than precursors by Dodge or Alcott, in that they show an almost desperate readiness to merge with the monied, urban class, and to acquire its advantages. *Five Little Peppers* concerns a widow, Mrs. Pepper, and her five children, who live in a "little brown house." The family is full of "jollity and fun," but since the death of the father, Mrs. Pepper has "had hard work to scrape together money enough to put bread into her children's mouths, and to pay the rent on the little brown house." She takes in sewing and gets by, but is troubled by the fact that her children are not being educated. As she puts it light-heartedly: "they haven't had any bringing up, they've just scrambled up!"[5] But money is insignificant in comparison to her main priority, which is to maintain her children in her own home: "Mother's rich enough . . . if we can only keep together" (p. 20). The suggestion of better things to come is introduced with the appearance of Jasper King. He is staying in a hotel with his rich but bad-tempered father. Lothrop was a great admirer of Alcott, and Jasper, like Laurie in *Little Women*, yearns for the domestic hubbub of a less wealthy household. Eventually he prevails upon his father to visit the Peppers. This leads to the most telling exchange in the novel:

Mr. King had been nervously putting his hand in his pocket during the last few moments that the children were together; but when he glanced at Mrs. Pepper's eyes, something made him draw it out again hastily, as empty as he put it in. (p. 229)

The crucial point that Lothrop makes here is that though one family is poor and lives on bread and potatoes, and one is rich and drifts from resort to resort, both are still – just about – of the same class. There can be no "betters" on the social plateau of gentility, even though there may be richer and poorer. Had Mr. King offered money, it would have been on the supposition that the Peppers were "inferiors" to whom he might offer patronage. Mrs. Pepper's eyes tell him that she will not surrender her claim to gentility to her present need for money. Here as elsewhere there is a tension *within* the middle class, or rather, a recognition that, with rapid but uneven economic development, the middle class embraced considerable disparities of wealth. These tensions resurface when Jasper, having returned to the city, falls ill and wishes Polly Pepper to visit him. Mr. King begins by offering Mrs. Pepper a kind of bribe. He will ensure "every advantage possible" for Polly, including "the best foundation for a musical education that the city could afford; also lessons in the schoolroom under the boy's private tutor" (p. 275). But Mrs. Pepper will not allow her daughter to accept the invitation while it is construed as being to the child's advantage:

[N]othing broke Mrs. Pepper's resolve, until, at last, the old gentleman wrote one day that Jasper, being in such failing health, really depended on Polly to cheer him up. That removed the last straw that made it "putting one's self under an obligation," which, to Mrs. Pepper's independent soul, had seemed insurmountable. (pp. 275–76)

This delicate negotiation between independence and patronage is managed so well that the whole Pepper family ends up living in the Kings' city mansion. For all that the Peppers seem to become indebted, their lack of a fortune is offset by the observation that "there's good blood there" (p. 309). This sense is confirmed when it is discovered that Mrs. Pepper is the long-lost cousin of Mr. King's equally wealthy son-in-law. Mrs. Pepper had avoided making herself known because she had heard that her cousin was rich. She felt that she could not revive the kinship without seeming self-interested; and of course, to be self-interested is to be "common."

Lothrop's novel exemplifies the same bad faith or hypocrisy that one finds in *Little Women* and elsewhere. Gentility is defined as a moralized behavioral code, but the narrative hastens to ensure that the genteel are also wealthy. Once again there is an insistence on the merger between old money and new, between class as conduct and class as financial power. The girl-reader is encouraged to see beyond material wealth to a different kind of status. But she is also shown, especially in *Hans Brinker* and *Five Little Peppers*, that those without money are socially endangered. An obvious social paranoia is at work, as the narrative explores the fear of being excluded, before stooping to rescue the virtuous. The fact that this drama was reworked time after time in the great bestsellers of the "golden age" of children's fiction suggests its potency not only for girls and other readers, but for female authors – women who often used their writing as a means of lifting themselves above the very dangers that they describe. Fiction becomes a rectifying, a tidying up, a mission to ensure social justice. But in this instance, social justice involves an imaginative appropriation of the good fortune that was also being presented as questionable. The ultimate message of this fearful and envious fiction is that while money is not everything, the good ought to have it. And in *Hans Brinker* and *Five Little Peppers* in particular, there is the suggestion that, in a shifting and treacherous financial environment, the good cannot be expected to make their own fortune. If they are "deserving," the narrator will bestow it upon them.

PART II
Fulfillment

4

Romantic speculations

Much of the fiction discussed so far, though it attempts to negotiate social and economic change, remains pre-consumerist in its overall tendency. It is aware of growing prosperity and the democratization of polite culture, but its response is often ambivalent. It exhibits a fear of loss of caste, especially in relation to the rise of a mobile urban class. There is a corresponding sense that democratization involves vulgarization: new money pays for the shows of gentility, but misses out on its values. But there is also a possibility of critique from within the pre-consumerist model: an early heroine such as Jo March is hungry for alternative worlds, in which radically different identities may be imagined and performed (and this is to be found in other contemporary texts, such as *Gypsy Breynton* [1865] and *What Katy Did* [1872]). A restless, theatricalizing spirit manifests itself, and is never entirely quelled by a reformative, rule-bound ethos. The writers of Alcott's generation value the restless element, and relate it, in Romantic fashion, to the child's connectedness to Nature. Jo loves to run and to climb trees, and girls more generally are shown to have a spontaneous and unself-conscious love of "romping." This first generation of writers was strongly influenced by Romantic ideas, but a conformist morality is still the primary context of the girl's self-exploration. However attractive Romantic "wildness" may be, it is also the sign of an unregenerate nature. Women writers do not wish to stifle the wild self entirely, but they want to show improvement via a series of disciplinary scenarios. The first generation writes in relation to a Romantic–Calvinist dialectic, except that, as we saw with Alcott, "modesty" is construed in social and moral rather than religious terms. There is an attempt to strike a balance between discipline and play, introspection and adventure, cathexis and spontaneity. But ultimately, the girl must internalize adult precepts: she must become self-governing. What I want to suggest now is that the Romantic tendency is the means by which the girl will be brought more fully into line with a consumerist ethos. A paradigmatic figure here is Kate Douglas Wiggin. She was the most influential of the second generation of writers for girls, and is best known for *Rebecca of Sunnybrook Farm* (1903). This novel was one of the outstanding bestsellers of the turn of the century period, and it also proved a phenomenally successful model for other writers to follow: one thinks especially of Canadian writer, Lucy Maude Montgomery's *Anne of Green Gables* (1908), and Eleanor H. Porter's *Pollyanna* (1913). *Rebecca of Sunnybrook Farm* was also the basis for a series of successful spin-offs, including a play, a film, toys, games, and girls' social clubs. Through Wiggin and her most famous creation, we can trace very clearly the Romantic impetus that takes us from first to second generation, from constraint to consumption. Also, *Rebecca* brings back into focus the sense that girls' fiction intersects with and mediates the genres of adult fiction. Wiggin's Romanticized novel was presented as the acceptable face of realism, in contrast to some of the more grimly deterministic treatments of girlhood and early womanhood that emerged at the same time, such as Crane's *Maggie: A Girl of the Streets* (1892), Norris's *McTeague* (1899), and Dreiser's *Sister Carrie* (1900).

It is appropriate to begin this exploration of Romanticism, girlhood, and consumerism with a theatrical moment. On 8 April 1911, Wiggin's stage adaptation of *Rebecca* played for the three-hundredth successive night at the Republic Theatre, New York. To mark the occasion, Wiggin wrote an epilogue to be spoken by the star, Edith Taliaferro. Wiggin used this as an opportunity to tease out the supposed reasons behind her audiences' love of the play:

> Did just a whiff of wholesome country air,
> Blowing o'er clover-fields and wayside flowers,
> Drift to your velvet-covered seats down there,
> And set you dreaming of dear, by-gone hours? –
> Or did the spirit of the eternal child,
> That works such magic in the human heart –
> Did youth, with just its native wood-notes wild,
> Charm and beguile, without conscious art?[1]

The poem sets a "wholesome" pastoral activity against a lesser, in-doors passivity. The unselfconscious child moves among natural beauties, while the fallen adults can only watch and remember. Rebecca induces in them a melancholy awareness of lost innocence. But the oppositions are not, after all, completely fixed. Although the play presents Rebecca very much as a child, in that she is supposed to be ten years old, Taliaferro was actually seventeen when she took the part.[2] Also, the "whiff of wholesome country air," however distant, does penetrate to the city theatre, and adult nostalgia only serves to prove that the eternal child is alive and well within them. Despite the plaintive note, Wiggin's verse reassures the audience that what has been lost is recoverable. It further suggests that the present has its pleasures, as all sit in their "velvet-covered seats" and dream of the "magic in the human heart." This epilogue is as much about continuity as it is about loss, and it assumes a sophisticated audience which suffers its nostalgia in comfort.

Wiggin's natural child is wholesome, free, and magical, and her Wordsworthian affiliations are clear. The child represents the means by which adults may glimpse once more their earlier, better selves. But there is an important element of compromise. Wiggin congratulates herself and her audience on how far they have come from a dusty, rural background, even as she pretends that they all yearn for a return to "native wood-notes wild." For all the nostalgia, there is an implication that the exchange of "clover-fields" for "velvet-covered seats" is a fair one. This link that Wiggin suggests between Romanticism and turn-of-the-century comforts is not entirely haphazard or inappropriate, in that cultural historians have argued that Romanticism and middle-class aspirations were mutually reinforcing. While older, more sternly religious forms placed emphasis on the surrender of self before a fearsome god, Romanticism's emphasis on the transcendent self – on the "magic in the human heart" – gave license for self-expression. The individual becomes more important, containing his or her own measure of divinity. In the American context, Emerson has a special relevance. In what is one of his most famous conceits, he writes of the restorative powers of Nature, and imagines himself as "a transparent eye-ball." His vision expands to encompass – to consume, indeed – the entire scene: "I see all." This corresponds neatly with Rebecca who, we will learn, is "all eyes."[3] The subject looks at Nature, and feels a correspondence with it. Such a moment initiates – and legitimates – the desire to possess. There is always this potential sympathy between Romanticism and modern consumerism, in that each prizes images of self-fulfillment and self-determination. This is not to say that Romanticism caused consumerism, but that at the least, consumerism could avail itself of Romanticism as a culturally esteemed validation of personalized desires. Romanticism's stress on the need for imaginative space, for constructive uncertainty, coalesced quite neatly with an entrepreneurial ethos. To have Romantic inspiration was to "indulge" in "the most high-flown speculations." The importance of recreation or imaginative renewal was a legitimation of the individual's right to pleasure. Without ever intending such a thing, Romanticism permitted the autonomous self to take part in the kind of self-theatricalizing hedonism that is essential to modern consumerism.[4] To trace the specific form this process took in Wiggin's career, we might look at her work as a teacher who had been inspired by Froebel's Romantic pedagogy of "guided play."[5] But Wiggin presents Romanticism in its most dynamic relation to consumerism in *Rebecca of Sunnybrook Farm*, in which the reader is introduced to the fiscal Romance of venture capitalism. In doing this, Wiggin also moves far beyond her predecessors. And yet, this urge toward fulfillment will also raise again the question of whether consumerism really does liberate or empower the girl, or if it is merely the form that her Foucaldian entrapment will take.

In *Rebecca* Wiggin establishes a series of juxtapositions, bringing to the fore racial, generational, and cultural differences. Initially there seems to be a preference for the Romantically marginal figure, the untamed racial other, or the free-spirited youth. The heroine, Rebecca Randall, is a disruptively "inspired" character living in a repressive New England society. The landscape itself is studded with reminders of thrift and morality: she is from the town of Temperance, and lives near Moderation. Rebecca has been sent to live with two spinster aunts because her mother cannot afford to raise all her own children (Mrs. Randall has given birth to the Wordsworthian number of seven). The encounter between Rebecca and her aunts figures the encounter between Romanticism and Calvinism, and a crucial aspect of this is that it brings into focus two different ways of understanding wealth. The spinster sisters, Miranda and Jane, represent conservative values. They have led careful, hard-working lives, and retain the status of living in "the brick house." But while Miranda is a rigid, oppressive figure, Jane is in secret sympathy with what Rebecca represents. In Jane there is "the faint echo of that wild heartbeat of her girlhood" (pp. 17, 27). Rebecca will be the means by which the liberatory truths of childhood will be revived, as the figure of the heroine will again be used to achieve a compromise between a residual Calvinism and an emergent Romantic consumerism. In her parentage Rebecca already seems to embody the tensions that she will reconcile. Her mother is from solid old New England stock, and is trying to manage a farm and pay off a mortgage. But her father, who died young, represents an infusion of the strange and wonderful. Lorenzo Randall was a half-Spanish, "dark-complected" teacher of music and dancing. The frivolity or pleasure-oriented connotations of his background were borne out in his person: he wore his hair a little longer than was usual (Miranda tells Rebecca that her father was a "Miss Nancy" [p. 78]), and was generally considered to be "handsome and luckless." This Latin, Catholic figure has had an altogether ruinous effect on the meagre profits of New England caution: he managed to squander his wife's inheritance. Rebecca's mother "had made what she called a romantic marriage, and what her sisters termed a mighty poor speculation."

Rebecca partakes of her father's wild and exciting foreignness. When she first arrives at Riverboro, she is thought to be "black as an Injun, what I can see of her – black and kind of up-an'-comin" (p. 18). The racial theme seems to take on a different aspect here, in that Rebecca and her father correspond more to the Romantic notion of the "Noble Savage" than to an inconvenient, diseased, or ignorant other. And yet, as we will see, the novel's interest in "soap" serves as a reminder that the heroine conflates both whiteness and cleanliness. At the start, however, Rebecca, in the clarity of her innocence, sees what older people have managed to hide from themselves and others. She is the "queerest" child, evoking repressed but undead sensations with a face that is, as noted, "all eyes." These eyes carry "such messages, such suggestions, such hints of sleeping power and insight, that one never tired of looking into their shining depths, nor of fancying that what one saw there was the reflection of one's own thought" (p. 7). Rebecca signifies the untrammelled and spontaneous power of the natural, or rather, of a power that seems "natural" but that has also been conditioned by her Romantic reading. But there is a hint of the consumer even at this early stage. The fact that Rebecca is "all eyes" reminds us of other heroines who were "just looking," or whose hungry gaze attempts to "take in" or consume all before it.[6] Perhaps also, being "all eyes" sidesteps the question of the body. Rebecca is a restless *spirit*, and so Wiggin seems to recognize Hall's fear of the girl's physiological incoherence, while also eliding the body altogether. This is, as we will see, a feature of the tradition. Whereas we know that Jo March is uncomfortable in her own body, later heroines have bodies that are insistently "tidy" or "trim," or more or less unmentioned. The attempt to address the problem of the girl's body, then, results in an avoidance of the very subject, while boy's bodies are often impressively and unproblematically present.

The subversively "natural" heroine is to be found in novels by Alcott and first-generation contemporaries such as Coolidge or Ward. Wiggin sets the stage for another negotiation between puritanical self-governance and Romantic self-expression. But in this later variant of that conflict, it is the pecuniary that comes to the fore, and Rebecca will be the means by which a new and dynamic control of money is achieved. The thematics takes on a more unusual, turn-of-the-century cast with the appearance of Adam Ladd, whom Rebecca will call "Mr. Aladdin." He represents the magic of money, much as she represents the magic of youth. He is a prosperous middle-aged businessman who falls in love with Rebecca, and who, we are led to suppose, will one day marry her. Adam Ladd is "handsome" and "well-fed," but he is also tired and dispirited. His career as an entrepreneur has taken him from his small-town background to the commercial hustle of the city. He exemplifies the disillusioned man of the period: his middle-class prosperity has produced little more than a feeling of "weightlessness," and, until he meets Rebecca, he seems to be headed toward the contemporary illness of "neurasthenia." He suffers from nostalgia for the harsher, more intense realities of his youth, the "breathless audacity" and "uncouth forms" of the pre-modern. Rebecca will provide an infusion of the elemental spirit that he has lost. But the paradox is that the course of her life will confirm and approve the softening quality of modern experience. Previous heroines often suffered under the austere obligations of the "chastening rod," in that they had to acknowledge the rightness of a patriarchal social and symbolic order in which they were "little women." Wiggin's heroine will not have to prove her moral submission in quite the same way, and her worth will be established more in a financial context. Rebecca must live with her monied aunts if she is to have a genteel education, and she must turn this education to profit to pay off the mortgage on her mother's farm. In her increasingly secular society, Rebecca must not so much cultivate her virtue as make a shift to avoid the shame and powerlessness of poverty. Adam Ladd has already succeeded in overcoming childhood poverty, but has been left enervated and unfulfilled by his material comfort. Each approaches the central material fact from a different direction, she seeking to progress and he to return. With her re-authenticating natural energy, and his capitalist well being, they were made for each other. The wide network of his commercial influence mirrors her Romantic expansiveness. His ability to manipulate the world of things corresponds with her imaginative ability to recreate the world for herself and for those around her.

This sense that Romanticism and consumerism were made for each other is something that Wiggin plays with in the course of the novel. In the events leading up to her first encounter with her "Mr. Aladdin," Rebecca befriends the poor and marginalized Simpson family. But she does not copy the March sisters in extending an improving patronage to the poor. Her desire to help the Simpsons finds a characteristically contemporary expression: she joins with them to market Excelsior Soap. If she can sell enough soap, it will enable them to acquire one among a number of more or less useless luxury items:

The premiums within their possible grasp were three – a bookcase, a plush reclining chair, and a banquet lamp. Of course, the Simpsons had no books, and casting aside without thought or pang the plush chair, which might have been of some use in a family of seven persons (not counting Mr Simpson, who ordinarily sat elsewhere at the town's expense), they warmed themselves rapturously in the vision of the banquet lamp, which speedily became to them more desirable than food, drink, or clothing. (p. 111)

In this comic moment of commodity fetishism, the girls are completely caught up in and enthused by the possibilities of selling at commission, and choosing their reward from a mail-order catalogue. This exercise in late nineteenth-century consumerism is a long way from the virtuous accomplishments sought by Rebecca's literary antecedents. The emphasis is not on making, or on use-value, but on the gratification made available via a capitalized network of exchange. The preservation of the domestic sphere has been swapped for a speculative venture that will take the heroine out into the world. Wiggin satirizes this new culture of advertizement and exchange, especially in the hyperbole of the sales patter provided by the Excelsior Company:

Can I sell you a little soap this afternoon? It is called the Snow-White and Rose-Red Soap – six cakes in an ornamental box; only twenty cents for the white, twenty-five cents for the red. It is made from the purest ingredients, and if desired could be eaten by an invalid with relish and profit. (p. 113)

Wiggin keys into the way in which the basic commodity has been brand-named and differentiated from rival products. The soap is given moral and romantic associations – the purity and desire of Snow White and red roses – and so the purchaser is being offered a symbolic property as much as something with which to do the washing. But however much Wiggin satirizes the unlikely promises of consumerism, it is symptomatic of her heroine's nature that she is supremely successful in the enterprise. When Rebecca and a friend go on a marketing expedition, we are told that "lucky Rebecca accomplished with almost no effort, results that poor little Emma Jane failed to attain by hard and conscientious labor" (p. 115). In the world of this novel, it is not enough to be "deserving"; one must also have the natural spark that draws the customer. And of course the lover too is a kind of customer. It is at precisely this point of marketing soap that Rebecca meets Adam for the first time, and makes her greatest sale. He buys all that she has. But the scene also hints that he has bought her too. In being inducted into the consumerist order, she has become part of the businessman's empire:

"Oh, I must know that soap," said the gentleman genially. "Made out of pure vegetable fats, isn't it?"
"The very purest," corroborated Rebecca.

"No acid in it?"
"Not a trace." (pp. 118–19)

The joke here is that Rebecca is selling this man's own product back to
him. In a light-hearted and commercialized version of the patriarchal scenario of "kissing the chastening rod," she is speaking his lines, and representing him in the market.[7] The good daughter has become the proprietary
child.

There is, then, nothing here to trouble Hall and other contemporary
socio-sexologists. Rebecca is a heroine because she is "tumultuous"; she
is Hall's classic adolescent. But she has a story because Wiggin, like Hall,
wishes the adolescent to be disciplined. The process of vaunting the inspired
energy of Romantic wildness while guiding that wildness into prescribed
forms, is something that will mark later Rebecca novels, as Adam Ladd sends
her to a stylish boarding school to be "finished." For all that Wiggin finds a
new and dynamic function for the girl, she also offers implicit recognition of
the liabilities of adolescence. But the romantic commerce between Rebecca
and "Mr. Aladdin" has further contemporary significations. It draws attention to the way in which the means to wealth is changing. Rebecca's
mother is working to pay off a mortgage on Sunnybrook Farm, and her
investment in land seems old-fashioned and unprofitable. When wealth
does come, it is in the form of an ambitious new project, more in keeping with Rebecca's expansive imagination. Adam Ladd causes a railroad to
run across Sunnybrook Farm, and for a station to be built there. In what
amounts to a form of insider-trading, the otherwise relatively worthless
land is transformed into valuable real estate. Rebecca's mother can sell up
for $6000. This event takes us back to the phoney nostalgia of the epilogue
written for the stage version of *Rebecca*. Rebecca's success lies in the sale
of her revitalizing pastoral energy, represented by herself and Sunnybrook
Farm. Both fall to the buying power of the modern venture capitalist. But
this sale and purchase also signals the demise of nature. The novel cel-
ebrates the uninhibited zest of rural childhood, but it also converts this
same commodity into something more profitable. The farm will become
a station and Rebecca, as noted, will be schooled in poetry and propriety.
When she completes the education for which Adam Ladd has paid, she
asks a question which is part-sentiment, part-customer survey: "[T]ell me,
Mr Aladdin, [are] you satisfied?" (p. 246). It is hard to see how he can be.
As with other therapeutic forms of recreation for businessmen, there is a
circularity whereby the modern interest has a modernizing influence. Adam
Ladd's investment in nature has transformed it: Sunnybrook Farm is no

more, and Rebecca too has been "developed." She retains her imaginative power, but she has also learned to make it pay. The Romantic impulse, in alliance with the forces of consumerism, has provided the heroine with the power to make her own future. In *Rebecca of Sunnybrook Farm* as in earlier novels, all apparent contradictions must be brought into productive association via the agency of the heroine. Rebecca accommodates herself supremely well to the new order of money, but she also learns to appreciate the old, thrifty intelligence of her Aunt Miranda. As Rebecca later acknowledges of her former antagonist, she had "been the making of me" (274). Miranda wills the brick house to Rebecca. At the end, Rebecca symbolizes the union of old, inherited property with the new patterns of enterprise.

The happy ending of *Rebecca*, as with so many popular novels, lies in the reconciliation of dissonant elements. But this kind of reconciliation is never achieved without some form of loss or distortion. Rebecca presents us, her latterday metropolitan readers, with a rejuvenating burst of outdoors "reality." She springs into the reader's life in the same way that she walks round the corner of a house into the life of Adam Ladd, the bored and unfulfilled capitalist. Wiggin characterized the writing of the novel in the same way. She began work on it during a convalescence at a "Southern health resort," and the process served as a therapeutic jolt to the rather grandly ailing authoress (*Garden*, p. 352). A similarly therapeutic effect was claimed with regard to the readers. Wiggin's sister recalled:

[P]hysicians, hospital attendants, and trained nurses were eloquent in Rebecca's praise and – rather dubious but heartfelt tribute – the Superintendent of a State Lunatic Asylum wrote, on duly labelled paper, from the Office of the Superintendent: "I have given 'Rebecca' to a number of my patients to read and they have derived great pleasure and benefit from it."[8]

Rebecca, it would seem, could awaken almost anyone from mental or physical torpor. But this wild and spontaneous energy is of course anything but wild and spontaneous. Rebecca is above all a "good" girl, whose impulses are always helpful and kindly. Wiggin gives us a narrowly idealized kind of natural freedom, and in doing so she imposes very clear restrictions on what could or could not appear in her work. The novel drew approving notices precisely because it avoided the systematic and often grim detail of the more ambitious realist and naturalist writers. As the *Atlantic Monthly* noted, *Rebecca* "is obviously not the realism of the critical, and, as it were, scientific observer, which is now so much with us. It is, rather, the creative realism of Dickens, of the creative sentimentalist."[9] Wiggin was under no illusions about how her fiction related to prevailing literary taste, and she sided with "creative sentimentalism" in a very knowing and calculated way. In an interview she gave to *The Lamp* at the height of her fame, she entered into the widespread turn-of-century debate about what fiction ought and ought not to do. She praised a realism that is a "faithful reflection of current life," but which lacks "temperament." She distinguished this from a more critical realism, and from naturalism or "what are colloquially known as 'strong books.'" While she maintains that her preferred realism is a faithful reflection of life, she undermines this in a subsequent comment: "If the 'anæmic' condition of our fiction be the price we pay for our high standard of morality, by all means let us pay it."[10] Wiggin believes that social well-being is more securely maintained through ignorance than through confronting the less pleasing aspects of modern life. She offers the girl as an infusion of red-blooded spontaneity in an over-civilized culture, an eruption of the natural in an artificial age. But at the same time, she urges a moral filtering process, and more or less admits that her heroine could only pass for red-blooded in an "anaemic" culture. The role of the girl in debates over whether fiction should be "clean" or "dirty," "red-blooded" or "anaemic," is developed in chapter 7. With regard specifically to Wiggin, the drive is always toward a somewhat weakened state of purity. How appropriate that, when her heroine becomes involved in the world of trade, the commodity is soap.

What might be the effect of this kind of fiction on the girl-reader? She might be flattered by her own centrality to the world of the novel, and her ability to smooth the contradictions that adults seem unable to manage. There is even a sense that the girl has an aptitude for the new world of consumerist exchange. But all the while, the child-reader is being informed of what she is needed to be: naive, innocent, and available to the world of commerce. The novel sells her "own" nature to her in the form of a cheeky, enterprising, but ultimately conformist self. The fictional girl and the actual girl-reader are akin to each other in the same way that white snow and red roses are akin to soap: there is no "real" or necessary relation at all. But *Rebecca of Sunnybrook Farm* offers the girl in a symbolic relation to her culture which is attractive and important. It is in her interest to buy.

5

Preparing for leisure

The advert shows a number of elegantly dressed, slender white women. It is twilight, and they saunter in peaceful college grounds. Each young woman is escorted by a handsome man in evening dress. The accompanying text tells us why four hundred and fifteen girls at Wellesley and Barnard, and five hundred and twenty at Smith and Bryn Mawr, use Woodbury's Soap (see illustration 1). This advert, which was published in *Ladies' Home Journal* in September 1925, shows how important the college girl had become in her first half century. She was beautiful, privileged, a leader of fashion, to be envied and copied. Her deployment by Woodbury's indicates the extent to which higher education for women had been incorporated into the myths and processes of consumerism. This chapter focuses on fictional representations of that incorporation, particularly in the work of Jean Webster. But first let us trace the progress of the college girl, from her feminist origins to her consumerization.

It had seemed so threatening at the beginning. The campaign to gain access to higher education grew alongside the female suffrage campaign: the issue was predicated on women's active dissatisfaction. Men's colleges resisted admitting women on an equal basis, but from mid-century on there were some small co-educational colleges, and some women's "annexes" to the major men's colleges. The dangerously independent all-female institutions began with Vassar in 1865, to be followed by Smith and Wellesley in the 1870s, and Bryn Mawr in 1883. Commentary in the press, from clergymen and educators, was often critical. A girl who was educated beyond the level required for raising children would be discontented with her lot as a housewife. It would damage her physiology and make her unfit for child-bearing. The living arrangements that prevailed at women's colleges would lead to "mischiefs" that were as "unnatural" as they were unnamable. As an article in an 1873 issue of *Scribner's Monthly* proclaimed:

JUNIOR PROM NIGHT AT COLLEGE

We interviewed nearly two thousand girls at Smith, Bryn Mawr, Wellesley, and Barnard on the kind of soap they use for the care of the skin. Their answers brought out the fact that Woodbury's enjoys more than double the popularity of any other soap among these young college girls.

Four Hundred & Fifteen Girls
at WELLESLEY and BARNARD
tell why they are using this soap for their skin

She is one of the most charming things America has produced—the American college girl.

No other country has a type that at all compares with her. Eager, fearless, inquisitive—naïve, and at the same time self-possessed—joyously alive in mind, nerve, body—she has the flavor of America itself, a fresher, keener flavor than one finds in older countries.

HOW does the American college girl take care of that smooth, clear skin of hers? What soap does she use? Why does she choose it? What qualities about it especially appeal to her?

To get their own individual answers to these questions, we conducted an investigation among nearly two thousand college girls at Wellesley, Barnard, Smith, and Bryn Mawr.

Nearly two thousand college girls answer our questions

Of 804 girls at Wellesley and Barnard, more than half were Woodbury users. The rest showed a wide scattering of selection over 51 different brands of soap.

At Smith and Bryn Mawr, out of 927 girls, 520 said they were using Woodbury's Facial Soap. Four hundred and seven girls used other brands of soap, their choice ranging over 56 different kinds.

Why is it that among these nearly two thou-sand college girls at Smith, Bryn Mawr, Wellesley, and Barnard Woodbury's enjoys more than double the popularity of any other soap?

Their answers, in their own words

The girls themselves answer the question—

"*The only soap that doesn't irritate my skin.*"
"*Seems to agree with my skin better than other soaps do.*"
"*Keeps my skin in better condition than any other soap I have used.*"
"*After trying other soaps, Woodbury's seemed to be the only one that helped me. Other soaps irritated my skin.*"

These were characteristic comments, repeated in varying language, over and over again.

Six hundred and forty-four girls spoke of the purity of Woodbury's Facial Soap, or its soothing non-irritating effect on their skin.

Many girls told at length how Woodbury's had helped them to overcome undesirable skin conditions and to gain a clear, flawless complexion.

Thirteen girls said they were using Woodbury's at the recommendation of their physician.

This Treatment will keep a sensitive skin smooth and soft:—

Dip a soft washcloth in warm water and hold it to the face. Do this several times. Then make a light warm-water lather of Woodbury's Facial Soap and dip your cloth in it until the cloth is "fluffy" with the soft white lather. Rub this lathered cloth gently over your skin until the pores are thoroughly cleansed. Rinse the face lightly with clear cool water and dry carefully.

Why Woodbury's is unique in its effect on the skin

A skin specialist worked out the formula by which Woodbury's is made. This formula not only calls for absolutely pure ingredients. It also demands greater refinement in the manufacturing process than is commercially possible with ordinary toilet soap. In merely handling a cake of Woodbury's one notices this extreme fineness.

Around each cake of Woodbury's Facial Soap is wrapped a booklet containing special cleansing treatments for overcoming common skin defects. Get a cake of Woodbury's today, and begin tonight, the treatment your skin needs!

A 25c cake of Woodbury's lasts a month or six weeks.

FREE—A guest size set, containing the new, large-size trial cake of Woodbury's Facial Soap, and samples of Woodbury's Facial Cream and Facial Powder.

1   Advertisement for Woodbury's Soap from *Ladies' Home Journal*, September 1925, p. 35

It is not necessary to go into particulars, but every observing physician or physiologist knows what we mean when we say that such a system is fearfully unsafe. The facts which substantiate their opinion would fill the public mind with horror if they were publicly known . . . Diseases of body, diseases of imagination, vices of body and imagination – everything we would save our children from – are bred in these great institutions where life and association are circumscribed, as weeds are forced in hot-beds.[1]

This type of material confirms the argument made in the introduction about the perceived incoherence of girls and women, and the threat this posed to social and biological reproduction – the arguments that would find sustained expression in G. Stanley Hall's *Adolescence* (1904). The idea that higher education distracted women from their "natural" function persisted into the twentieth century. As a headline in the *Boston Herald* declared in 1922: "Wellesley Fails to Teach Girls How to Bring Up Children."[2] In the face of such hostility, the early college women tended to be extremely committed, and were not ashamed of the radical nature of their ambitions. But the pioneering generation of 1860 to 1880 gave way to a more diverse group, which often had different goals. This was in part due to an attempt to make female higher education less threatening. For once the colleges were in place, they needed to attract students. Fears about independent women were offset by claims from the colleges themselves that they were designed for young ladies, and did not provide professional or vocational training. Effectively, they announced their own uselessness. At the same time, the press discovered that the witty, wealthy, fun-loving college girl was profitable material. Instead of publishing stern editorials on woman's place, they began to do photo-essays of "Fêtes of College Girls," "Float Day at Wellesley," "Daisy Chain at Vassar," and so on. The pioneering New Woman was joined by a less radical counterpart who had heard that college was amusing and stylish. This second generation of college girls could fulfill their educational ambitions – if they had any – without surrendering their marriageability. The ubiquitous Gibson Girl, who dressed well and was pictured on bicycles and in automobiles in all places of resort, was found to be equally at home in a lovely gothic quadrangle.[3]

With the making safe of college girls, higher education expanded, but it remained very expensive. The college girl became a member of a significant, select minority.[4] Once she had been established as part of an enviable élite, she became very useful for marketing purposes. By the time we reach the Woodbury's Soap campaign, the college girl was in place as young, white, beautiful, wealthy, and an active and discriminating consumer. Her college courses, her essays, her reading lists and professors, do not figure. Her only thought is that Woodbury's does not irritate her skin like other soaps. She had been taken up as a devoted consumer and an important marketing target, but also as a symbol through which to influence the choices of other consumers. And, as was also the case with *Rebecca of Sunnybrook Farm*, the immersion of the college girl in consumerism produces her as an item of consumption. As the Woodbury's text tells us: "[s]he is one of the most charming things America has produced." At once free but not independent, she was above all available, transparently convenient, for would-be husbands, readers, consumers:

Eager, fearless, inquisitive – naive, and at the same time self-possessed – joyously alive in mind, nerve, body – she has the flavor of America itself, a fresher, keener flavor than one finds in older countries.

What could the bachelor, reader, or shopper do but try this new flavor, the college girl? She, like the soap, would refresh without irritating. This ties in with Henry James's observation in *The American Scene* (1907) that the American girl had been transformed into a commodity, an "appliance" that exemplified the new consumerist order to the rest of the world:

[H]er manner of embodying her sex has fairly made her a new human convenience, not unlike fifty of the others, of a slightly different order, the ingenious mechanical appliances, stoves, refrigerators, sewing-machines, type-writers, cash-registers, that have done so much, in the household and the place of business, for the American name.[5]

In this process of standardization and branding, of America as girl, and girl as America, clearly the college girl occupied a special place, as a top-of-the-range model.

From the turn of the century on, we find an interpenetration of college and market, whereby learning is like buying, and buying is a form of education. Higher education was itself something to be consumed. Those who could afford it might actually attend a college. Many more, who were too young, too old, or too poor, could vicariously enjoy its pleasures in their reading of novels and magazine stories. Or indeed, they could buy Woodbury's Soap. The match-up of college and market is also found in such magazines as *Frank Leslie's*, *Collier's*, *Good Housekeeping*, *Munsey's*, *The Century*, and *The Ladies' Home Journal*. These journals published numerous photo-essays on the college girl, her surroundings and her activities. The essays resemble very closely the Woodbury's advert, with images of landscaped grounds and moments of leisure.[6] Colleges themselves, aside from welcoming the fawning attentions of the journals, generated their own sales literature. The early college catalogues tended to be straightforward lists of courses, professors, and students. But even these, with their competing ranges of artistic and musical "electives," are setting out a series of choices for the students who can afford to attend. The publication of the names and places of residence of the alumnae might also be seen as a sort of advertizing: it allows the girls and their families to promote their educational acquisitions, while enabling the college to publish its own growing connectedness to the well-to-do. Colleges also began to produce different kinds of promotional materials in the form of illustrated pamphlets or "view books." A Bryn Mawr pamphlet of 1905 deals in the same negotiation between rural and urban class values that was a feature of much girls' fiction. Bryn Mawr, we are informed, stands on "a fair green hill conspicuous for its beauty," but if this seems a little too rustic, we are reassured that the "original farm houses have now in many places been replaced by big stone mansions, and simple country folk by denizens of the city who have turned the countryside into a park." And if this turn seems too "improved" to be truly reviving to the depleted urban spirit, we are again assured that "in certain corners well known to the youthful pedestrian, the farmer is still to be seen driving his plough with its patient, slow-moving horses; cattle graze in the deep grass; and sheep graze all day long under gnarled apple boughs." The same pamphlet makes it clear that there is no snobbery or financial discrimination among the girls, but it does avow that Bryn Mawr graduates "will everywhere with surprising rapidity begin to set standards, social, intellectual, and moral." Indeed, the Bryn Mawr product will "be looked up to by simple communities as exponents of culture." The college offers to re-tool the gauche student after a standard model:

Her attention is called to the provincialisms and inaccuracies of her individual pronunciation, and exercises are given to help her to correct her faults... When mimicked by her teacher, her way of vocalising a sentence leaves her no possibility of self-delusion.[7]

As such marketing would suggest, it tended to be the newly rich who bought into this kind of status. The old social élites of Boston, Philadelphia, and New York continued for a while to educate their daughters privately, but to the newly wealthy it was a means of confirming and refining one's sense of having made it. A self-made man was not necessarily a gentleman, but his money could ensure that his daughters acquired upwardly mobile manners and contacts.[8] The daughter was the figure that, above all others, must be prepared for the ascent to the leisure class. Nowhere is this phenomenon more emphatically confirmed than in a critical voice from the provinces. In

1898, the "Homestead" column of the *Hampshire Gazette* reported under the heading, "TONY EDUCATION," that it was "Becoming Fashionable to Get an Education, and Book Learning the Lesser Part of It." According to "Homestead," the girls were learning "Taste in Appearance." It noted that an "influx from wealthy homes has set a higher standard of dressing and social customs." In its characteristically begrudging tone, "Homestead" concludes: "There is always money enough to provide the American girl what she wants. Not the least among her wants is a college education."[9] Doubtless "Homestead" would have agreed with William Dean Howells's statement that the "pride of caste" was becoming a "pride of taste."[10] New money bought old things, paying with hard cash for what had not been inherited. Susan Porter Benson's description of the department stores might equally fit the colleges, in that both were "dynamic museums of a constantly changing way of life attuned to style and propriety" (p. 22).[11] The notion of the "dynamic museum" captures the way in which everything has been removed from the context of its origin. As befits a move from an ethos of production to an ethos of consumption, there is a sense in which things are not made – they do not exist before they are on display. There is no prehistory, no struggle, no factory, no workers. The emergence of a consumerist middle class was simultaneous with the redesign of social space, as factories and workers' districts were relocated to outskirts. Labor and laborers were rendered as invisible as possible. There was only the object – refrigerator, cash-register, girl – in all its symbolic glory. And the college girl fits this notion, in that her origins too are obscured. As with the Woodbury's Soap advert, although she is offered to us as a kind of product, she is not so much manufactured, as "the flavor of America itself." Her learning, her social and intellectual work as a student, is not seen. She appears, fully formed, on a float at Wellesley, or in a daisy chain at Vassar. This hiding of the means of production carries through into the fiction, in that the girls are described in stylish dresses, and with all the other accoutrements of modern taste, but they are seldom described in the act of shopping or studying. Their style is allowed to be integral to their very being, a natural expression of self, rather than a new thing that has been willed and paid for.

How does this self-proclaiming and self-disguising culture manifest itself in fictional representations of the college girl? The world of college became immensely popular as a setting for series fiction. Shirley Marchalonis, in her recent study of the genre, notes that in its heyday, the college story refers to a sort of world elsewhere. As with all formula fiction, college was a realm with its own rules, preoccupations, and repertoire of characters. This was part of the consumer's privilege, to move into a place that was immune to normal necessities and obligations. The "green world" of college – and especially of the girl's college – was enchantingly small and self-determined.[12] I want to focus on one particular author who both exemplifies the college formula and who also departs from it. Jean Webster's early "Patty" stories allow us to see how class and taste operated in the allegedly closed world of college. Her later and most successful novel, *Daddy-Long-Legs*, is interesting because it embraces more than the formula would allow.[13] *Daddy-Long-Legs* suggests the way in which the college-consumerism nexus was haunted by spectres of poverty and social injustice – of, in Jacob Riis's famous phrase, "How the Other Half Lives."[14] For the prosperous, there was a kind of vertigo whereby, as Robert Bremner suggests, "people had risen so high that the possibility of plunging down seemed so frightful."[15] If the Woodbury's college girl seemed to be the acme of modernity, poverty seemed to be the flaw. This had particular relevance to the lives of children. They, even more than adults, demonstrated the emergent truth that the poor were more victims than villains: child-labor was a transparent ploy to maximize profits. The "green world" of college may have seemed all the more attractive as an escape from the unavoidable spectacle of the "Other Half." Certainly in Webster's early fiction there is a retreat to the world of college. But she was also to develop her work in a way that confronted social problems, that sought some constructive interplay between the cleanly college girl and the filthy urban waif. Webster herself was from new money, was educated at Vassar, and married a Standard Oil millionaire. But she tried to remain true to the New Woman sympathies that had led to the creation of the college girl in the first place. Her fiction attempts to take a Progressive approach to social issues, in that she investigates the possibilities of social re-engineering along the rationalized lines of "scientific philanthropy." But as we will see, she found Progressive ideology unsatisfactory, and her ultimate disposition seems reactionary. She is similarly ambivalent with regard to contemporary debate on the nature and role of fiction. In fictionalizing pressing social issues, especially those to do with urban struggle, Webster was verging on late realist and naturalist topics. But like Wiggin before her, Webster's fiction was taken up by mainstream commentators as an acceptable way of representing social problems. Her girls' fiction moved towards controversial adult genres, but in doing so it mediated them for a broader market. There is, then, an element of social and generic daring in Webster's work. But it remains for us to ask if she achieved anything more than the preparation of her representative orphan for life in the leisure class.[16]

As with advertizers and magazine editors, Jean Webster was quick to turn the interest in privileged girls' lives to account. By the late nineteenth century, the college story was already in place, with *Harvard Episodes, Princeton Tales, Smith Stories* and *Vassar Studies,* and Webster too enjoyed considerable success placing stories of girl-life in the magazines. When still a student, she had made money writing a column on the Vassar girls' doings for a local Poughkeepsie newspaper. The character with which Webster established herself was Patty Wyatt, who, like Webster herself, goes from a private boarding school to Vassar. Beginning at school, the stories collected in *Just Patty* (1911) revolve around the doings of a set of mischievous but honorable girls. These girls subvert the rules, but they still manage to affirm the basic values of their class and gender. The scenario permits a liberatory exploration of life beyond adult dictates, but in a non-threatening way. The three friends, Patty, Priscilla, and Conny, are clearly drawn from monied backgrounds, and yet they represent a force for social compromise. Although their school careers have been blemished by stereotypical pranks, they have never overturned or ignored the more important underlying principles of their educational milieu. For this reason, the headmistress gives them the task of moderating the excessive behaviour of other girls. Keren, a daughter of missionaries, must be made less tiresomely pious; Irene, a very large girl, must be persuaded to become thinner; Margaret "Kid" McCoy from Texas must be made to become more lady-like. So although Patty and her friends are presented as bordering on rebellious, they actually serve as a behavioral police. They parody and undermine excesses, which has the effect of cementing the fundamental characteristics of their social realm. Patty is especially treasured by the headmistress because, although she breaks "every minor rule," she does not "flirt with the soda clerk."[17]

Although Patty's power is to enforce the values of her class and gender, she also has the less convention-bound performative powers of some earlier heroines. The most telling demonstration of these comes with Patty's decision to reform Mae Mertelle Van Arsdale. Mae is an heiress and a beauty, who is rather too preoccupied with her reputation as a lover. Her romantic charisma threatens to distract all the girls from the concerns that are appropriate to their time of life, namely sport and scholarship. Mae has claimed to have a secret aristocratic lover, disapproved of by her parents. Patty and her friends seek to undermine Mae's pretensions by sending Mae gifts, allegedly from this same pretend lover. Mae is of course surprised to receive gifts from a lover who had only existed in her imagination, but she enjoys the confirmation of her mysterious amours. But then Patty sends gifts that denote a showy, not to say lower-class lover. Mae receives sunflowers rather than violets, and cheap chocolates. Worst of all, Patty, in her guise of pretend-lover, sends the wrong sort of books:

His taste in literature was as impossible as his taste in candy. He ran to titles which are supposed to be the special prerogative of the kitchen. "Loved and Lost," "A Born Coquette," "Thorns among the Orange Blossoms." (pp. 48–9)

Mae is shamed by the impression that her lover is undiscriminating and beneath her own class. Patty, as avenger, by no means rejects romance, but shows herself to be a true expert in the nuances of the code. The dual lesson that she gives Mae is that romance should neither distract from sport and study, nor cause one to move beyond the boundaries of one's class. But the lesson with regard to Patty herself is rather different. She has the ability to reinvent herself regardless of the social structures that surround her. Even as she polices Mae, she reveals her own radical mobility and her potential for critique. This is confirmed in an episode that centres on the characteristic contemporary preoccupations of labor relations and shopping. In this episode, the girls all wish to go to town, but they are obliged to stay in and listen to a suffragist lecturer give an account of a strike by female laundry-workers. Patty absorbs the radical lecture unwillingly, and takes her revenge by applying its lesson in reactionary form. She organizes a strike amongst the girls, on the grounds that they should not be made to translate more than sixty lines of Virgil per day. Recycling the lecture she has been made to listen to, she tells her teacher:

We can't allow ourselves to be exploited. Singly, we are no match for you, but together, we can dictate our own terms. Because two or three of us can keep up the pace you set, [this] is no reason why we should allow the others to be overworked. It is our duty to stand by one another against the encroachments of our employer. (p. 68)

After some "arbitration," Patty calls off her strike. She wins, again by demonstrating her ability to assimilate and re-use conventional forms.

The reader may feel that Webster has cast up the notion of working-class women's struggle in order to make a rather thin joke, and certainly there is much ambiguity in Webster's recurrent but fumbling engagement with the social questions of the day. This is most apparent in the episode in which she portrays a plutocrat. Patty has decided to play truant, and in a further act of rebellion, she trespasses on the estate of Silas Weatherby. Weatherby is "celebrated in the neighborhood, in the United States, for the matter of that," as the multi-millionaire "originator of a great many Wicked Corporations" (p. 188). Weatherby's estate is famous for its sumptuousness, with its conservatories and Italian gardens. Webster is clearly fictionalizing Frederick Vanderbilt who, in Webster's time at Vassar, had his famous mansion built in nearby Hyde Park. Equally, the Vanderbilt fortune was widely perceived to have been derived from a series of "Wicked Corporations." In her trespasses, Patty encounters a gruff gardener whom the reader rapidly surmises is none other than Weatherby–Vanderbilt himself. Patty's pert and unabashed manner strikes through his reserves; the tycoon and the girl end up gardening and lunching together. There follows an exchange of opinions. She questions his ill-tempered attitude to the interfering public, and he overcomes her preconceptions as to his "heartlessness." She discovers that he makes a practice of employing former convicts who cannot gain work elsewhere. In a scene that bears resemblance to Rebecca's meeting with Adam Ladd, they go on to debate the correct relation between labor, capital, and the state:

She discussed at some length upon whether or not the corporations should be subject to state control. She stoutly agreed with [an] editor that they should. He maintained that they were like any other private property, and that it was nobody's damn business how they managed themselves. (p. 192)

This in itself might seem a rather adult exchange for children's fiction. Certainly it obliges us to think about Webster's intended readership. We might suppose that this is, to use Hendler's argument, an example of "children's fiction for adults," in that the child's perspective gives the adult a fresh (and perhaps remoralized) approach to familiar issues. If we look at the contemporary reviews of the Patty stories, however, we are left in no doubt as to the primary audience. Patty's adventures at school and at college were seen as the "kittenish pranks" in which, reviewers assumed, "every girl of school age will delight." Patty was promoted and read as "gay," "sparkling," and "innocent." She was suitable for girls because her life was seen to be "healthy in its fun." Her adventures as a "healthy, enthusiastic college girl" were thought to make "essentially a girl's book."[18] Of course Webster's fiction, like much other girls' fiction, attracted both adult and child readers. Perhaps she flatters the girl-reader with the fact that the girl-heroine is granted opinions on adult topics, and is listened to by an influential man. At the same time, many adults might readily have identified with Patty in this situation, bravely refusing to be overawed by the presence of a much more powerful figure.

Webster toys with the possibility of a frankly political confrontation, but then shies away into humour. When Patty criticizes Weatherby to the "gardener," he defends himself by attacking the hypocrisy of his critics:

All the world's against him – when people are decent, he knows it's because they're after something. Your teacher, now, is polite when she wants to see his conservatories, but I'll bet she believes he's an old thief!

To which Patty replies: "Isn't he?" The millionaire breaks into a roguish grin at this point. The fact is that the girl's mischievousness and the millionaire's are presented as more or less equivalent. She is troublesome but honorable; he is rich and prickly, but humane. The girl and the businessman find they have more in common with each other than they would, say, with a striking female laundry-worker. The reader, whether child or adult, is let down gently with the assurance that the depredations of the system are no worse than the flaws of the individuals involved, and that such flaws are relatively minor. Later on, Patty encounters a harmless, ineffectual burglar, whom she sends on to Weatherby for help. She too has been inducted into a personalized world of private philanthropy.

Patty enabled Webster to succeed in the magazine market at a time when her family depended increasingly on her income. She was able to use the girl-heroine to explore pressing social themes, even if there is an overwhelming sense of caution in her treatment. Webster was still buying into modernity, and had not yet found a suitable vehicle to express her anxious awareness of what lay behind the successes of enterprise capitalism. Patty and her friends may seem likely New Women in their desire for higher education, but they do not study hard. The fictionalized Vassar has a finishing-school air, and Patty pretends to be unsure whether Swedenborg "got up a new religion" or "a new system of gymnastics." Playing down the more exciting implications of higher education for women, she characterizes herself and her friends as "nice American girls," who are "interested in golf and basket-ball and Welsh rabbit [sic] and Richard Harding Davis stories and Gibson pictures."[19] But Webster's most successful novel by far was *Daddy-Long-Legs* (1912), which sold more than five million copies in its first four years and was converted into a massively successful stage hit. This novel offers a rather more complex commentary on how the figure of the girl might ensure a smooth incorporation of consumerism and Progressive concerns.

Daddy-Long-Legs begins in the John Grier Home, an orphans' asylum. This mistrustful, hard-driving institution is marked by the Progressive practice of scientific philanthropy. The obsession with rationalized orderliness, and the absence of any quasi-paternal nurturance, means that the charges live dull, pinched lives, in which they are never supposed to be anything more than scrubbed and grateful. Jerusha or Judy Abbott is a prime example of the children's obligation to be deserving, in that she has been allowed to stay on at the Home and study at a local high school on condition that she works long hours cleaning, mending, and looking after the younger orphans. In the spirit of science, she is warned by the head of the Home that her imagination "would get her into trouble if she didn't take care" (p. 3).

As it happens, her ironic humour and her imagination will prove her redemption. She is bought out of her Home life by a wealthy benefactor. His "immoderate sense of humor" causes him to appreciate the "originality" of one of Judy's English compositions. The implication is that having talent is another way of being deserving. The benefactor, "John Smith," whom Judy is told she will never meet, pays for her to go to college on the understanding that she will write him letters describing her life. She has only seen him in the form of a long shadow cast against a wall, and so she writes to him as "Daddy-Long-Legs."

We might take this scenario as an instance of a broader cultural shift from the stern, moralist father of earlier fiction to the sugar-daddy. In this respect later fictions such as *Daddy-Long-Legs* and *Rebecca* stand apart from *Little Women*. But Webster wishes to attempt something more subtle and ultimately more feminist, both in regard to the "daddy's" intentions, and the "daughter's" response. We quickly understand that the unknown benefactor holds an ambiguous view of his own wealth and social power. He sends an awkward, satirical girl to a fictionalized Vassar in order to improve her, but also so that he may, through Judy's letters, enjoy a sly commentary on establishment conventions. His motives are mixed. He wishes to transform her, to make her his own proper and finished creation; but he also wants, vicariously, to push the boundaries of propriety. From Judy's point of view, moving from one institution to another, her life is to be completely different. From living in repaired, handed-down, ugly charity clothing, she is sent off to college with six new dresses, including an evening dress of "pink mull over silk," a "blue church dress," a "dinner dress of red veiling with Oriental trimming," and another of "rose-colored challis." She is thrilled by her own clothes, her own room, her educational opportunity, and, not least, money to spend: "I assure you, Daddy dear, I do appreciate that allowance."[20] And yet, in moving from the institution of the Home to the institution of college, Judy's career will raise the possibility that each institution shares certain key assumptions. She must please her Daddy with letters much as she had to satisfy the requirements of the "mother" of the Home. But college gives her skills and opportunities that enable her to reject her Daddy's help. She realizes that what she really wants is the means to independence. Her desire to graduate is also a desire to throw off the need for either mother or father. Judy knows that her own satisfaction will lie outside of the institutions, public and private, that define an unmarried woman as dependent.

Judy succeeds, in that she wins a scholarship, and is offered employment tutoring another girl over the summer holidays. In both instances, her benefactor wishes her to turn the chance down. This is the repeated pattern of their relationship. He seeks to play the plutocratic role of domineering philanthropy, while she seeks the power that will give her freedom. Beyond putting her on an "allowance," he smothers her with gifts. These include five gold pieces, pink rosebuds, furs, a necklace, a liberty scarf, gloves, handkerchiefs, books, a purse, and, on one occasion, seventeen assorted Christmas presents. Pleased, but not fooled, she tells him: "I'm a socialist, please remember; do you wish to turn me into a plutocrat?"[21] Equally, she is resentful when he tries, after the manner of Adam Ladd with Rebecca, to make her conform to the Romantic vision of the purity of nature. He decrees that she must spend summer after summer on a farm, but she becomes restless in an idyllic backwater. She begins to refuse any more money from him than she needs, as she intends to repay him at some point in the future. Finally, when she receives payment for a magazine story she has written, she sends him all that she owes.

Judy manages to avoid the potentially disabling aspects of entering into a monied and consumerized realm. In going to college, she might have become too refined, too "ivory tower," to make her own way in the world. The danger is that she will exchange her former position of helpless exploitation for a position of equally helpless privilege. This fearful exchange is powerfully conveyed if we turn aside from the novel momentarily, and look at the promotional photographs made for the stage version of *Daddy-Long-Legs*. They form a "before" and "after" narrative, in which the supposedly triumphant "after" has a troubling aspect. Judy, as played by Ruth Chatterton, was pictured as the poor, working orphan, in rough, serving clothes. This "before" figure looks tired and sad, but, with her sleeves rolled up, she also looks active, and strong. In the photograph of Chatterton as Judy after she has been discovered and improved by her benefactor, she is pictured in a very pretty silk and lace dress, a bouquet at her waist, ensconced on a sofa, reading Bayard Taylor. This "after" Judy is smothered in luxury, surrounded and overwhelmed by large chintz cushions. Seated, reading the undemanding Taylor, craning forward submissively and looking up at the camera, she seems shy, pallid, and proper (see illustrations 2 and 3).

In the play, we are not supposed to question this polarized transition from one form of powerlessness to another. But the novel does explore such ambiguities. We learn of the dangers that Judy has passed in her developing relationship with her sponsor. With his resentment of her scholarship and her earning strategies, it is clear that he did not intend her education to be quite so liberatory as it proves. Daddy is so charmed with Judy that, unbeknown to her, he enters her life under his real name of Jervis Pendleton.

2 Ruth Chatterton as Judy in *Daddy-Long-Legs, c.* 1914

3 Ruth Chatterton as Judy in *Daddy-Long-Legs*, *c*. 1914

As with earlier paternal figures such as Adam Ladd, he is also to be the love-interest. Taking her from her Home, he wishes to place her in his own home. She falls in love with him, not knowing that he is Daddy. When, having discovered his secret, she does eventually decide to marry Jervis, it is a free and independent choice. She does come Home to Daddy, but on her own terms. Furthermore, her unusual relation to such terms as Home and Daddy means that she has an awareness of the performative or willed nature of such concepts. She remarks repeatedly on the gaps in her own experience, and of how, as a result, the most familiar scenes are, to her, moments of confusion and of possible self-invention:

Jerusha leaned forward watching with curiosity – and a touch of wistfulness – the stream of carriages and automobiles that rolled out of the asylum gates. In imagination she followed first one equipage then another to the big houses dotted along the hillside. She pictured herself in a fur coat and a velvet hat trimmed with feathers leaning back in the seat and nonchalantly murmuring "Home" to the driver. But on the doorsill of her home the picture grew blurred. (p. 2)

Traditionally speaking, she ought to understand what a home is as part of her essential womanly nature, but Judy is aware in this and other ways of the arbitrariness of what she is or may be. Her name was chosen by the mistress of the Home in the same way that all the other orphans' names were chosen, from the directory or from tombstones. Jerusha adopts her nickname of Judy out of a will to invent the childhood she did not have: "It's such a silly name. It belongs to the girl I'm not – a sweet little blue-eyed thing, petted and spoiled by all the family, who romps her way through life without any cares" (p. 20). As with her thrill in dressing up in upper-class clothes, Judy enjoys – but is slightly at odds with – her deepest thoughts and sensations. She seeks constantly to assess the distance between her various selves: her historical, tragic self; her lucky, redeemed self; her intellectual, careerist self; her sentimental, daughterly self. The lightness of tone, the comedy of the novel, is in large part derived from this sense that things are slightly haphazard and unstable. Webster uses the instability to depict a heroine who has powers of decision and self-creation: she is not simply subject to a process of education and consumerization, but evolves a critique of these processes even as they continue to form her. As with earlier heroines from Jo March onwards, she has the power to create and enact alternative meanings from within the prevailing system. Then again, while *Daddy-Long-Legs* may be a critical reappraisal of older models of eroticized daughterly duty, it is not entirely rebellious or "New Woman." Judy will marry into money and leisure, even if her path to that goal is more questioning than with many earlier writers. Above all, Judy is deserving. To borrow the terms of Michael Moon's discussion of Alger heroes, the chief quality of this heroine is her "legibility." With the inside view of the first-person narrative, the reader, as much as Daddy himself, may feel assured that there is no unknown or "lurking" trace of the "dangerous classes."[22] As Judy confides in one of her letters, the "whole secret is in being *pliable*" (p. 115). This pliability is confirmed by her eventual marriage. The reader may wish that she had fallen in love with her other suitor, a nice Princeton boy closer to her own age. But in setting up the narrative tension between the two suitors, Webster effectively circumvents the possibility that Judy might not marry at all, or that she might fall in love with an unmonied, non-varsity man. Webster's novel, for all that it bears the marks of the commitment and social energy of its time, nonetheless conforms to the half-denied goal of a dependent, materially gratified femininity.

Daddy-Long-Legs is, it seems, another description of a girl's maturation into an ambiguously defined independence. As with other novels in the tradition, it retreats from some of its more unusual implications. With its happy marriage, the heroine has once again found a satisfactory way of achieving a morally approved wealth and class status. Webster broached problems that ordinarily belonged to adult, naturalistic fiction, in that she has destitute characters, and she stages the growing inequities between different groups. But she also takes an optimistic, tidied-up view. This is apparent from the rather more frank accounts she gave to interviewers of the problems facing orphans:

[T]he majority of orphan asylum children are so painfully unprepossessing little things, they are thin and dull and anemic, and most of them use such horrible language. Why the way they swear would make your hair stand on end.[23]

Webster wished that there were some way to take the children and "fatten them up and polish them off" so that ordinary people might be more willing to adopt them, and this is precisely what *Daddy-Long-Legs* does.[24] Judy and all her fellows in the asylum are attractive and good. Webster's cleaned-up vision of child-poverty and its consequences caused her to be compared favourably with naturalistic treatments of the same theme. As the *Century Magazine*'s promotion averred: "In a year of murky and morbid fiction it came as a blessed relief."[25]

The success of *Daddy-Long-Legs* was such that, as with the generic college girl, Judy was widely dispersed and exploited within the culture of consumption. There was a Judy doll which became the centrepiece for a charity promotion known as the "Daddy-Long-Legs Brigade." In an effort to create an aura of fashion around the venture, it was advertized that "The Vassar Girls Are Doing It."[26] Throughout the period of its most intense success, the *Daddy-Long-Legs* excitement often seemed to turn on the spectacle of class and money. As with the breathless recommendation that "The Vassar Girls Are Doing It," the story of an orphan who becomes rich offered a voyeuristic peep into both upper and under classes. This sense is confirmed by incidents surrounding the play that was produced from the book. In the midst of its triumphant New York run, Webster went to give a lecture to an audience of working girls at the Jacob Riis Settlement. The New York *Sun* thought the encounter worth covering. The newspaper's commentary makes it clear that the event was defined by its bringing together normally disparate class and cultural identities. The reporter made great play of the question session which followed the lecture, in which Webster was assumed to expect difficult questions on "the dramatic unities or other abstract matters." In fact, she is asked: "Does Miss Chatterton wear her own hair?" The *Sun* finds its humor in the meeting between the educated, upper-class author and the uneducated, celebrity-hungry working girls.[27]

Webster's own position in relation to Broadway and its stars provides another instance of how the publicity phenomenon became a part of the process of social marking. It was Chatterton who became a star with *Daddy-Long-Legs*. Her name gradually moved up the billing, from near the bottom of the cast-list to the top, and finally to above the title. As the working girl's question would suggest, the play made Chatterton much more famous than Webster. In the illustrations accompanying the many interviews that she gave, Chatterton was most often pictured as the "before" Judy, in rough gingham. But that publicity still would frequently be set next to one of Chatterton as her own glamorous self. These photo-montages create an attractive continuity between character and star, as Judy progresses from the orphanage to wealth, and Chatterton progresses from anonymity to Broadway. Also, much as the fiction sought to allay fears of female radicalism even as it depicted female ambition, Chatterton was very careful to present a modest, not to say an infantile persona. The *Globe and Commercial Advertiser* happily reported to its readers that Chatterton "May Never Be Great, But Will Do Her Best."[28] In the meantime, Webster's own response to the world of Broadway, and to Chatterton in particular, revealed other nuances. She and the ingénue came to the theatrical world from very different points of origin. In her friendliness to Chatterton, she made it clear that she herself was at home in a milieu that excluded the naive and uneducated Broadway star. Chatterton may have been nationally famous, but this was not a guarantee of acceptance with the older cultural and social élite. When she visited Webster in Tyringham, a backwater haunt of the old literati, Webster wrote of the event in a way that made humorous play of Chatterton's ignorance of gentry style and manners. In a description of a visit to the cultivated home of Richard Watson Gilder, editor of the *Century*, the actress is made to appear vulgar and showy:

> We took her to the Gilders to tea in their garden Sunday afternoon – she wore, among other details, white satin slippers with diamond buckles – and it required all the finesse I possess not to have her go to the P[ost] O[ffice] in a pale blue embroidered negligée and pink and blue satin brocaded slippers.[29]

Chatterton may have corresponded to the working girls' idea of glory, but she was an embarrassment higher up the social ladder. Yet perhaps there was a certain cachet for Webster in being able to parade the dazzlingly pretty young woman of the moment. Webster could satisfy the passing curiosity of the grandees, and join them in observing the star's gaucheries. As much as the heroine she played, Chatterton's rapid ascent revealed how intensive were the demarcations in her culture, with respect to the proper regard for, and display of, money. Unlike Judy, Chatterton was not prepared for such an ascent by education. She was, quite simply, unlearnt. Her money was of the moment, and she had not yet assimilated the knowledge and codes that had enabled Webster herself to make the transition from a dubious western background, via Vassar, into Society. Webster knew how to acculturate her financial power, to the extent that it seemed simply the expression of innate good taste. She became a perfect example of how the education of the consumer, and the consumption of education, conspired to make all else disappear. She, more than the actress, was truly prepared for leisure.

6

Serial pleasures

Did girls' fiction register turn-of-century crises of overproduction? In part, I have suggested that it did, in that it produced confidently acquisitive heroines. But there were more wholesale changes as well. In other industries, the challenge had shifted from production to consumption, as people had to be encouraged to spend at a rate that would keep pace with industrial productivity. Entrepreneurs and capitalists had to develop the market; they had to "engineer consumption."[1] There was a growing preoccupation with "forward integration," as manufacturers took an ever-greater part in retail: in conceptualizing, packaging, and marketing their product. Historians such as Kelly, Ohmann, Scanlon, and others stress the importance of the magazines to this process. Publications like *Ladies' Home Journal* became an essential "handbook for the middle class," in that they educated people's tastes, telling them how and why they should spend their money. Aside from advertizing and other forms of product-placement, the magazines had other, more subliminal ways of encouraging a class-ed consumerism. Fiction was important, in that it was intended to reflect and entice the new professional–managerial class that had emerged to create and service the processes of consumption. This quintessentially modern class had pursued a path of "upscale emulation," and magazine fiction encoded their aspirational desires. The popular romances of the magazines, as Ohmann and others have pointed out, envisaged love-matches across the divide of old and new ruling classes, gratifying emotional longings and class interests at once.[2] But what about girls' fiction? Clearly novels such as *Rebecca of Sunnybrook Farm* and *Daddy-Long-Legs* perform similar ideological maneuvers. But from the early twentieth century onwards, there was another strand of girls' fiction which manifested "forward integration" in even more dynamic ways. This was the series fiction produced by the syndicates. In the "literary machine" of the syndicates we find the engineering of consumption in the pricing and packaging of the product, but also in the way that luxury modern items are foregrounded in the novels' thematic content.

That is to say that the series make great play of the allure of new technologies. In this chapter I look at the techniques of the leading Stratemeyer Syndicate, and then trace the impact of professional–managerial ascent within the subject-matter of series fiction.

In the nineteenth century, one "hit" would often spawn a series of sequels, as was the case with *Little Women*, but such series were owned and created by individual women. A different pattern of literary production emerged towards the end of the century, in the form of the dime novel. In the 1880s and 1890s, the demand for weekly stories of adventure and sleuthing was so intense that numerous writers would be employed in the literary equivalent of a sweatshop. Edward Stratemeyer was one of the outstanding literary piece-workers, who could assume whatever pseudonymous guise a publisher might require. When Oliver Optic and Horatio Alger Jr. died leaving unfinished novels, Stratemeyer completed their work. From the turn of the century onwards, he initiated a variety of series, and established his own writing factory or Syndicate. The Stratemeyer Syndicate would go on to produce over 1300 books, with sales of over two hundred million. The historian of the Syndicate, Carol Billman, estimates that Stratemeyer wrote two hundred of those books, and outlined and edited a further eight hundred.[3] He achieved this remarkable output in part through his enormous personal energy, but in him we also find an application of modern management principles. Coming to prominence at the same time as efficiency geniuses such as Frederick Winslow Taylor and Henry T. Ford, Stratemeyer used similar methods. The transformation is from independent literary artisans such as Alcott and Wiggin, to the division and depersonalization of labor in keeping with time-and-motion theory. In the past, the home-based craftsman would make an object from start to finish, and there was assumed to be a satisfaction and a job-security in this use of diverse skills. With industrialization, and especially in its final, Taylorized perfection, the work-process was fragmented. The employee would perform one very specific operation over and over again, as the human was expected to function like a machine. Under the systematization of production, a few people were designated thinkers and creators. Others, through endless and mind-numbing repetitions of one part of the process, were only required to be obedient.

Stratemeyer was the key thinker and developer in his syndicate, in that he designed or blocked out the narrative. Then he would assign the writing to one of his team of writers. This did indeed lead to "efficiency savings," in that a Stratemeyer book usually took no more than forty days to produce, from initial plan to typeset. The process was doubtless also speeded up by the fact that many Stratemeyer writers were or had been journalists, and were familiar with commissions, deadlines, and invasive editorializing. A further aspect of this renegotiation of the function of the author was that he or she would be paid a flat fee of $100 to $125, and had no right to be identified as the author. The reduction of the writer-craftsman to a writer-laborer was a further prompt to increased productivity in that, not being in receipt of royalties, the writer could only maintain and increase his or her income by writing more.[4] This was literally dehumanizing in that the author – "Carolyn Keene" or "Laura Lee Hope" – was no longer a real, identifiable person. Laura Lee Hope was at least six different people, each of whom was responsible for different elements of the Hope output.[5] On occasion, a novel published under a famous female identity might well have been written by a man, and *vice versa*.[6]

The industrialization of the literary process extended beyond redefinition of authorship. Stratemeyer also "integrated forward" in ways that were crucial to the success of his whole enterprise. A key innovation here was that he had his novels typeset within the Syndicate, and the electrotype plates would then be leased to a publisher.[7] In this way, he kept control over the product through further stages in its progress towards the market, with the advantage that he could have a stronger bearing on how it would finally be presented to that market. The most significant area in which he brought his influence to bear was in pricing. In 1906 he persuaded one of his publishers, Leon and Cupples, to halve their normal price for a series fiction. Hardback series tended to cost around one dollar, but when *The Motor Boys* was published for fifty cents, it went through thirty-five printings and became one of the bestselling series of all time. Stratemeyer broke the pattern by making publishers recognize that more money was to be made by going for volume of trade. Effectively, Stratemeyer had renegotiated the relation between producer and consumer: the series books were so cheap that they enabled the child-customer to bypass many of the usual adult "gatekeepers" of reading. Buying a series novel became more manageable to the juvenile budget. The series provoked a great deal of complaint from parents, teachers, and librarians, especially after the prices were dropped and the approval of these same adults was no longer necessary to the purchase. Despite objections, the statistics tell us that this was still a booming industry. Between 1900 and 1910, forty-six new series for girls were begun; between 1910 and 1920, there were ninety-four new series for girls.[8] There was a seemingly endless stream of new (though often very similar) narratives, and sales figures indicate that children loved them. As for the nature of adult criticism, it suggests that the series disrupted certain preconceptions of class. There was still the belief that stories for children should be improving, and should urge the values of courage, thrift, patience, and hard work. From this point of view, the series were "cheap gratification" – cheap to buy, but also "vulgar," "tawdry," and "trashy." The Chief Librarian of the Boy Scouts of America was typical when he complained that series novels made no effort to "confine or control" what were considered to be the "highly explosive elements" of childhood passion.[9] We should not assume though that the subject matter was "low life" as in the boys' precursor of Oliver Optic. The content or subject matter of the series was anything but proletarian. If anything, they resemble Ohmann's characterization of adult magazine fiction for the professional–managerial class, in that they too are in love with "upscale emulation." This conflict between established critics and rising producers and consumers serves as a reminder that the emulative drive of the rising classes was only approximate: those who were being "copied" did not recognize themselves in their mimics. And where the tastes and values of different classes did not coincide, the interests of the rising class would prove the ultimate determinant of success.

This social-industrial matrix, with its attendant tension of class interplay, is manifested in the fiction. The most obvious feature of the series is its surface allegiance to modernity. A declared investment in modern technology and modern freedoms is often a defining trait. Many titles, from Stratemeyer and other syndicates and authors, advertise the fact that the fiction is oriented around a specific invention and the liberty it implies: *The Motor Boys, The Motor Girls, The Automobile Girls, The Moving-Picture Girls, The Submarine Boys, The Sky Flyers, The Aviation Girls, The Motor Boat Club*, and so on. As the twinning of titles suggests – Motor Boys and Girls – the girls' series often represents a translation of boys' freedoms for girls' lives. Previously, boys' fiction tended to be more adventurous and girls' more domestic, but here the sense is that all may take part in the adventure of modern technology. Even where technology is not to the fore, there is a prioritization of spatial freedom, as with *The Outdoor Girls, The Campfire Girls, The Meadow-Brook Girls*, and the various Grace Harlow titles, *Grace Harlow Overseas, Grace Harlow's Overland Riders*, and so on. Compared to the interiorized, domestic subjugations of *Little Women* and other first-generation texts, this is adventurous indeed. Modern girls get to do things: to drive cars and even to fix them, to fly planes, solve mysteries, and foil the plots of international criminals. A scholar in the field, Nancy Romalov, observes: "Unlike the heroines in [earlier] novels, who were deprived of their ability to act directly upon the world outside the home, series heroines – however unrealistically – are movers and shakers in the world of education, commerce, and occasionally politics" (p. 3). Similarly, Billman takes the remarkable Ruth Fielding series as a paradigm of change from one kind of fiction to another. Ruth begins as a traditional endangered, orphaned "charity child," but in the course of one of the longest and most prolific series careers, she will become a detective, a playwright, and a film director. The pathetic orphan grows into a dynamic figure of command:

"There she is! That girl in the blue sweater is Ruth Fielding!"
    "You mean the one giving orders through the megaphone? She looks too young to be a moving picture director."[10]

But this rise to command is also a problem. Ruth Fielding in particular out-grew her genre, and her series lost its way. The lesson that Stratemeyer took from this was that he should allow heroines some of the privileges of adult-hood, but he should also ensure that they remained enclosed within net-works of adult approval. Perhaps this is the main drawback of series fiction: the apparent physical freedom is often conditioned by an intense and almost inescapable ideological control. There are attitudes and protocols to which the girls must conform at all times and in all places. While the March girls suffered from more obvious oppressions, they also benefited from "a little wholesome neglect."[11] The freedom of the series fiction girls can seem trivial when the unremitting presence of the imperatives of class is taken into account. Also, as we will see, this type of monitoring recognizes and serves the other factors of overproduction and the engineering of consumption.

    To look more closely at the nature of the fiction, we can begin with a persistent element in the series, of what I will refer to as "resort fiction." Many series have a defining attraction – car, boat, camera, or plane – but this is often twinned with an exotic locale. Indeed, the one follows on from the other: once you have your car, you can aim for a fashionable destination; once you have your camera, you can film it. Boys and girls often have their adventures in historic seaside towns such as Newport or Nantucket, or on the Great Plains, at the Grand Canyon, or, in the case of boys, at West Point or Annapolis.[12] The travel element is a gesture towards consumerism, in that the novels stand in for the touristic experience that most child-readers could not hope to gain at first hand. The same applies to the machines – the cars and boats and planes that, in the real world, were only available to a small part of the adult population. Reading a narrative oriented around a prize commodity becomes a subsidiary "buying into." In resort fiction, the locale itself is a luxury purchase. Among the clearest examples of this is the Automobile Girls, who in successive novels visit Newport, the Berkshires, Palm Beach and Coconut Grove, the Hudson River Valley, Chicago, and Washington. Each destination is emphasized as a place of expensive leisure and of "sights" and "attractions." One of the major sights is that of money and breeding, which are themselves on display. The resort is a place for the exhibition of class values, class "properties," and class assessment, and the novels themselves function in a similar way. Series fiction is both outside and inside wealth, offering a vicarious luxury to the reader while establishing the boundaries of the leisure class. Every novel has its good poor girls who assimilate the code and protect the boundaries – figures who, like the reader, are outsiders who are invited in. There are also the bad poor characters, who try to assimilate the code in order to exploit and undermine. The fiction, then, lays bare its founding contradiction: an enormous hunger for wealth and status is expressed, while climbers and interlopers are exposed and punished.

The Automobile Girls series exemplifies this tension. It pivots on a pair of sisters, Bab and Mollie Thurston. Their well-to-do father has died, and their mother has been swindled out of the father's fortune by a cousin. This swindler is father to the spoilt and snobbish Gladys Le Baron, so from the start a connection is made between ill-gotten gains and failures of etiquette. The Thurston girls now live in a cottage with their mother, and make a little extra money selling strawberries to the people who visit the nearby luxury hotel. The Thurstons are established as March-like characters, in that they are poor but virtuous, and have good breeding. Their modesty makes it plain that, though poor, they do not pose a threat to those that have wealth. They make friends in the right places because they show that they can fit in, that they will always know their place. In a world of relatively new money and new social adventures, such as the world of the resort hotel, behavior is of great importance. Upward mobility has disrupted traditional ties of community and extended family. The places of resort cast everyone into an exciting social vacuum in which antecedents are hard to establish. New forms of connectedness must be relied upon, and a new process of familiarization must be gone through, with certain authenticating tests being applied. Above all this involves obedience to the decorum of class. This fledgling leisure class is so vulnerable to exploitation that explicit obedience to a class-ed code serves as constant reassurance that one is "on the level." As in all girls' fiction, obedience is even more important than money (though, with poetic justice, obedience usually finds its reward in money). Bab and Mollie, by virtue of their proper upbringing, obey the code, especially its strictures on modesty and truthfulness. As one tells the other: "Let us not pretend we are rich, because everybody we meet seems to be." They do not blur their entitlements. Gladys, on the other hand, has the advantage of money, but fails to play by the rules. In the breakfast room of the hotel, she wears a "lingerie frock more appropriate for a party."[13] Even the world of conspicuous consumption has its moments and places of self-conscious modesty, and Gladys, in refusing to obey the rules, will prove a danger to herself and her class.

The dangers attendant on a lack of discipline become apparent when Gladys begins to flirt with a flashy stranger who will later be revealed as a famous international thief. The scenario with Gladys and the thief – he is known as "the Boy Raffles" – is typical, in that the mystery and detection work of these novels is nearly always tied up with preserving social and financial boundaries against the incursions of outsiders. To this extent Bab and Mollie belong to the servant class, in that they maintain and preserve the property of others. This preservation is often figured in explicit form in the plot: at some point in each novel Bab or Mollie will save a rich child from drowning, or from falling off a cliff, or they will intervene when a princess is being threatened by a man with a gun. It tends to be Bab who performs these daring acts, as she is rather tomboyish, and has a tennis serve which is "as swift and straight and true as a boy's."[14] More generally, the Thurston girls preserve the concentration of wealth by exposing plots. In this way, they express both the aspirations of the poor and the paranoia of the rich. To perform their tasks, they must be able to spot who does not fit in. The reader is given fairly obvious clues as to how to do this. Bad people dress too grandly; they flirt; they try to establish their social pre-eminence instead of letting it "materialize." In case the reader is insufficiently alert to such tendencies and what they signify, the narrative gives strong suggestions as to which particular characters to look out for:

No one can deny they make a good appearance but there's something about the mother that I distrust. She is not genuine, and although she tries to conceal it she's not well-bred.[15]

The woman in question dresses "perhaps a shade too elaborately for good taste," and though she claims to be from "an old Southern family" (p. 17), she is of course a lower-class swindler. Having made the assumptions urged upon her by the narrative, the reader's suspicions are triumphantly confirmed towards the end of each novel, when a charmingly modest, and truly wealthy character notes that he or she had suspicions all along: "I am not pretending I knew his special game. Only I knew he was not our sort."[16] At this moment, the reader joins the leisure class in a community of taste, for she too has learned to recognise who is and who is not "our sort."

This is also the meaning of the "club." The Automobile Girls' club – and all the other clubs in series fiction – is based on shared assumptions, common points of view, similar interests. The most obvious shared interest of the Automobile Girls is that of being "autoists," their love of the open road, and of arriving at beautiful and exotic places. More pervasively, however, clubbing together symbolizes the formation of newer, more modern processes of class recognition. The founding club of the Automobile Girls consists of Bab and Mollie; their closest friend, Grace Carter, who is the daughter of the local squire; and Ruth Stuart, a "rich western girl who quite recently had come to spend her summer at Kingsbridge."[17] Ruth's father is a "big, blue-eyed, open-hearted" man who has made his fortune mining out west, and who now deals in real estate in Chicago. What one notices about this club is that it combines the distressed gentility of the Thurstons, the reigning squireachy of the Carters, and the new money of the Stuarts. This marriage of old and new is also indicated in the hints that Mrs. Thurston and Mr. Stuart, both single parents, will fall in love. The series establishes the composition of the new ruling class, and the members of the club are defined partly, but not entirely, in terms of their relation to money: if they have it, if they had it. There is the mixing in of older forms of prestige with the new, the less affluent rural gentry with the cosmopolitan magnate. It is another accommodation between residual and emergent groups. Beyond the club formed by the girls, there is an ever-present sense that the upper class is a kind of club. All its members know each other, or know how to recognize each other. When the girls' car breaks down on the way to Newport, they are rescued by a group of Yale boys, one of whose mothers the girls have already met. Similarly, when the Motor Girls break down while driving through New England, they are rescued by the millionaire owner of the resort hotel they have just visited.[18] This millionaire, it transpires, was friendly with one of the Motor Girls' fathers. The message is clear enough: the upper class represents security and rescue; others constitute a threat. Further, the club looks after its own. Given this stark division between acceptable and unacceptable groups, the narratives incite a strong motivation in the girl-reader: she had better make sure that she belongs.

Although the club is defined by behavior, it is also defined by property, and by one's relation to property. The most secure members are extremely wealthy, and the others have a suitable appreciation of that wealth. This means that the narrative, or indeed the journey that the girls undertake, is a journey through luxury consumables, against a backdrop of purchasable grandeur. When the girls drive to Newport, for instance, they pass through New York, and stay at the Waldorf. Mollie loves to "gaze around her at the women in their jewels and wonderful gowns" (p. 67). She sees one lady "with a string of pearls round her throat, and a pearl and diamond butterfly that glowed and sparkled in her hair" (p. 68). This is Mrs. Cartwright, who will subsequently take the girls to a dance at Yale. Unbeknown to Mrs. Cartwright, the stunning butterfly she wears in her hair falls to the floor. In the first of many such acts of preservation, Mollie picks it up and discreetly returns it to its owner. In her gratitude, Mrs. Cartwright ensures that, once at Newport, the girls are included in all the activities of the rich. She invites them to the Casino, another club, where people of fashion meet for tennis and dances: "Nearly all the nicest people in Newport belong to it" (p. 117). Mrs. Cartwright also has them invited to other spectacular displays of conspicuous consumption, such as a Mrs. Erwin's "famous white and gold ball, long remembered in the history of splendid entertainment in Newport" (p. 131).

This novel and the others in the series are in love with the very heights of luxury. Jewels, yachts, dresses, mansions, limousines, are all lovingly described. The relatively poor Thurston girls are thrilled by their inclusion, but at the same time the narratives also generate excitement by bringing their inclusion into doubt. The drama always hinges on questions of social status, and Bab and Mollie's status in the mansions of Newport is questionable indeed. When a magnificent emerald necklace disappears, it almost seems that Bab will be held responsible. The boundary between respect and covetousness is easily overstepped, and suddenly Bab (and by implication, the reader too) is open to suspicion. The narrative reminds us that the power that makes the rich desirable is also what makes them frightening. Bab has no defence against the disfavor of those who surround her. Ultimately she will be instrumental in the return of the emeralds, but the scenario makes the point that Bab must make it clear whose side she is on. That is not an option for the servants: they are all automatically suspected, and their quarters are searched. So while the novels inculcate a positive love of wealth, they also bear this coercive sting, in that it is dangerous to "get on the wrong side" of wealthy people. This is equally suggested by the title of the chapter in which the lower-class villain will finally be caught: the epithet, "Brought to Bay," is drawn from blood sports. Those who do not serve the rich will be destroyed by them. Bab and Mollie manage to establish themselves on the right side of this divide, and are rewarded with tokens of luxury: a gold watch set in a circle of emeralds, and a pearl butterfly. Having proved that they have the right behavioral characteristics, they are, as it were, welcomed once more into the club.

The alternative to submission to the rules of the newly agglomerated leisure class is either arrest or, if one has been a member, exile. The lower-class villain usually aims to steal not merely the goods of the rich, but also to swindle the affections of the girls themselves. The material paranoia is accompanied by a social-sexual paranoia. In a crude re-working of *Daisy Miller*, and as if to affirm contemporary fears over the white, middle-class adolescent's incoherence, when the Automobile Girls go to Palm Beach, they witness a young heiress being dangerously free with a young man who is not "our sort." They suddenly remember a series of cautionary tales of "foreigners with no money and plenty of title," and "waiters who pretend that they are real counts." They call to mind a particular instance in which a rich American girl married a "title" who turned out to be a waiter who was wanted by the police for forgery. The friends reflect: "Just think girls how dreadfully she must have felt."[19] Well-to-do girls must always be on guard against allowing their hearts to betray their class and its financial investment in them. Yet the fiction also makes it clear that they should not marry for gain. When various attractive Yale boys are dangled before Bab and Mollie, they like best a boy from a family that has lost its fortune. The mother observes of his friendship with Bab:

"It's just like Ralph," she complained to his father, "to pick the poorest girl of the lot, when the rich ones are so much more charming. A great way for him to retrieve the family fortunes!"

"We will hope," said Ralph's father quietly, "that Ralph will not try to restore our fortunes by marrying for money."[20]

Similarly, when they go to Chicago, the girls learn that the beautiful and well-bred Olive Presby could restore her family's wealth by marrying the "Young Napoleon of Finance." But as the "Young Napoleon" is dishonest, and as Olive does not love him, the family will face ruin. They are saved when a long-hidden treasure is rediscovered – by the Automobile Girls. The critical point here is that the narrative is all about getting and retaining money, but that this same material appetite must also be disavowed. To be too hungry is automatically to define oneself as poor and unsuitable. In this way, the characters with dubious status, such as Ralph and the Thurston sisters, must, like the climbers and swindlers, "put on a good show." The theatricality of the leisure class makes it accessible to the deserving poor, and vulnerable to the criminal poor. Bab and Mollie, like other heroines before them, have a performative power that is essential to their ability to "make good." They – and their readers – become involved in the learning and playing out of a code, and their success will lead to seemingly endless resources for performance and reinvention.

Romance is always the element that threatens to destabilize the system. Younger girls like Bab and Mollie are happily seen as too young for love, which they regard as "foolishness." They develop "friendships" which give assurance of romantic success at some point in the future, when the time is right. For the slightly older, marriageable girl, money alone is not important. But class is, in that class indicates morality and correct behavior, and a good girl does not fall in love without these. Also, if a man is of the right class, his family's fortunes may be low, but he has his Yale education and his connections to the web of millionaire businessmen: he is, to quote Alger, "bound to rise." The treatment of romance varies from one series to another, and some are more adventurous in this respect than are the Stratemeyer series. A good example of this is the Motor Girls series. Whereas the Automobile Girls travel with only a female chaperone, and a large part of each novel focuses on adventures that the girls have without boys, the Motor Girls are accompanied everywhere by boys. This is at once more and less daring. More, in that it becomes the grounds for a surprising amount of sexual banter; and less, in that there are few of the anxieties about these girls meeting the wrong kind of man, for they are followed everywhere by boys of their own station. The focus of the Motor Girls is very much on the interplay between boys and girls, and the sexual tensions tend always to surround Walter. He is described in a tantalizing and directly physical way, something that we do not find in the Automobile Girls: "Walter was looking his best, which was always very good, for the brown boy was now browner than ever, with the tan of beach, sand and sun." His attractiveness is also signalled by the homoerotic horseplay of his friends:

"Sometimes he's Walter, but when it comes to the possibility of our losing him, he's Wallie," declared Jack, clasping his arms around the other boy's neck.[21]

In stories that are at least as much about the boys as the girls, Walter always falls in love with each new girl that they meet. When the group is stranded on a sand bank and Walter swims from the boat to shore to get help, he returns with a girl who has helped him, but he is now dressed "only in a bath robe!" His brownness, his good looks, his lively sexual impulsiveness, and his past and future nakedness are all advertised. This adolescent sexual daring does not really extend to the girl characters, who are not embodied to the extent that Walter is – the girl's body is taken for granted to the point that it becomes invisible, and perhaps unmentionable. But the hints of sexuality – embodied in the boy – are particularly interesting when one places them in the context of the politics of the fiction as a whole. The more chances that the narrative takes in this, the more punitive it is of transgressions in other areas. For the Motor Girls fiction also has a much cruder, and even vindictive ruling-class politics than does the Automobile

Girls series. It is tempting to read *The Motor Girls Through New England* (1911), for instance, as a parable on the dangers of Progressivism. The girls meet an attractive young woman who tells them of her brother, a beautiful and well-bred young man who has gone astray:

[H]e got interested in social problems, and got to thinking that the poor were always oppressed, and all that sort of thing...He went down there among the foreigners to study actual conditions. Did you ever hear of anything so idiotic? (pp. 185–86)

The narrative tells us very clearly to trust in the kindly common sense of the plutocracy, and to steer away from new-fangled notions of social improvement. More importantly, the lower classes are figured as foreigners, immigrants, "Bolshevists," uncouth workmen, and so on. This is a world in which white girls are chloroformed and abducted by marginal others. The Anglo-Saxon whiteness of the middle class, always implicit, becomes explicit here with danger coming from "whiteness of a different colour" as represented by gypsies. Indeed, the unplaceable foreignness of "gypsies" allows them to stand in for the ethnic and racial other more generally. Sexuality is invoked by the presence of the other, in that the other is nearly always libidinal and "primitive." The sex that Walter represents in a light-hearted way is counterbalanced by a more predatory and violent appetite. Nancy T. Romalov explains the role of the gypsy in series fiction in this way. Drawing on bell hooks' discussion in *Black Looks* (1992), she argues:

These white girls may for a time flirt with desire for the primitive and fantasize about living gypsy lives, but their infatuation with the exotic is soon manipulated and transformed into a cautionary tale about the limits of independence and into lessons on sexual knowledge.[22]

This seems absolutely right, except that the message in the Motor Girls might be seen not as a rejection of the sexual, but a rejection of the sexual insofar as it involves venturing outside of one's own class. But Romalov's most telling perception for me is that, the more eroticized the narrative, the more strongly the menacing other will feature. This is akin to my earlier observation that the rich are as frightening as they are attractive. As with earlier girls' fictions, the material seems to invite a Foucaldian reading: through its permissive lures, the narrative instigates the attraction and the guilt that will enable future discipline. What we learn by placing the Motor Girls series next to the Automobile Girls, however, is that, within a very restricted formula, there are significant differences. The Automobile Girls stories remain at an innocent, pre-sexual level, whereas the Motor Girls series permits a racier, eroticized pleasure. But what all the novels affirm is that wealth is pleasure: it is things, places, experiences, power, respect, indulgence, love, and non-threatening sexual allure. The fiction inculcates a desire for power over the commodity, and it gives an aspect of the commodity to all human trans-actions. In this sense the series serves as a further example of engineering consumption or, more pervasively, of engineering consumerism.

I have focused on some of the series that deal most explicitly with "upscale emulation." But even where the series do not reproduce the same extrav-agant consumerist spectacle, they offer the same subliminal motives and principles, the same social structuring of consumerism. They are still about the pleasures and entitlements of class. To give one example, Stratemeyer introduced Laura Lee Hope's *The Moving-Picture Girls* in 1914 to com-plement Victor Appleton's *The Moving-Picture Boys* (1913–22). Obviously both were designed to capitalize on the sudden development of the cinema as a popular spectacle. The Moving-Picture Girls novels are geared to a younger audience than are the Automobile Girls, in that the girl characters are younger, and their father is present in all their adventures. The social focus is not as rarefied as in the other series, in that the film company represents a more inclusive realm – indeed, a microcosm. Ruth and Alice DeVere work as actresses for the Comet Film Company. Alice has a nascent love-interest in the male lead, Paul Ardite, whereas Ruth seems destined for the likeable and ingenious cameraman, Russ Dalwood. The father, Hosmer DeVere, is troubled by an "affliction" of the throat, which means he can no longer work in "legitimate drama," where he "had formerly been a leading player."[23] Rather as with the Alcotts and their fictional alter egos, the nar-rative signals an anxiety over loss of caste. Appearing in film seems to be a latterday version of taking in washing, except that in this case the narrative sympathies are very firmly in favour of trade as a form of progress. Of Mr. DeVere's attitude to film-acting, we are told:

At first the veteran actor was much opposed to the idea, looking down upon moving pictures as "common." But his daughters induced him to try it, and he came to like them very much. The pay, too, was good.[24]

But this gradual adjustment is off-set by more reactionary forces within the company. Mr. DeVere's authentic status as decayed gentry is contrasted with the belated pretensions of others. Another actor, Wellington Bunn, com-plains endlessly about being reduced to film-acting, even though "he had not made a success in Shakespeare."[25] Also present is the ethnicized impli-cation of class. In a comic revision of the relations between the Marches and the Hummels in *Little Women*, the De Vere girls interact with immigrant figures in the form of the genial comedian, Mr. Switzer, and Mrs. Maguire, who takes the "old woman parts." They are welcome additions to the troupe, but also signaled as inferior. The most significant point of contrast for the girls, however, is with the company's two ingénues. Pearl Pennington and Laura Dixon are "from the vaudeville stage, and you could see this without being told."[26] The new technology of film, then, is acknowledged as a positive force that can encourage and accommodate social adjustment, but it does also permit the emergence of a new hierarchy, which reproduces many of the attitudes of the old one. The vaudeville actresses provide an updated version of the vulgar, *nouveau riche* city girls of fifty years earlier. Through them the series expresses an on-going fear over theatricality and display. Although the series deals with the usual kinds of conspiracy (people being tricked out of their property) the continuous conspiracy is that of the vaudeville actresses to displace Ruth and Alice as the "leading ladies." Pearl and Laura are always at hand to grumble about casting, to deride Alice and Ruth's efforts, and to resent the vicissitudes of the profession. This is a modernized restaging of the battle between a dominant rural class, and a flashier, more consumerized urban class. Ruth and Alice will prevail because they manage to strike a proper balance between old and new. They love the energy and even the slang of the film world: "[I]t's this moving picture business. It just makes you want to use words that *mean* something." But they also love the country and its traditions, while the vaudeville girls complain when the quiet of the country begins to "get on their nerves." That Ruth and Alice represent a perfect modern compromise is suggested by the fact that they are chosen to play country girls in film. Alice performs in "a simple little drama, concerning a country girl and boy," in which she and Paul Ardite are the "chief characters." Ruth "was to represent a country maid of a generation past – and very pretty she looked, too, in her wide skirts and poke bonnet, covered with roses." Subsequently both are cast as "Quaker Maids."[27] Repeatedly they are permitted the thrills and diversity of modernity, but in such a way as to confirm their traditional worth. They, like Wiggin's Rebecca and Webster's Judy, are post-pastoral heroines.

The Moving-Picture Girls maintain their social seniority via their training and their background, but they also get to travel, to dress up, to embody a series of different possibilities. They also maintain their power over upstarts from lower classes and other races. For all that this series has less of the worldly paraphernalia of the Automobile Girls and other series, these girls do learn all the skills and codes that will enable them to do and to have more. They still get to play the "chief characters." And all these girls, from whatever series, get to go on to further adventures. In this respect, the series is always a perfect instance of consumer culture, as reader and characters alike can go on from one volume to another, from one series to another, in a seemingly endless process. This hunger for narrative reminds us once more of the definitive hungry heroine, Sister Carrie, who also "wanted more – a great deal more." The advent of series fiction ensured that, in her reading life at least, the girl's desire for more would always be fulfilled.

PART III

Revision

7

The clean and the dirty

In some of the key bestsellers of the turn of the century, including *Rebecca of Sunnybrook Farm* and *Daddy-Long-Legs*, the girl represented a modified version of Romantic nature. With the spontaneity of youth, she seemed a model of Wordsworthian authenticity amidst the artificiality of the modern age. But the nature that she could represent was limited. Certainly it excluded such things as sexuality or predatory violence. In her nature took naive and harmless forms, so she could serve as a preferred image for a society that was ever more deeply immured in the guilt and dirt of industrial urbanization. But far from being an antidote to the modern, in reality the girl was one of its defining symbols. She stood for a consumerized pastoralism. Through her, natural values could be transformed into a spectacle to beguile the successful city-dweller. There was, though, a reaction against the consumerist idealization of girlhood. With the success of *Rebecca of Sunnybrook Farm*, Wiggin became embroiled in what Howells referred to as the "realism wars." She intervened in the debate as to whether the privileging of the girl and her cleanly nature had led to an anemic culture. Similarly, Webster's girl-oriented work was occasionally excoriated for infantilizing popular taste. The girl was caught up in the argument as to what fiction should attempt to do. Even from its early days, girls' fiction was set up as a sort of cure to what were perceived as overly critical and sensational realist tendencies. In 1870, a reviewer for *Lippincott's Magazine* praised Alcott for being one of the "honorable exceptions to the present literary degeneracy." As early as 1867 the "Books for Young People" column in *Riverside Magazine* interpreted the emergence of children's literature as a necessary response to the development of an increasingly frank, "scientific," and distressing realism:

The birth and growth of a special literature for the young is the result of a reaction from the tendencies of modern literature. Just as the tired father, jangled with the disturbances of his day's toil, flees for refuge to his prattling children and finds an inexpressible soothing in their free nature; so, weary with the push, the sweat, the burden of a literature which believes in no atmosphere that cannot be weighed and measured, men have begun to turn to what children read, hoping to find there more faith in what is above the mean faculty of understanding.[1]

From Alcott on through Wiggin and Webster, girls' fiction offered a realism that was heavily conditioned by polite sensibilities. These writers took a parental responsibility; they did not wish to disturb their reader with a detailed knowledge of misery or depravity. Other writers, though, wished to affront that same reader, to make him or her fully aware of the shameful consequences of American modernity. Beside the wistful pastoralism of *Rebecca of Sunnybrook Farm*, one might set Crane's *Maggie: A Girl of the Streets* (1892); beside Judy's ascent to the leisure class might be placed the more compromised trajectories of Dreiser's *Sister Carrie* (1900) or Norris's *McTeague* (1899). All of these novels, both "anemic" and "strong," were written with a recognition of the security and power of wealth, but they operate under very different understandings of nature and the natural. Writers like Crane and Norris reveal the influence of French naturalism, in that they present nature as a series of social and biological determinisms. With them, nature has become a scientific logic of recurrent traits and unavoidable destinies. In their "dirty fiction," nature is the force of the individual's inherited social and racial characteristics, including propensities to alcoholism, violence, and illicit and perverse forms of sexual expression. Webster's Judy is the pristine individual of dubious provenance, as orphaned from her background as from her parents. In naturalist fiction, though, the underclass individual is much less likely to escape the perceived degeneracy of poverty.[2]

Novels such as *Rebecca of Sunnybrook Farm* and *Daddy-Long-Legs* were praised for providing "blessed relief" in contrast to the "murky" and "morbid" works of the naturalist school. The girl was a paradigmatic figure in the contest over fiction, nature, and social reality, and Wiggin and Webster were influential combatants. I want to build on this sense of contest by looking at the work of Gene Stratton-Porter. Although she is now largely forgotten, Stratton-Porter was among the most famous and the best-paid of American writers in her heyday of 1905 to 1920. She is of interest here because she shows some of the same tendencies as her precursors: in her we find an engagement with the pleasures of modern consumerism – an engagement that is tempered by fears of the artificiality of modern life. But Stratton-Porter also betrays a growing uncertainty over the "clean nature" of earlier heroines and the "dirty nature" of the naturalists. She belongs in a discussion of buying into womanhood because in her the issue of determinism – of social and biological inheritance – is closely bound up with the right to wealth and spending power. I focus on two of her novels, each of which offers a slightly different perspective on these central concerns. In *A Girl of the Limberlost* (1909), Stratton-Porter assesses the girl's right of access to American wealth, as it is symbolized in the dangerous but attractive swamp of the Limberlost. In *Her Father's Daughter* (1921), the white heroine's control of money is presented in relation to the claims of other races, and especially in relation to the "Yellow Peril" of Japanese immigration. And in spite of Stratton-Porter's declared dislike of "strong" fiction, both novels suggest a naturalistic social vision. The girl's powers and rights of acquisition serve as an expression of her legitimacy in relation to predatory others.

All the foregoing would suggest that Stratton-Porter occupied or explored a different fictional realm than earlier writers of girls' fiction, and clearly she does represent a new and revisionist impulse. But she can be integrated into the tradition more easily than we might wish. Her girls are buying into womanhood in that they acquire consumerist powers and skills, but Stratton-Porter construes the process in a much more overtly political way. No other writer offers such explicit support for the socio-scientific narratives of adolescence. She picks up not so much on the moral tumult of adolescence, as on the endangerment of white, middle-class power. Following Hall and other more pointedly racist sources, she fictionalizes the imperative that the girl be socially and racially coherent. A crucial part of this is that the girl prepares herself to submit to the duties of reproduction. While Stratton-Porter's girls are buying into womanhood, she is much less concerned with individualized means of self-expression, than with the girl's need to subjugate herself to urgent political necessity. But perhaps Stratton-Porter's work is simply a more extreme version of what is implicit elsewhere. In *Little Women* and other early classics, the white, middle-class girl must learn to manage rather than to befriend the racial or ethnic other. The girl has a duty to aid and even improve the other, and while this may seem benevolent, it always assumes and confirms a hierarchy. In the series fiction, the same racialized thematic emerges in more paranoid form, as "gypsies" and underclass others threaten the white girl with abduction and ruin. The other has come to seem an intractable problem, and management must take ever more aggressive forms. In her representation of underclass and "foreign" others, Stratton-Porter is unusually extreme, but she is not without precedent.

It would seem strange to the critics of Stratton-Porter's own day to discuss her or her work with any seriousness. For much of her career, she was derided for her romantic and idealizing tendencies, but defended herself on the grounds that her fiction was true to her own experience. When she wrote of strong, trustworthy, and loving people, she claimed that they were based on men and women that she had known. Arguing from an explicitly anti-naturalist position, she stated that critics would only believe that something was true to life if it was also the worst in life. It was symptomatic of distorted "literary" preoccupations that they could not believe that anything "clean" might also be true. She claimed to take her fiction from life itself, with her role merely that of a "transmitter." She became a major campaigner against what she saw as the "muckraking" tendencies of the age, and wrote articles on "Why I Always Wear My Rose-Colored Glasses." Characteristically, when she became involved in film-making, she chose to work with Thomas Ince, whose slogan was "Clean Pictures for Clean People."[3] Contemporary dust-jacket notes promote her on the grounds that "[g]enerations of readers have grown up with these delightful, wholesome romances." Stratton-Porter seems, on first view, to belong on the side of other "clean" or "anemic" writers such as Webster and Wiggin. That one "grows up" with Stratton-Porter captures the by-now familiar theme that juvenile fiction is not only "for" or "about" one particular group. Rather it is for readers, whether adult or child, who wish to trace the progress towards adulthood. The juvenile novel may safely be given to the young reader, but the older person is equally welcome: if "it's been a long time since you re-read [them]," you can "dip into one today for a lasting literary treat."[4] The recreational value is literally that; it is a fiction of return, of going over, of rescue. Stratton-Porter was keenest to rescue what she took to be the purity and good sense of a farming life in the country. In novel after novel, and also in the editorials she wrote for *McCall's*, she extolled the vigour and usefulness of farm lives, and decried the artificiality of the modern age. The outdoors was clean and authentic; the indoors was unhealthy and tainted. She warned repeatedly of the dangers of dancing, smoking, and immodest clothing, and she boasted of the boredom that she felt at society events.

Stratton-Porter typifies a conflict of authority between a basic rural background and modern consumerist splendor. In a magazine article, "Why I Wrote *A Girl of the Limberlost*," she presents us with a series of scenes of reading:

First, a wealthy club woman of a great city wrote me that she had read one of my books to a company of tired clerks, while they lunched at their noon rest hour, and it had brought to them a few minutes of country life so real that they had begged for more. A nurse wrote from a hospital ward, for a man who had always lived in and loved the open and now, from spinal trouble, would never walk again, that my pictures of swamp and forest were so true he had lost himself for an hour in them, and would I please send his address to my publishers, so that he might be informed when I wrote again. The warden of a state reform school wrote that fifteen hundred sin-besmirched little souls in his care, shut for punishment from their natural inheritance of field and wood, were reading my books to rags because they scented freedom and found comfort in them.[5]

In this version, fulfillment is to be found in the return to nature that Stratton-Porter can provide. Her motive is to "carry to workers inside city walls, to hospital cots, to those behind prison bars, and to scholars in their libraries, my story of earth and sky."[6] She plays upon contemporary notions of "over-civilization," with tired clerks and city workers, and the idea that the solution for the exhausted and the corrupted is a return to nature. The structure of address is always hierarchical, with a powerful figure advocating Stratton-Porter's fiction to a needy and ingenuous readership. She envisages a deserving reader in the same way that philanthropists envisaged a deserving poor. One senses a secret pleasure in the spectacle of the needy readership, in that their hopeless submission confirms the necessity and the conspicuousness of her success.

A Girl of the Limberlost (1909) is indeed about the superiority of a country background, but it is equally about the need to leave such a background behind. The heroine's triumph lies in gaining access to cosmopolitan largesse. The country proves to be as much the scene of in-bred madness and criminality as it is of wild, romantic beauty. The story is that of Elnora Comstock, a girl who lives on a farm bordering on the Limberlost swamp. Shortly after she was born, her father fell into the swamp. Her mother, weakened by childbirth, was unable to save her husband, and she has blamed and hated her daughter for this failure ever since. Mrs. Comstock, in a prolonged madness of grief, spends her nights in the swamp, lamenting her husband. From this background, the narrative projects a familiarly modern and urbanizing course for Elnora: "Behind her lay the land on which she had been born to drudgery and to a mother who made no pretence of loving her; before her lay the city through whose schools she hoped to find means of escape and the way to reach the things for which she cared."[7] This narrative vantage-point hinges on the generational difference between Elnora and her mother. As with the relationship between Rebecca and her thrifty Aunt Miranda, this is a difference that manifests itself particularly in different ways of understanding wealth. Mrs. Comstock is tied to old forms of wealth, in that she is obsessed with paying the taxes on her land. This means that she and her daughter never have any money to spend. Meanwhile, her daughter makes efforts of her own to attend school, only to find that she is laughed at and ostracized for her country eccentricity. Seen as backward and unsophisticated by her citified peers, Elnora must overturn the meanness of her agricultural past, and the liminal dangers of the swamp. She achieves this social redemption via a meeting with the moth woman, a character that Stratton-Porter based on her adult self. The moth woman is interested in the swamp because it is the habitat of many rare and beautiful specimens. She wants to gather as large and comprehensive a collection as she can, and she pays Elnora for any moths she can bring to her. The swamp, then, is presented as a rich natural scene, and it is all the more to be valued because it is disappearing. Lumbermen are draining, felling, and clearing the Limberlost to make way for the planting of more corn and potatoes. But aside from its natural wonders, the Limberlost swamp is also the meeting-place of the loafing, criminal Corson gang. So the central motif of the novel is used to ambiguous effect. The swamp signifies madness, confusion, the past, brutality, the criminal, but also beauty, individuality, and rarity. Elnora herself occupies a rather uncertain position in relation to this. She can escape from all that the swamp implies by turning its natural resources to profit. Like the lumbermen, she "industrializes" her environment with the collection of rare moths for pinning. She uses the money to buy books, clothes, and the "treats" that win her favour at school. The novel never pauses to lament this business of plucking the moths from their nocturnal half-life, to be exposed on the entomologist's board. There is the implication that the narrative is ultimately more in love with order and productivity than with the festering strangeness of the swamp. As one character expresses it in another Limberlost novel: "I feel dreadfully over having the swamp ruined, but isn't it a delight to hear the good, honest ring of those axes, instead of straining your ears for stealthy sounds?"[8]

Ultimately, Stratton-Porter banishes the nature she loved and that made her famous, in favour of a consumerized and metropolitan modernity. Yet, in keeping with the divided response to nature, much of the novel is equally concerned with reversing this tendency. The more firmly Elnora establishes herself in the city life of dresses and soda-fountains, the more her narrator vaunts what has been left behind. Even Elnora's mother's abusive treatment is seen to have had its improving effects. Elnora is well-mannered in a submissive, old-fashioned way. As one city matron notes of this "unusual case of repression," Elnora "waits on her elders and thinks before she speaks" (p. 98). Also, a relenting Mrs. Comstock makes various delicacies for Elnora to share with her schoolfriends, which have a freshness and novelty that store-bought candy lacks. After its initial yearning for modern consumption, *A Girl of the Limberlost* balances itself by exploring the things that, as Mrs. Comstock says, "money can't buy." This reversed course is most fully developed with the introduction of the love-interest. In keeping with contemporary fears over the emasculating tendencies of in-doors, modern living, Philip Ammon is an ailing scion of a wealthy Chicago family, who has come to the country to recover his health and his sense of the natural fitness of things. He corresponds to the jaded modern readers whom Stratton-Porter claims to have refreshed in "Why I Wrote *A Girl of the Limberlost.*" As his name suggests, he represents the potency of city wealth, but with something missing ([M]ammon). It is through going to the Limberlost, and through his encounter with Elnora, that he will re-virilize his body and his mind. He is engaged to marry Edith Carr, a selfish socialite who will never be able to give him the kind of support he needs. The contrast between Elnora and Edith, as each tries to win American wealth in the form of Philip Ammon, allows Stratton-Porter to represent both her preferred view of nature and her fundamental understanding of the natural world. In a repeat of *Rebecca of Sunnybrook Farm* and like novels, Elnora's backwardness becomes the strong but modest womanliness that the "Man of Affairs" must find. Meeting an active and self-reliant girl like Elnora teaches Philip to despise the "strictly ornamental" types like Edith. We might have assumed that Elnora as child of nature would be wild and irresponsible, but in fact it is Edith who is closer to the swamp, in that she has never learnt to curb her wishes. She is, we are told, an "unrestrained woman" (p. 303). Her grace is described as "inborn," meaning that it is inherent, but also suggesting the onset of the degeneracy of inbreeding (p. 286).

The crucial point here is that nature operates differently on different characters. With some it is naturalistic, with others it is Romantic. It has produced in Edith a sort of *fin de siècle* degeneracy. But in Elnora it has inspired a transcendent morality: the beeches have taught her to "be patient and to be unselfish," while the oaks "say 'be true,' 'live a clean life,' 'send your soul up here and let the winds of the world teach of what honor achieves'" (p. 254). Similarly Elnora's dead father is idealized as a dreamy, outdoors figure, but we later learn that "no woman was ever safe with him" (p. 191). Nature is glorified as an epiphanic moral force, but it also subsists as a violently opportunistic sexuality. If for no other reason than that she was a keen botanist and entomologist, Stratton-Porter did not deny the evolutionary theories that informed naturalism. Nature was for her the sign of depredation and amorality, even though it also remained the scene of transcendental inspiration. She is a classic instance of what Mark Seltzer has called the "transmutation of the natural," in that the boundaries between what counts as nature, what counts as artifice, and what counts as technology, are all shifting. She presents us with "melodramas of uncertain agency," in that her characters are at once individualized entities, and biological machines.[9] Through Elnora, Stratton-Porter attempts to moralize an otherwise amoral struggle for predominance between biological machines: she makes her heroine both good and strong. But ultimately their relation to the wealthy suitor makes both Elnora and Edith appear in the light of commodities. Elnora has a simple, provincial charm, whereas Edith is the fetishized, leisure-class *pièce de résistance*. Philip will, of course, opt for Elnora.

A further complication occurs with Stratton-Porter's attempt to represent social hierarchy as evidence of naturalistic truths. Underlying the call for modesty, there is in this fiction a desperate thirst for power and recognition. Although Stratton-Porter makes much of the humility of her favoured characters, they prove to be among "nature's aristocrats." This tendency is rendered even more literally in the "prequel" to *A Girl of the Limberlost*, Stratton-Porter's first big success, *Freckles* (1904). The orphaned and abandoned Freckles's name suggests a mongrelized, betwixt-and-between quality. But when an upper-class girl falls in love with him, she deduces that he must be from a background at least as exalted as her own: "Thistles grow from thistles, and lilies from other lilies" (p. 273). Sure enough, she soon discovers that Freckles is descended from Irish lords. In life, Stratton-Porter invented a coat-of-arms for herself to lend some spurious substance to family myths about noble ancestors; in fiction, she could not quite value her characters without doing something similar. Meanwhile, anyone without the right breeding is condemned to poverty, and is seen to be naturally fitted for this lowly estate.

There is, then, a naturalistic and ethnicized sentiment at work, whereby one type of blood is recognized and rewarded as superior and clean, and another is rejected as irredeemably corrupted. Elnora, the clean-minded, country-bred girl, proves the natural inheritor of American wealth, as is signified by her marriage to Philip Ammon. She will have a cosmopolitan life in Chicago, while the degenerate Edith will retire to the country with a man who understands her weakness. But Stratton-Porter also confirms the naturalistic vision in unintended ways, in that the novel itself has a kind of predatory energy, as Edith is laid bare, punished, and exiled. The narrative exemplifies a kind of evolutionary violence, as Elnora gains everything and others are destroyed. Although Elnora makes the transition from rural hardship to consumerist power, there is a concurrent reactionary element that is concerned with possession and preservation, not expenditure. The logic is that of competition for limited resource. The novel does not quite believe in the modern myth of abundance, and Stratton-Porter means to see that her fictional alter ego gets her rightful share. This competitive drive for limited resource would find its fullest and most explicit form in *Her Father's Daughter*. In this later novel, it takes on a broader and more political aspect, in that Stratton-Porter suggests that the white race can only thrive via a struggle for pre-eminence with other races. Her work exemplifies the fears that we have seen elsewhere: that the modern white woman's claiming of independence led to a decline in the birth-rate, and that this was tantamount to "race suicide." White victory was thought to hinge upon controlling and increasing white reproduction, and so there was a need to re-engineer the white girl's attitudes as she approached child-bearing age. In *Her Father's Daughter*, the girl becomes involved in a racist and nationalist competition. Much as Elnora would prevail at Edith's expense, in this subsequent fiction we discover that the wealth of the "clean American" will be at the expense of a "dirty Jap."

Stratton-Porter's later novel deals with widespread fears over the "rising tide of color."[10] Like many other long-established immigrants – white, largely Protestant people from Britain, Germany and Scandinavia – she tended to see her own race as useful, civilized, and assimilable, while "new" immigrants – Catholic, Orthodox, Jewish, from Italy and Middle Europe – were less desirable. This distrust of "whiteness of a different color" was matched by her fears over the "rise of the Negro." She is characteristic of the nativist atmosphere that legitimated lynching, political disenfranchisement, and "deportation delirium."[11] Having acquired fame and money, she moved to Los Angeles, and took up the West coast variant of nativist politics. The long history of anti-Chinese discrimination had already led to the ending of Chinese immigration. However, there was small-scale Japanese immigration from 1880 onwards, and so fears of "the Yellow Peril" were kept vividly alive. Immigration from Japan was particularly feared because Japan was seen as a "strong" nation. It had its own imperial interests, and had recently won a war against Russia. With the American acquisition of the Philippines, the United States itself was a player in Asia. Japan and the United States were already verging on a predatory contest for pre-eminence. The white backlash against Asia was evident in various nativist tracts, in newspapers, and in electoral campaigns. In the opening decades of the twentieth century, the San Francisco *Chronicle* ran articles with captions asserting that "Crime and Poverty Go Hand in Hand with Asiatic Labor," "Brown Men Are an Evil in the Public Schools," "Japanese a Menace to American Women," and "Brown Asiatics Steal the Brains of Whites," all ideas that Stratton-Porter would exploit in *Her Father's Daughter*. In 1906, the San Francisco Board of Education directed that

Japanese children be taught in segregated schools, and when, in 1919, James D. Phelan was coming up for re-election to the Senate, he campaigned under the slogan, "Keep California White." The Hearst newspapers conducted anti-Japanese campaigns in 1915–16, and Irish-dominated trades unions were actively anti-Japanese throughout the period. Wallace Irwin, in *Seed of the Sun* (1921) would warn that Americans had better watch out because "[t]here's standing room only in Japan." The emerging cinematic culture of Hollywood was equally sensitive to the excitement surrounding the figure of the Japanese immigrant. With silent films such as *The Yellow Menace* (1916) and the Fu Manchu series, and in the various Hollywood versions of *Madame Butterfly*, Japanese and Asians were represented as dangerously exotic, fiendish, rapacious, but occasionally child-like and sympathetic.[12]

There is a dual tendency at work in this period, and it is exemplified in Stratton-Porter. On the one hand, there is the imperial approach to and intrusion upon the other, as with the draining of the Limberlost, or indeed ventures in the Philippines. Such imperial intrusions are accompanied by self-purifying strategies. After forcible contact with the world, America must be on guard against counter-intrusion: the urge toward expansion brings in its wake a concern with racial and territorial integrity.[13] In *Her Father's Daughter*, Stratton-Porter would bring these issues to the fore, but within the familiar rubric of the girl's acquisition of money and power. The novel offers us a dual struggle, as the heroine must compete with her sister for the right to spend their father's legacy, and white children must struggle with Japanese and all other races over the right to enjoy the wealth of America. It is the story of Linda Strong, daughter of a famous "nervous specialist" (*sic*). The seventeen-year-old Linda's parents have died in a car accident, and she now lives with her sister, Eileen. This is less than ideal, as Linda was close only to her father, and Eileen only to her mother. As with the hated mother and the demonized rival in *A Girl of the Limberlost*, there is a strong competitive drive for precedence in relation to the father. With her father, Linda led a healthy outdoors life, observing nature, while Eileen was spoilt by her socially ambitious mother. Eileen now leads a hedonistic, jazz age existence of smoking, dancing, and spending to excess on fashionable clothes. Given their different dispositions, Linda is secretly convinced that she is indeed "her father's daughter," but that Eileen and the mother are not her blood relatives. The novel will bear this out, revealing that Linda and Eileen are only step-sisters, brought together in what was a second marriage for both parents. Linda is proved to be the only truly "Strong" character.

There is a clear opposition between Linda's sturdy values, and the modern, racially "tainted" jazz culture of Eileen. The novel engineers a distinction between a girl who has been reared to make a "well-dressed, cultured, and gracious woman," and a girl who has been "reared for society." The good girl should avoid "rouge, lipstick, hair-dress, and French heels" (p. 103), and above all, she should aim to be a mother and a support to her husband. She should be unconscious of any selfish or pecuniary opportunity that life presents to her, even though, at the same time, she will not marry beneath herself. She must be restrained, and semi-consciously naive. *Her Father's Daughter* will become a contest between the two sisters, and between the two extremes of traditional and modern femininity. Linda tells Eileen:

If Daddy were living I think he would say we have reached the limit with apartment house homes minus fireplaces, with restaurant dining minus a blessing, with jazz music minus melody, with jazz dancing minus grace, with artificial progress minus cradles. (p. 34)

Eileen lives in an "atmosphere of georgette and rouge," while Linda wears breeches and can cook a meal in the desert. As the good Irish servant, Katie, declares, youngsters like Eileen miss out on the "natural joy the good God provides" because they are in a "scrabble to wring artificial joy out of life" (p. 45). Although Linda is independent in that she can survive in the wild, she looks forward to the day on which she will subjugate herself to a husband. Her strength lies in her natural resignation to the re-virilization of American values. Her sister, like Edith in *A Girl of the Limberlost*, has more selfish will than is appropriate to a woman, and again like Edith, she will be humiliated.

The re-authentication of an essentially masculine national identity takes on a racial form in that white America must reaffirm its superiority over other races and nations. Stratton-Porter takes up this theme at the start when Linda chides a popular, well-bred boy, Donald Whiting, for failing his race. She tells him that:

[A] boy as big and as strong as you and with as good a brain and your opportunities has allowed a little brown Jap to cross the Pacific Ocean and in a totally strange country to learn a language foreign to him, and, with the same books and the same chances, to beat you at your own game. (pp. 4–5)

Donald asks her for advice on how he can "beat that little cocoanut-headed Jap" (p. 85), and their subsequent friendship is built on her helping him to rediscover and reimpose his racial superiority. Linda argues that white pre-eminence lies in the constructive or inventive faculty. Other races are merely imitative:

I know of a case where a little Indian was picked up from a tribal battlefield in South America and brought to this country and put into our schools, and there was nothing that any white pupil could do that he couldn't, so long as it was imitative work... when a white man is constructive, when he does create, he can cut circles around the colored races. The thing is to get the boys and girls of today to understand what is going on in the world, what they must do as their share in making the world safe for their grandchildren.

And as elsewhere in Stratton-Porter's work, proof is to be found in the natural world:

There is no better study than to go into the canyons or the deserts and efface yourself and watch life. It's an all-day process of the stronger annihilating the weaker. The one inexorable thing in the world is Nature. (p. 89)

Whereas other races are savage, the white race is intelligent. But this same intelligence, it would seem, must be used to savage effect: "[W]ith our brains we must do in a scientific way what Nature does with tooth and claw" (p. 90). In the meantime, Linda makes money writing a series of articles on "Aboriginal Cookery" for a magazine. She describes "Indian Salads" and other dishes for her readers, but Stratton-Porter's virulent prejudice prevents her from seeing Linda's imitation as problematic. This kind of racialized false consciousness is in evidence throughout. Linda claims white superiority on the basis of rational, constructive power; but privately, she acknowledges a more visceral sense of motive: "[I]n all my life I have never seen anything so masklike as the stolid little square head on that Jap. I have never seen anything I dislike more than the oily, stiff, black hair standing up like menacing bristles." She finds "something repulsive" in his eyes (p. 122). Although the narrative cannot quite recognize this, whatever is attributed to the other is also to be found in the self. Every aspect of "Japanese" identity is unconsciously reflected in the seventeen-year-old heroine's own attitudes. She resents the Japanese for their perceived impassiveness, detecting behind it an "oily" or calculating intelligence. This is confirmed by her belief that they form a brotherhood to look out for each other's interests, even to the point of murder. Meanwhile, in a moment of calculation and conspiracy of her own, she forms a pact with her school friend, Donald, to help him beat their Japanese class-mate, Oka Sayye. She perceives a "deviousness" in the Japanese, but no one is more disingenuous than she. And for all that she deplores the murderous brotherhood, she herself declares that a white woman would stab or club to death a foreigner when her native interests were threatened.

The narrative, which Stratton-Porter described as "just a plain little story cut clean from the pages of life,"[14] will dramatize and vindicate the heroine's nativist impulses. Oka Sayye follows Linda, Donald, and Katie on a cooking and botanizing expedition into the desert. He tries to murder Donald, his natural rival, by rolling a rock down onto him, but only Donald's foot is trapped and broken. Linda and Katie go after Oka Sayye, and Katie kills him: "'Get him?' [Linda] asked tersely, as if she were speaking of a rat or a rattlesnake" (p. 331). Linda finds in herself all the aggression and envy that she projects onto other races. Her polemic anticipates violence as a way of justifying violence:

People have talked about the 'yellow peril' until it's got to be a meaningless phrase. Somebody must wake up to the realization that it's the deadliest peril that has ever menaced white civilization ... If California does not wake up very shortly and very thoroughly she is going to pay an awful price for the luxury she is experiencing while she pampers herself with the service of the Japanese, just as the South has pampered herself for generations with the service of the Negroes. When the Negroes learn what there is to know, then the day of retribution will be at hand. (pp. 88, 280–81)

Stratton-Porter takes up arms in the interest of a spuriously deterministic logic whereby the northern Europeans are seen as clean, pure, ideal, and superior. Yet the white self, embroiled in racialized hatred, seems no more ideal than the projected dirty, sensual other. This kind of projection is particularly familiar to us in the wake of studies of imperialism, and it is a notion that Christopher Lane took up in his recent study, *The Ruling Passion*. The point of Lane's evocative title is that the ruler posits a gap between the rational, intelligent self and the childish, passionate other. But the "ruling passion" is precisely that – a passion. As such, it is driven by the same powerful and subjective urges that it attributes to the other. All of those visceral wishes, fears and loathings that Linda herself feels, she represents as characteristic of the Japanese and the Black. Desire is cathected as racial violence, a violence that assures the ideality – the whiteness or cleanness – of the self.[15]

This twinning of race and desire is brought out more fully in the treatment of romance. Although Linda could marry Donald, a boy from a wealthy and leading family, she will not. But her alternative is equally safe, in that she will marry a rich author, Peter Morrison. Like a good juvenile heroine, she does not recognize her own burgeoning attractiveness, and never understands sexual feeling to originate within herself. She is aroused in relation to the "menace" of the racial other. We are told, for instance, that Peter Morrison writes articles and stories that "have horse sense, logic, and humor, and he is making a lot of money" (p. 20). He reads one such article to the receptive Linda, about how the United States is "threatened on one side by the red menace of the Bolshevik, on the other by the yellow menace of the Jap, and yet on another by the treachery of the Mexican and the slowly uprising might of the black man." Soon Peter is "thundering his best-considered arguments" while Linda sits back "with parted lips and wide eyes." Indeed, she "gaze[s] at a transformed Peter with aroused eyes" (p. 185). This scene shows very clearly how racism permits the otherwise orderly white subject to express an erotically primal nature. Rather than own a passionate energy, Peter and Linda are righteously aroused by the spectacle of the other. Oka Sayye becomes the excuse for and focus of arousal. With his death, he also serves as the means by which desire can be expelled and disavowed.

Linda's solution to the "Yellow Peril" is for good, clean white women to have six children each, and to raise them "with the proper love of country and the proper realization of the white man's right to supremacy" (p. 112). It is because modern woman has asserted her right to a life beyond and outside of her maternal potential, that white America has fallen prone to its enemies. Linda is determined to reverse this process. She will marry Peter, have children, and support him in his supremacist ventures. In the meantime, she succeeds in reclaiming her rightful inheritance, the fortune that Eileen had attempted to usurp. Eileen goes to live with some *nouveau riche* relations, only to discover that those who have become rich "by accident" are insupportable in their vulgarity. She returns, chastened, to her step-sister. Linda is the "deserving rich," the rightful white inheritor of private and national wealth. This right is always conditional on her submission to the values and authority of the paternal other: her father, her husband-to-be. Stratton-Porter wanted to create a heroine who was "Strong," but she also wanted to argue that racial theme does not alter the need for the girl-heroine to be a "little woman."

In *Her Father's Daughter* money is again important, and the heroine is rewarded with wealth, but the concern is not so much with spend and display as with effective management. Both this novel and *A Girl of the Limberlost* are about possession. In confronting competitors for wealth, Stratton-Porter presents the reader with dark, criminal others. She uses nature to romanticize the girl as figure of American purity, but she also uses "dirty" nature to demonize the indisciplined, predatory other. The girl once again is central to the justification of white American self-enrichment. Her perceived beauty and moral quality – her fetishized "cleanness" – is the conceit that permits and even necessitates the continued mastery of a white middle class. But Stratton-Porter represents a reactionary tendency, not just in her nativism, but in the attitude to economics that it implies. She does not have faith in the abundance that might be achieved via endless growth in production and consumption. She does not want to embrace all races and classes as potential consumers who might ensure such growth. Rather, her understanding is of wealth as a static entity, and possession must come not as a result of growth, but through predatory struggle. In this sense, Stratton-Porter represents a revision of the consumerist confidence to be found in *Rebecca of Sunnybrook Farm*, *Daddy-Long-Legs*, and the series fiction. This is perhaps enough to make Stratton-Porter of interest. But the question might be asked as to why, given the deeply offensive aspect of her work, she should be brought forth once more from obscurity. There are, I think, several reasons. One is that her work makes explicit the exclusionary, nativist thematics that is implicit throughout the tradition of girls' fiction. As we have already noted, from *Little Women* through to the series fiction, the point of view is always class-ed and racialized, that the role and importance of the American girl is modulated in relation to others who are perceived as marginal, problematic, threatening, or quite simply diseased. This aspect seldom becomes a central aspect of other narratives to the extent that it does in *Her Father's Daughter*, but it is nonetheless a persistent presence. Although I have at times stressed the liberatory, performative potential that women writers locate in girlhood and in consumerized progress, there are limitations that, however obvious or self-evident they may appear, should still be commented upon. The intensely objectionable example of Stratton-Porter forces me – a white reader – to notice what I might otherwise take for granted: that the American girl – the one that is seen to matter – is white. Also, if we allow ourselves to forget about someone like Stratton-Porter, does that become a way of pretending that she and what she represented did not exist? Does it become a way of assuring ourselves that the whiteness of the American girl is nothing more than a historical circumstance? To revive Stratton-Porter is a way of remembering that historical circumstance is never merely circumstantial in the sense of being without political value or intent. To re-read the canon of girls' fiction with knowledge of Stratton-Porter is to read with a renewed sensitivity to the racialized and ethnicized biases that are found in the tradition as a whole.

8

"Black Tuesday"

Wall Street crashed on 29 October 1929, and thereafter it seemed as if there was not much left to "buy into." By 1931 there would be between four and five million people without work; by 1932 the unemployment rate would have risen to 50 percent in some cities, and there would be over two million vagrants across the country; by 1933 five thousand banks would have collapsed, the unemployment rate would be 25 percent, and the national income would be half what it had been in 1930. Despite Federal works projects, the Depression would continue throughout the thirties. But, to put things facetiously, two girls would succeed where the Work Progress Administration failed. Nancy Drew and Laura Ingalls beat the Depression. Both first appeared in the early 1930s, and would flourish throughout the next ten years, and indeed, to the present day. Although the Nancy Drew series and the Little House series are very different, each seeks to rescue consumerist possibilities for the girl in an age in which they are endangered. They are revisions in that they take a step back in order to move forwards. Nancy is a quietened down, suburbanized outgrowth of the earlier syndicate series, while the Little House books take the heroine away from the metropolis once more, and back to the farm.

Entering into the world of the early Nancy Drew, it is as if the Depression is not happening. Nancy still has her "snappy little roadster," her fashionable travelling outfits, and money to spend. It seems that now money is scarce, fiction must make it more visible. Nancy has charge accounts at all the downtown stores, and will unhesitatingly suggest to a friend that they "have a shopping orgy."[1] Her home town of River Heights is unmarked by tragedy. It is not in a dust bowl, nor does it have lots of redundant factory workers. Vagrants are few and far between, and they are still "bad" rather than "economically disadvantaged." The surrounding country clubs, resort hotels, and golf clubs continue to thrive. Nancy's handsome, amiable boyfriend, Ned Nickerson, has not been taken out of college by a bankrupted father. But then again, most of the Nancy Drew stories turn on lost or stolen fortunes. One might say that these are, however obliquely, Depression novels, in that they repeatedly ask the question: Where has all the money gone?

I want to look closely at Nancy's world – her relation to money, work, her father and others – to theorize how and why it offers a response to economic uncertainty. But I also want to include a very different kind of Depression writing in the form of Laura Ingalls Wilder's "Little House" books. They are contemporary with Nancy Drew (Nancy first appeared in 1930, the Little House books from 1932 onwards) but Wilder takes the reader back to the 1870s and 1880s, and to much earlier droughts and panics. Wilder reversed the buying into modernity that we have traced in other writers, and in looking at how previous generations dealt with hard times, she suggests that latterday Americans have been disempowered by progress. They have learnt to depend on others' inventiveness, and on the spreading network of exchange. Having lost the know-how that was necessary for survival on the frontier, the later generation is not able to withstand changes in their circumstances. Perhaps in this sense, Nancy Drew and the Little House books are akin, in that they prioritize ingenuity. Wilder, certainly, was scornful of Federal attempts to mitigate economic hardship, and her fiction is a deliberate attack on Roosevelt's policies. One of the chief pleasures of the Wilder books is that they tell the reader how to make and do without outside help. Through her reading, the modern girl is inducted into a different kind of womanhood. Yet, even as Wilder takes the girl back, she also brings her forward: we get to buy into modernity all over again with Laura and her family. Does the greater satisfaction lie in going back to basics? Or, having gone back, does it lie in coming forwards? There is a tension here between the naive pleasures of the past, and the thrills of emergent consumerism. Wilder always draws us on even as she makes us want to stay behind. The narrative pauses at various optimal moments of fullness and safety, which is why occasions such as Christmas are so important and so lovingly described. In taking us back from one hard time to another, the narrative hunger is always for the space in between. The unwanted irony is that we long for the moment of excess; we long to surrender to the abundance that the narrative simultaneously warns us not to count on. The dream of emotional and material plenty is kept alive, but it is also disavowed and postponed.

To begin with Nancy Drew, controversy has hovered over her for most of her existence. She was one of Stratemeyer's last creations, but the question as to her "true" author has remained open. In fact the question is somewhat misguided. Stratemeyer wrote – or at least, blocked out – the first three Nancy titles shortly before his death in 1930. She was then taken up by

Stratemeyer's daughter, Harriet Adams, who managed the syndicate after her father's death. Adams claimed a particular interest in Nancy, a sort of maternal care, and this is hardly surprising when one looks at this "daughter's" success. Adams controlled Nancy in that she provided the plots, and had the final say as to everything that Nancy said or did. But another woman, Mildred Wirt Benson, actually wrote most or all of the first twenty-five books. So the named author, "Carolyn Keene," was always to some extent a composite or collaborative creation, with various people contributing story-lines or an occasional volume, or taking up where another had left off. One of the reasons it is hard to know who Carolyn Keene is at any given time in her history is because all Stratemeyer authors signed a contract containing a confidentiality clause, enabling the Syndicate to preserve the myth of the real, individual author. Although Benson broke this confidentiality on a couple of occasions, to this day Carolyn Keene is only allowed to speak to her public under her alias, whoever she or he may actually be. At a recent public conference on Nancy Drew, a current Keene was permitted to talk about her work, but her real name was not revealed.[2] What this means is that the debate as to what a heroine can and should do may still take place within the fiction, but it also takes place beforehand. With numerous writers working under changing editorial supervision in a series that has now run for seventy years, the argument as to content and message takes place between authors, editors, and publishers. Particular authors have struggled to identify with aspects of Nancy in order to help them think themselves into writing as Carolyn Keene, but this attempt to specify is precisely what editors work against. A syndicate is best served by uniformity of product, so that the myth of the single author is preserved across the series as a whole. Also, the legitimacy of the Stratemeyer Syndicate's ownership of Nancy depends on uniformity. If she is reinvented by a particular author, then in a sense that author becomes the "mother," not the editor. The Syndicate must protect its legal possession against the imaginative possession that might be asserted by an author. This is not to say that Nancy cannot be reinvented at all. In such a long-running series, she has constantly been updated and modernized. She must always change with the world as it seems to be for Middle America. Before the Second World War, Nancy's opponents were assorted spivs and fraudsters, jewel thieves, international smugglers, and various other kinds of outsiders on the make. During the Cold War, they were frequently Communists who were taking orders from the Soviet empire.

The fluidity of Carolyn Keene, of River Heights, and of Nancy again points towards the performative aspect of the girl's tradition. There is always something assumed and pretended in the production of the series. The reader may choose to believe that Keene is one real person, that River Heights is an actual place, and that Nancy is the essential, unchanging girl. Perhaps the reader even needs to believe in Nancy and her world. But the vast numbers of titles and the numerous, unlikely, but often similar adventures perhaps also invite the reader to acknowledge that this is a "good product" as much as a "good story." The claim to the "real" is sustained within the narrative, but so thinly that the reader may feel more free than usual to re-specify and editorialize her experience as she goes along (and as we will see, certainly readers testify to having done this). For the moment, though, the performed and provisional nature of the Nancy series can be seen as a source of struggle – of political contest – as much as of choice and reinvention. Nancy represents the dominant notions of an older editor, and the radical, emergent feminism of a young writer. This is a further example of the way in which the historical context is always an unfinished debate rather than a completed "period." Although the stories themselves are nearly always constructed of a similar handful of elements, they represent a complex interaction over women's agency within a consumerist society. The question of Nancy's power was one of the most contested aspects of her early development. When Harriet Adams took over editorship of the series, she made changes on the grounds that Nancy had been "too bold and bossy." Subsequently, the housekeeper, Hannah Gruen, was given a slightly bigger part, and Nancy began to treat her more considerately. This was to give domesticity an enhanced role. Stratemeyer himself had felt that Benson's writing up of his heroine was a departure from the old style of the Syndicate. Benson recalls that Stratemeyer found her version of Nancy "too flip, she was too vivacious – she was not the namby-pamby type of heroine that had been dominating series books for many years."[3] Somewhat ironically, Benson was only allowed legally to express this opinion when a court case was brought to establish ownership of the series. When the Syndicate transferred Nancy from Grosset and Dunlap to Simon and Schuster in 1978, Grosset and Dunlap sued, and Benson was called to give evidence about the Syndicate's methods of production. With regard to her own work, Benson felt that Stratemeyer and Adams had attenuated the strength and modern attractiveness of her heroine. Stratemeyer thought that Nancy should be toned down, and Adams sought to achieve this by insisting that Nancy have companions – Bess and George – and a boyfriend. The editorial directors wanted to mitigate the sense of Nancy as a confident lone figure, so they humanized – or rather, feminized – her with traditional social contacts and supports. Eventually the differences between Benson and the Syndicate became so great that Benson stopped writing as Carolyn Keene.

Nancy would continue to change, and, according to Carolyn Heilbrun, for the worse. Before the Second World War, Nancy was a prototypical feminist heroine, but during the Cold War she was made safe: "Where Nancy drove policemen in her car, they now drive her. At camp, in the new versions, the girls are supervised by a chaperon. What Nancy once did for herself is done by her boyfriend Ned in the revised version, or else she is carried off by him to rest after combat."[4] But was the Nancy under consideration here, the pre-War Nancy, really feminist? If so, what kind of a feminism does she represent? Most importantly in this context, how does her feminism relate to her economic position? With the recent academic rediscovery of Nancy Drew and of popular culture more generally, and with the "coming out" of Nancy Drew fans, the debate over the meaning and value of Nancy as a role model has been hard fought. At the Nancy Drew Project public conference at the University of Iowa, some elderly women spoke of how, in their youth, they had loved Nancy for her independence, her practical bent, her freedom and power, her ability to do things. Bess only served as a reminder of a weak, contemptible womanhood; Ned only got in the way, and was never considered important.[5] The tomboyish George, who can perhaps only be read as a cautionary example to girls who get above themselves, is forgotten about. From Nancy, we are told that girls learned "to see adventure in solving problems and the joy of self-reliance."[6] But one wonders whether the stories might not work with an already present curiosity and sense of independence, acting in a way that is both permissive and disciplinary. Romalov, who writes so astutely about the conventions surrounding Nancy, brings a note of caution to the celebration: "Our assumptions about Nancy as liberated, competent, powerful – as having ultimate control and freedom of movement – are not invalidated by a consideration of her limits, but these limitations need to be explored more thoroughly if we are to come to a fuller understanding of her cultural meaning."[7]

The point that Romalov chooses to stress is that though Nancy does have a certain kind of power, one should still ask, at whose expense, and at what cost to herself? The focus should not be on whether Nancy wins or not – of course she does. We need rather to look at how power is constructed in Nancy's world. In *The Girl Sleuth* (1975), Bobby Ann Mason draws attention to the way in which Nancy's power is always subservient to senior, élite others. Nancy has the power of middle management, of the entrusted inferior. Like the traditional woman who was expected to rule the home except when she was submitting to her husband's superior judgment, Nancy's willing acquiescence in the perception of her inferiority allows her a vindictive power over certain lesser others. As Mason puts it: "[S]olving a mystery is like tidying. You can't have a perfectly laundered neighborhood as long as uncouth strangers are hanging about."[8] Nancy's ambitions are strategically curbed, and the narrative encourages girls to look for power in enclosed spaces. Mason interprets the settings in this light, suggesting that we see them as "enlarged dollhouses" (57). They are presented as "enchanting": we know they are safe even when we are told that they are dangerous. As with most formula fiction, the narrative encodes its own limitations in the opening pages, even though it sets itself before us as an adventure. Mason's most urgent point about Nancy and other girl-sleuths is that they subject girls and women to contradictory discourses about themselves. On the one hand, the Nancy Drew mysteries are "helplessly entranced by wealth, status, and glamor." On the other, they judge with severity any woman who steps outside traditional feminine boundaries in pursuit of wealth, status, and glamor. Girls, and the women they will grow into, are invited to be discontented with their lot, and yet they are still expected to settle for it. They are led to yearn for unlikely treasures, rather than to focus on more immediate problems and desires. Mason does not allow for the reader who reconstructs the text in keeping with her own disposition (as, for instance, with the women who blanked Ned as an unwanted intrusion). But does her fundamental point hold, that girls are rewarded and discouraged at the same time? Whether the reader perceives Nancy Drew and like fictions after the manner of Mason, or of other, more positive critics, may depend on that reader's sense of the possibilities of women's social power. For now, though, let's look more closely at how Nancy operates.

The reader is immediately confronted with the autonomy of the early Nancy Drew. She drives a car that is described as her own; and she fixes it herself, happily, automatically, and with a perfect understanding of the mechanics of it. Nancy's life is one of conspicuous control and choice. She seems always to be in motion, and if her destinations are not as glamorous as in earlier series fiction, they are also less prescribed. Nancy's life is not an exhausting journey from one leisure class playground to the next; she goes where she wants to. Another sense emerges from her constant activity: that her life and her character are always entirely present. Nancy lives in and through her adventures, and there is no sense of another, introspective Nancy, a Nancy who thinks about her dead mother, or who wonders if her boyfriend really loves her. I would argue that this enhances the reader's sense of Nancy as a performance in which we may join. She is theatrical in that she is, as it were, a "well-lit" character, one who manifests herself fully to her audience (one also thinks again of Michael Moon's point that the good child character must be "legible"). But perhaps the subsequent, creeping perception is not of independence and volition, but of tremendous social hunger. This hunger – for recognition, for pre-eminence – is so intense that it takes the most extreme forms. The narrative voice is always complicit with this: however much Nancy may deprecate herself, the narrator continues to reassure us that she is a winner. We get frequent and heavy-handed reminders that we should see through Nancy's modesty to her true worth and glamor:

"I'm sure I look a fright," Bess panted.

"None of us looks especially like a page from a fashion magazine," laughed Nancy, running her slim fingers through her wavy, blond hair.[9]

As the overweight friend pants beside her, Nancy pretends to suppose that she too is far from looking great. Meanwhile and seemingly incidentally, we are told of Nancy's slim fingers and wavy blond hair, which suggest that actually Nancy does belong in the pages of a fashion magazine. Nancy can afford, in every sense, to dress her intrinsic glory in a discreet fashion. Whether she is "neatly dressed in a blue traveling suit, her golden hair bound snugly beneath a modish little hat," or whether she wears "a simple and inexpensive dress of white silk," Nancy is always an oxymoron, at once simple and straightforward, but elegant and calculated. This, though, raises again the question of the girl's embodiment. Nancy is a late arrival in terms of the turn-of-century debate over adolescence, but she still seems to be written as a paranoid response to adolescent physiology. Jo March is explicitly uncomfortable with her girl's body, to the extent that she wears masculine clothing or masculinized women's clothes whenever she can, and she uses her body to strike masculine poses. But with many later heroines, we have noted that the fiction often responds to the problem of the adolescent girl by sidestepping the body. Girls are "all eyes": they are restless minds that desire and look. In earlier series fiction, boys are physical entities as much as is Jo March. Walter in *The Motor Girls* is the classic instance, and his handsome body is mentioned frequently. This makes the girl's body seem correspondingly problematic and even unmentionable. Nancy is characterized in a similar way. As we will see, her boyfriend is offered to us as a bodily presence, whereas Nancy is "trim," and "tidy," as though her body were indeed "tidied away." This may represent the fear of female adolescent incoherence in the tradition of Hall. More specifically, the "trim" body suggests a fear of or shame over biological womanhood. To put it directly, Nancy and heroines like her have never and will never menstruate.

As one would expect, Nancy negotiates the often contradictory rules of class and gender with consummate skill. Notionally, she is equal, one of a set of "chums," but all the details tell us otherwise. From her roadster to her looks, to her discreetly famous father, to her splendidly available, handsome, vacuous boyfriend, Nancy stands in possession of everything a superior person could possibly have. She has the best physique, the best car, the best clothes, the best father, the best boyfriend, the best times – the best of everything. She combines all pecuniary and non-pecuniary symbols of status. Others are drawn irresistibly to her understated but unmistakable glory. Even at the most fashionable resort or the most prestigious university, she is the centre of attention:

> Without making the slightest effort, Nancy became popular with everyone. She met so many new students that she could not remember the names of half of them. However, Ned's fraternity brothers remembered her, and that evening at the formal party held in the chapter house they annoyed the young man exceedingly by constantly cutting in upon his dances.[10]

The contradiction of Nancy's quiet, dainty grandeur carries through into the treatment of her fame. The important distinction that the narrative wishes to make is that Nancy's professional expertise has not declassed or defeminized her. Small-town sheriffs and minor crooks can only stammer or gaze when they discover that she is the celebrated daughter of a celebrated father, but she remains untainted by careerism. Nancy, and perhaps the girl-reader, longs to command small people, while still looking up to others. Given a place within an established hierarchy, Nancy's responsibilities never become frightening: she always has a senior other to whom she may defer. Similarly, her sleuthing never takes her towards independence. Whereas the Hardy Boys get substantial rewards for their endeavours, Nancy gets small, attractive tokens.[11] One of the most obvious examples of this double-dealing, of fame and power within a suitable feminine shelteredness, occurs when Nancy goes to Washington and meets, not the President, but his wife:

> The distinguished first lady told Nancy that Mr. George had spoken of her work as an amateur detective, and she asked many questions about the girl's famous cases. She introduced her to a small group of personal friends who had gathered to do honor in an informal way to the celebrated young detective.[12]

Nancy provides endless consolation for the girl-reader who does not command, who is not ceded respect and authority by her elders, and who perhaps has no contact with "leading" adults in the first place. But the crucial distinction here and throughout is that Nancy manages to have it all while remaining "amateur." She is still defined by her relation to money she has access to it, but she does not possess it and she does not earn it.:

The sense is that Nancy is a "natural winner." Her intelligence, her straight thinking, and her good looks bring her the attention she deserves. But if her power is signified as natural and automatic, it is also mystified. That is to say, the sources of her power are always present, but they are never named as such. They are – familiar terms – race, class, money and gender. To begin with race, Black people are scarce in River Heights, and they are scarce wherever Nancy goes. They are servants – maids, lavatory attendants, country club menials – and they have no words. Nancy has nothing to do with them. They make her existence possible by cleaning, grooming, and fixing her various locales, but this common ground with Nancy as "tidiers" is not allowed to become manifest. The same is true of other, white menials. Whenever Nancy's status is jeopardized by her similarity with someone beneath herself, the narrative becomes overtly aggressive in placing a marker between her and them. Nancy is her father's helper, but she is not allowed to be confused with her father's other helpers. She is not high-handed with her inferiors, but she is high-handed about them:

"I shall ask [father] to have some clerk in his office start a search."

And:

"This isn't a case for the police in my opinion."[13]

Similarly, businessmen and lawyers do not discuss matters with the police, they "give orders" to them. To be wealthy and middle class is to be the law; to be a policeman is to be a minion of the law. This is where the patriarchalism of the fiction becomes most visible, for Nancy's power is bound up with her relation to her father, a well-to-do, famous, and well-connected lawyer. Carson Drew is the necessary guarantor of Nancy's power, and people's fear of or respect for Nancy is determined by her daughterly relation:

"My father is Carson Drew." Frank Semitt's face turned a shade paler, and he swallowed heavily two or three times.

Or, even more simply:

"If you're his daughter, there's no need for explanations."[14]

This is perhaps a manifestation of period anxiety: in an age of "failing" and "collapsed" men, this series gives us a fantasy about the father, and about the need for his fearsome, seductive, and reassuring authority. Nancy is often flattered with the observation that she is a sort of partner to her father in his legal business. She knows not to take seriously the various offers of work that come her way: she knows that she does not want to exchange the privileged subservience of the daughter for the waged subservience of a clerk. Her power is always with and through her father. Going about his business will always ensure his crushingly magnanimous attention, if, in the meantime, he does let her "get on with it." Significantly, Nancy's mother has died in the novels' prehistory, and nothing – certainly not plain old Hannah Gruen – can come between the daughter and her Oedipal bliss. Carson Drew is handsome, youngish, and more than solvent; we might expect him to marry again. But the father–daughter plot will never be disrupted. Nancy, for her part, will never presume to be her father's equal. She will always defer to his opinion, seek his guidance, and lay her rewards at his feet:

After discussing the events Nancy seated herself upon an arm of her father's chair, and playfully tweaked his ear. "As my legal adviser, how would you suggest that I spend my gold?" she asked.[15]

As is always the case, when a girl's or a woman's power is at issue, men's power must also be accommodated and dealt with. But not all male power is legitimate. We know that Nancy assumes power over poorer, lower-class men. Her challenge is always to locate herself appropriately, flatteringly but non-threateningly, in relation to men. This takes several forms. There is her relationship with her father, and there is her superiority to lower classes and other races. Then there are the more complex categories: criminals, and the boyfriend. Male criminals are nearly always social climbers. They dress too well, and seek Nancy's company too insistently. The conservatism of early Nancy Drew is very clear. There is a sense that wealth rests with the middle and upper classes, varsity men like Carson Drew and Ned Nickerson. This order of wealth and social exclusion is moralized and naturalized. The fraudulent characters want things for which they do not have the proper breeding; crime always involves the breaking of class boundaries, and criminals are interlopers in matters of sex and class, as well as property. Mason notes, "Nancy's job is to preserve the class lines, and for her defense of property and station are inextricably linked with purity and reputation. She defends beautiful objects, places, and treasures from violence – the sexual violence of nasty men who want to stifle her energy" (p. 73). The directness with which social judgements are conflated with crime and justice is – one assumes – both shocking and laughable to the modern reader. Nancy wonders, for instance, if the lovely and well-bred Margaret Judson could possibly be "a member of an international jewel-theft gang":

"Yet if I am any judge of character she didn't look the type," Nancy reflected in bewilderment. "She appeared like a very fine woman who might have suffered intensely."[16]

Of another dispossessed member of the ruling classes who has been claimed by self-interested others, Nancy tells us: "I believe this timid girl is much too refined to belong to such a common person." The narrator confirms Nancy's social–criminal sense: "There was an air of daintiness and refinement about the young waitress, which was apparent despite Sadie's cheap clothing and menial position."[17]

It is telling that the dispossessed are often women and children, and one wonders how this positions the reader. The girl who does not enjoy Nancy's advantages is perhaps encouraged in the fantasy that style and wealth are rightfully hers, but that she has missed out by a tragic quirk of fate. The pleasure lies in the fact that in Nancy's world, having cheap and mean guardians or parents is only a temporary limitation. Nancy can ennoble all with whom she comes into contact, readers and characters alike:

"Always in my heart have I known that I was born to rule," he said quietly. "But without your help I could never have done it."[18]

The reader joins Nancy and her rescued princelings and heiresses in that splendid, romantic realm where we all, in our hearts, know we belong.

If the novels locate themselves in the paternalized security of childhood, they also look forward to the way in which Nancy might preserve her position as a privileged amateur into adult life. She is effectively married off from the outset to a younger, more ebullient version of her father. As we have noted, Nancy has the best boyfriend in the same way that she has the best outfits and the best car. There are constant reminders of Ned's attractiveness: the reader is told of his muscular arms, his sunburn, his footballing prowess, of how he keeps "in perfect form." One can but agree with Nancy on this: "How thrilling, Ned, and how commendable!"[19] Ned is always available, but never center-stage. Whenever Nancy looks away from her own doings, there is Ned to give confirmation of what they both will still have when the story is over – money, looks, prospects:

Turning, she saw Ned Nickerson . . . very handsome indeed in a well-pressed grey suit of collegiate cut, and as always his eyes were for Nancy alone . . . Ned smiled warmly. "It's surely great to see you again, Nancy. You're looking like a million dollars!"
"I feel that way too, Ned."[20]

This sense of Ned always being on hand to assure her of her worth does not belie our sense of what their marriage will be. For, however devoted Ned is, Nancy must always manage rather than command him. Bursting with athleticism and sexual energy, Ned's impetuous drives must be channeled by Nancy to serve the needs of her story. Bright, strong and ready, he will always leave his own interests to one side to help her. But he is subject to inconvenient fits of jealous anger which might, if Nancy did not know how to restrain him, upset the all-important process of detection. Mason argues that, in a way, the mystery is always about sex, not least because, for adolescents, sex is the great and fascinating mystery. In this light, we should read the fiction as a sublimation. Ned is transfixed by the sexual possibility that Nancy represents, but she, Mason points out, "diverts his attention towards sleuthing" (p. 63). In this way, Nancy both "pursues sex and runs from it" (p. 67). What she seeks is pleasure on her own terms, with a good prospect like Ned rather than one of the conmen in sharp suits. But she also needs the commitment of all Ned's future love and earning power. Until then, her heart still belongs to her father.

Sex may indeed be the hidden key that unlocks the mystery, but as I argued earlier, the narratives are calculated to elide the girl's body altogether. Furthermore, the mystery serves another important purpose. It must hide the actual banality of Nancy's life. What would she do if she did not have criminals to track down? She would shop, play golf, have tea with George and Bess, and wait for Ned to call, or for her father to get home. What the mysteries hide – and also give oblique expression to – is the tedium of a girl's life in River Heights. In order to make the consumerized leisure of her ordinary existence seem attractive, it must be threatened with violence and social chaos. From that endangered perspective, the neat, tame pleasures of tea, shopping, and waiting for men may start to seem enviable once more. Making trouble in River Heights is a way of making sure that Nancy will stay at home – she is needed there. The novels present the reader with the security and pleasure of class and money, and then refuse to let us see beyond that. The girl-reader, and the heroine herself, will never gaze into the distance, because there is always trouble in the foreground.

To return to the context with which we began, these 1930s fictions provide reassurance that there is still security in wealth, and that some collapsed fortunes may, with Nancy's help, be resurrected. If they do indeed ask, where has all the money gone, we can rest assured that the girl-detective will come up with the answer. Once again, the subliminal goal has been to make the girl central to the processes which normally exclude her: control of money and goods. But where does this leave most girls? To some extent, it invites them in, and this is the secret to Nancy's "intelligence." The fact is that even the slowest reader is given emphatic hints as to how to construe the evidence. This means that when Nancy seizes on the truth, the reader does so at least as quickly. When someone turns to Nancy and says,

"Oh, Nancy, I wish I were as smart as you are," the reader is fully included in Nancy's smartness.[21] And if the reader may so easily share in Nancy's smartness, who is to say that she may not also share, at some point, in all the other aspects of Nancy's good fortune: her access to money, her stylish clothes, her glorious looks, her handsome boyfriend? Wealth and status are made to seem close at hand, but in another way they are distanced and mystified. For Nancy's possession of these things is represented as her natural and moral right as a white, middle-class girl, rather than something she may aim for and achieve. The mystery of wealth is that it has its own unstated logic. Possession is indirectly naturalized, gendered, racialized, and class-ed. It is not offered as something the girl can ever hope to control through her intelligence alone. She must respect it, and dream of its power.

The Nancy Drew mysteries are what happens to girls' adventure romance. It quietens down and suburbanizes. Nancy does not have the advantage of immense wealth, but she has a middle-class controlling intelligence, a knowledge of her own position and its scope. Laura Ingalls Wilder's fiction continues the more realistic strand of girls' fiction. Throughout the early part of the twentieth century, as the series took hold, there was also a tradition of serious or approved fiction; or, perhaps, of more truly middle-class fiction. This is the era of the Book-of-the-Month Club, with its massively successful promotion of an anti-modernist, socially responsible if somewhat naive, realist fiction. We find a girls' equivalent in such writers as Doris Gates, Eleanor Estes, Carol Brink, and Elizabeth Coatsworth. There is a strongly neo-Alcottian aspect in much of this fiction, in that the focus tends to be on middle-class family life. The emphasis is less romantic and less sentimental than many earlier novels, but questions of emotional truth and moral responsibility are to the fore. Anne Scott MacLeod, one of the few critics to give this new realist fiction serious consideration, makes two very interesting points in relation to morality and class. Firstly, she observes that the "bad" characters have gone. In their place, we have the "impersonal forces" of a destructive nature or of economic decline. Secondly, although poverty is frequently present, it is also softened. MacLeod writes: "It was not a very grinding form of poverty the fiction described. It caused neither bitterness nor severe deprivation, and it rarely set the poorer children apart in any important way."[22] Perhaps children's fiction must always mitigate the extremes of poverty to some extent. Either its horror must be passed over, or it must be projected back onto a safely distant epoch. Other critics such as Billman and Lestvik note the tendency in the 1930s of sending the heroine of realist fiction back to the frontier farm of the nineteenth century. This, alongside the heroine's frequent tomboyishness, is read as symptomatic of ambivalence over the role of the modern woman.[23] Heroines such as Becky Landers and Caddie Woodlawn suggest a widespread ambivalence, not to say disapproval, of the more flapperish evolutions of the New Woman. At the same time, they should be read as a historical projection of the hardship of contemporary life. Furthermore, we can pick up my argument about genre – about the way in which girls' fiction is in dialogue with realism and naturalism – at this point. The other advantage of going back is that issues concerning of urban squalor and naturalistic representation can be sidestepped. Latterday realists can go back to the gentler realism of the immediate post-War period, and avoid the debates that had beset the careers of Wiggin, Webster, Stratton-Porter, and others. The most lastingly successful of these realists, Laura Ingalls Wilder, had a complex and highly political attitude to her past. She had spent virtually all of her life on farms, in Kansas, Minnesota, South Dakota, Florida, and Missouri. She came to professional writing quite late, beginning as contributor and then Home Editor on the *Missouri Ruralist* in 1911–1912, by which time she was in her forties. Articles such as "The Farmer's Wife Says" (1919) and "My Ozark Kitchen" (1925) brought her to a wider readership in *McCall's* and the *Country Gentleman*. The Little House series did not begin until 1932, when Wilder was in her sixties. Her intention, as she expressed it in a speech in 1937, was that she had "wanted the children now to understand more about the beginning of things, to know what is behind the things they see – what it is that made America as they know it." But this asserted historical transparency is disingenuous. What Wilder chose to tell of the beginning of things was significantly reshaped to reflect her political understanding of the Depression and the New Deal.[24] She aligns her own realism with the resourceful vigor of the past, and sets both against the artificiality of the modern age. But realism is, of course, an alternative mythology, and in rewriting her past, Wilder seeks to enshrine a social vision of much later vintage.

Wilder believed that living in a consumerized modern age had deprived young people of constructive resources. In taking the reader back to agricultural hard times in the 1870s and 1880s, the relief is that there is always something to be done. In the midst of drought, plagues of grasshoppers, blizzards, heat-waves, crop failure, loss of livestock, the Ingalls survive almost entirely unaided. Whether she puts out fires in summer, twists straw for fuel in winter, or works as a dressmaker and teacher to earn money, Laura's is an active struggle. But what, in the thirties, could anyone do about the domino effect of margins not being met and of banks failing? The problem lay in the virtual reality of over-capitalization. How could the modern child or adult respond constructively to a problem that was both pandemic and invisible; real, but also only numbers and percentage points? One might suppose that there is a "preferred Depression" in evidence here, in that Wilder takes us back to the simple hardship of natural forces. In fact, her response to hardship, to past and present is more fraught. She did romanticize the energetic simplicity of the past, even as she dared to show how unremittingly difficult life had been. She also implies a certain scorn for the enfeebled modern generation. Yet through it all, her narrative hungers for the same pleasures that come with consumerized modernity.

From the start of the Little House books, and throughout, there is a fascination with making and doing. Wilder begins with a spell-binding description of the various processes of pioneer life. In the first chapter of *Little House in the Big Woods* (1932), a pig is slaughtered and butchered, and we are told of the different stages of scalding, scraping, hanging, cutting up and eviscerating, salting, pickling, smoking, blowing up the bladder, cooking the tail, and making "head cheese." An apparently brutal act is transformed into an exhibition of great skill and ingenuity. Every part of the process, and every part of the animal, is seen to have a perfect logic or use. This sense of orderliness is enhanced by the wonderful simplicity of Wilder's prose, as it carefully takes us from one step to the next, until the process is complete. The days of the week have a similar structured rationale: "Each day had its own proper work." Ma has a different task for each day:

> Wash on Monday,
> Iron on Tuesday,
> Mend on Wednesday,
> Churn on Thursday,
> Clean on Friday,
> Bake on Saturday,
> Rest on Sunday.[25]

This compartmentalization of tasks and roles creates a tremendous sense of control over self and environment. The practicality of the arrangement takes on its own propriety, so that the necessity of washing, cleaning, and mending seems inseparable from the natural morality and gentility of being clean and tidy. Work is always accompanied by this sense of moral and aesthetic accomplishment. All the while, Laura, her sister, and the readers, learn to understand and predict the world of the narrative. For all that these are poor people leading "backward" country lives, the impression is of power born of a kind of practical erudition. We develop a knowledge of how to make butter, how to clean a rifle and make bullets, how to sew, how to collect maple sugar, and so on. Each time that their power is tested, the family will confirm its ability to maintain its moral and material equilibrium. But the pride and even pleasure that Laura derives from the family's independence is offset by a rather different one: the thrill of shopping. The girls wait in an agony of anticipation when their father takes furs to the store to trade. They know that he will return with "beautiful things from town," as the store is "full of candy and calico and other wonderful things" (p. 75). The fascination with "boughten" things continues throughout, and one of the girls' favourite games is playing at going to town. Consumerism, at however humble a level, explodes the control and prudent structures of normal life with a bewildering excess: "Laura could have looked for weeks and not seen all the things that were in that store. She had not known that there were so many things in all the world" (pp. 122–23).

These two polarities of a self-made sufficiency and a tantalizing excess will take different forms in the rest of the series. On the one hand, there is an anti-materialist slant. Wilder stresses the emotional gratification to be won in the simplest of lives. This is contrasted with the emotional meanness of material lives. When they move to the banks of Plum Creek, finding a bought broom makes the girls think that there is "no end to the wonders in this house."[26] But we and they are soon given a cautionary figure in the form of Nellie Oleson, the storekeeper's daughter. Nellie has ribbons and fancy clothes, and looks down on the Ingalls sisters as "Country girls." Her home has a carpet and china, and she herself has breath-takingly impressive dolls, toys, and magazines. But this does not assuage Nellie's awakened hunger for recognition and power: "Don't you wish you had a fur cape, Laura? But your Pa couldn't buy you one. Your Pa's not a storekeeper" (p. 158). The lesson is clear. Things are thrilling, but only the good will know how to enjoy them. To take pleasure in this world, one must also have a sense of other, more important things that lie beyond. As the girls are taught to sing:

> It is not much this world can give
> With all its subtle art;
> And gold and gems are not the things
> To satisfy the heart;
> But Oh, if those who cluster round
> The altar and the hearth
> Have gentle words and loving smiles,
> How beautiful the earth!

But once the moralized terms of enjoyment have been established, the narrative can allow its devouring appetite to manifest itself again. The cry goes out: "There's more, Ma!"[27]

Although, or perhaps because, the girls are taught to look askance at worldliness, the experience of going shopping remains intensely dramatic. The sheer terror of going into a shop without her parents gradually becomes one of suspenseful excitement for Laura – the excitement of choice in a world in which all tasks and processes are as predetermined as the days of the week. Even buying name-cards, and deciding between colours and designs, is described in close detail.[28] But the undertone warns of the liability of the modern technologies that commerce makes available. Pa hires a "wonderful machine" to do his threshing but he also warns against railroads, telegraphs, kerosene, coal, and stores: "they're good things to have but the trouble is, folks get to depend on 'em."[29] Shortly after this warning, the community is visited by unusually harsh winter weather, forcing them once more to realize and exploit their personal resilience. The struggle brings a kind of perverse pleasure in concentration and defensive pride that anything can be withstood. But this alternates once more with expansive pleasure, as the people – and Wilder's syntax – stretch once more in the spring sunshine:

The Chinook was blowing. Spring had come. The blizzard had given up; it was driven back to the north. Blissfully Laura stretched out in bed; she put both her arms on the top of the quilts and they were not very cold. She listened to the blowing wind and the dripping eaves and she knew that in the other room Pa was lying awake, too, listening and glad.[30]

The progress of the novels, despite fond backward glances, is always towards the power of buying. Laura discovers her own consumer-power in *These Happy Golden Years* (1943); indeed, what makes these years golden and happy is that the family achieves prosperity. They buy an organ, which is lovingly described, and Laura herself is able to buy clothes of an elegance she has not known before. Almanzo Wilder, with his fine horses, buggy, and "faint scent" of cigar smoke, comes to call. Money, love, and happiness all come at once. Meanwhile, Nellie Oleson is reintroduced. This far-fetched narrative twist reveals the aggressive aspect of pioneer hardihood. Nellie is brought back in order to be humiliated. Her family has lost its money, and has had to break up. The now pre-eminent Laura triumphs over Nellie, who must live on, unappreciated and unwelcome among undesirable relatives, far from genial society. As in Stratton-Porter's work, there is an Oedipalized conservatism at work here: wealth is necessarily limited, and the heroine's access to it must be at the expense of another. Wilder can never quite believe in the modern dream of democratized luxury, and so as Laura rises, Nellie must fall. Nellie's fate also reminds us of what can happen to desire in a realist world: the excess that she gains from having a storekeeper-father, and her continued hunger for more, brings her downfall. Eventually even Laura must learn the same lesson. In a final volume that was unfinished at Wilder's death in 1957, Laura has married Almanzo. The couple are excited by buying things on credit and through mail order, and are soon beset with financial crises. Their pleasures are paid for with impossible mortgages, ill health, and final disaster with the panic of 1893.

The paranoia over rivals and over the dangers of pleasure is also suggested by the way in which Wilder's fiction turns on ambivalence as to the full and the empty. The past is at once deprived and full; the present may be materially full, but emotionally empty. This moral–material problem is projected onto the landscapes. The family leaves the woods of Wisconsin because the excess of settlers has emptied them of game. Once on the prairie, the emptiness is full:

> There was only the enormous, empty prairie, with grasses blowing in waves of light and shadow across it, and the great sky above it, and birds flying up from it and singing with joy because the sun was rising. And on the whole enormous prairie there was no sign that any other human being had ever been there before.
> In all that space of land and sky stood the lonely, small, covered wagon.[31]

Laura will soon learn that this apparently empty space has been the essential habitat of Native Americans for centuries, but for the moment the emptiness is full of opportunity. It is, in more senses than one, a vast prospect. But even as the narrative once again enshrines the family's disconnected survival in the open space, the impetus is still towards the golden years of socialized prosperity.

Although I have separated the two series on the grounds of generic difference, with the Stratemeyer in the tradition of adventure romance, and Wilder in the tradition of social realism, in terms of their underlying ideological point of view, the similarities are more important. Both series are about the concentration of wealth, and both advocate a social isolation, a careful guarding of privilege and opportunity. Wilder spent most of her adult life on an unprofitable farm, often relying very heavily on her daughter, Rose Wilder Lane, to help her with money and with her writing. As Anderson and Fellman have shown in fascinating biographical studies of the relation between the two women, both were increasingly fierce proponents of laissez-faire capitalism. Both saw the Little House books as a way of propagandizing against Roosevelt and the New Deal. Even as they grudgingly depended on each other, they vaunted old-time individualism, and belittled the difficulties of the poor of the 1930s. As the publicity for one of Lane's own novels stated: "What these two heroic young pioneers went through dwarfs your present hardships and makes you ashamed to complain."[32] In recreating the Ingalls–Wilder past, they suppressed various instances of help that they had received. In spite of Wilder's claims to historical accuracy, Fellman argues that there is much settling of old scores in the books, and Wilder also casts a golden glow over certain aspects of the family's life. Above all, Fellman finds that Wilder and Lane exaggerated the "economic separateness" of their pioneer life (p. 557). The spectre of the impoverished "weak" people of the 1930s are akin to Nancy Drew's gypsies and fraudsters, in that there is an underlying impulse to keep American wealth in the hands of a deserving few. This occurs at the level of Nancy's suburban delights, and at the Ingalls' more basic level. Perhaps unsurprisingly, in the aftermath of "Black Tuesday," the narratives share a preoccupation with maintaining property in the face of less worthy others. Each series registers the political and cultural presence of "welfare," and in negative terms. These are hungry and defensive narratives. They exhibit a fierce desire for prosperity, but also a belief that access to prosperity should serve as a moralized proving ground. This is the problem with abundance in a residually puritanical culture: when material wealth is truly abundant, it ceases to be a marker of righteousness. Abundance means enough for everybody, and not just for the "deserving." To the economically righteous, welfare can seem a profane simulation of abundance; it is a foolish attempt to counteract the higher imperative to separate the wheat from the chaff. The financial traumas of the 1930s could be seen to vindicate this point of view: the ensuing chaos would force people back to their own resources, and the strong would prevail. So the legitimate business of the family is carried out in something of a cut-throat atmosphere, and the daughter is encouraged to believe that she has everything to gain, and everything to lose.

Conclusion

Given the way in which girls' fiction evinces a hunger for conspicuous wealth, the reader may be left in weary agreement with the James character who supposes that society "can never have been anything but increasingly vulgar." Vulgarity is wealth that has not yet been refined and assimilated; it is a social power that still bears the marks of newness, crudity, self-interest and self-congratulation. Although the character to whom James gives these words – Mr. Longdon in *The Awkward Age* (1899) – is one of his most sympathetic, the reader may feel that it is Longdon's privileged background that allows him to view "vulgarity" as decline. Longdon's financial well-being – symbolized by his home – is of such long standing that its origins, or even the fact that it is financial, have been forgotten or disguised: "Everything on every side had dropped straight from heaven, with nowhere a bargaining thumbmark, a single sign of the shop."[1] James seems to encourage us to identify with Longdon and the novel's "girl," Nanda Brookenham, who strive for personal integrity in a corrupt environment. We can assume the outlook of the graceful Longdon, whether we ourselves are from old money or not. Or we can try out Nanda's courageous, self-defeating and self-affirming honesty, as she rejects the wealthy suitor her mother wished her to accept. But in refusing to be "vulgar," Nanda is left with no agency beyond the power to say no. She never becomes active, and she never has – or never dares to express – any particular hunger or desire of her own. As Mizruchi notes in her reading of the novel, Nanda exchanges one restrictive norm for another.[2]

James explores the possibilities and limitations of the girl's agency, and he leaves us with a more equivocal vision than we would expect to find in most girls' fiction. His work is too questioning, too hesitant and too precise to offer reassurance. It was girls' fiction that achieved mass popularity and widespread critical approval in what we might otherwise think of as the age of the Jamesian girl. Girls' fiction approached the same issues in a more optimistic and a simpler way, and in doing so it could stand apart as having its own function and values. And yet, girls' fiction also presses against its own limitations. Many of our texts have sought to achieve a balance between the self-satisfied and the lamenting. The process of "buying into womanhood" has at times been an exciting, creative process, and if its dangers cannot be entirely thrown off, neither are they altogether ignored. The more interesting novels have explored the awkward process of conforming to the materialized order of power, while noting the need to establish some measure of independence within or apart from that order. The fear remains that to be very independent, to be "at odds," is to surrender power and to be nowhere. With this in mind, I want to conclude with the most tellingly ambivalent of moments in girls' fiction, and one in which an immensely powerful woman writer is cited. This occurs in *Daddy-Long-Legs*; the scene is a classroom at Vassar. A teacher has written a poem up on the blackboard, and Judy and her classmates have been asked to write an essay on it. The poem reads:

> I asked no other thing,
> No other was denied.
> I offered Being for it;
> The mighty merchant smiled.
>
> Brazil? He twirled a button
> Without a glance my way:
> "But, madam, is there nothing else
> That we can show today?"

Judy and her class-mates have no success in making sense of it: "I don't know who wrote it or what it means... The rest of the class was in the same predicament; and there we sat for three-quarters of an hour with blank paper and equally blank minds." Judy formulates an interpretation, but then rejects it as unthinkable: "When I read the first verse I thought I had an idea – the mighty merchant was a divinity who distributes blessings in return for virtuous deeds – but when I got to the second verse and found him twirling a button, it seemed a blasphemous supposition, and I hastily changed my mind" (48).

The poem is in fact a tidied-up version of Emily Dickinson's poem 621.[3] One wonders why the girls cannot read it, and why Webster incorporates this unattributed, uninterpreted verse into the middle of her narrative. For both character and author, it seems barely comprehensible, but also somehow unignorable. For all that it may lend itself to a metaphysical reading, in which the pompous merchant is God, Dickinson is also exploring the discourse of consumerism. She places the woman speaker in open and direct contradiction with the marketplace. At least, she envisions an awkward relation to money and spending. The woman is cast in the notionally powerful role of buyer: the "mighty merchant" is nothing more than a retail clerk, at the service of "madam." But "madam" sets out to test this man's ability to provide for her happiness. In asking for Brazil, she asks for something vast, spectacular, and exotic. She seeks something of immense promise – something, moreover, that could not possibly be contained in a shop. The poem suggests that that which is to be truly valued cannot be bought and sold.[4] The woman-buyer in this poem may seem confused, but she is also challenging the commodified and gendered entrapments of her society. Dickinson anticipates the argument made by Ann Douglas, to the effect that women were "bought off" by a masculine world that had little use for them. The reward for acquiescence in a male-ordered society was a material, aesthetic, and spiritual indulgence.[5] But Dickinson also confounds that argument in that her speaker's response to the bribes of consumerism is, in the words of another poem, to "ask too large," to "take – no less than skies –" (352). The poet subverts the consumerist order by pretending to expect more from it than it can ever deliver. The "mighty merchant" can show his contempt, and try to fob her off with his own designs for her happiness. But in the end each is defeated, and no transaction takes place.

Judy is dumbfounded and even shocked by the poem's "blasphemy": its anti-Christian, anti-consumerist, and anti-patriarchal implications. But she and her author nonetheless feel compelled to make a space for it. They cannot accommodate, nor can they forget, this queerly recalcitrant piece.[6] Dickinson's work, then, is both included and rejected. The poem draws attention to – but also places a limit around – the heroine's willingness to be a satiric and rebellious figure. For the novel seems to be at odds with the poem, in that although Judy makes a play of gaining her independence, she nonetheless marries the Daddy who has showered her in furs, jewels, and gold pieces. Perhaps Judy – and Webster – were to some extent "bought off." Is it then the case that Dickinson does not provide a clear or viable alternative? Perhaps it is naive to expect her to do so. Her poetic vision is not likely to translate into a coherent and equitable social order. And Dickinson's resistance to the order of commerce is, as with Longdon in *The Awkward Age*, a sign of her privilege. She was a daughter of the "Squire" and an inhabitant of the fine "Homestead." And yet, though Dickinson was rich in status, there is evidence that she did not have much in the way of disposable cash. Dickinson is an interesting citation for Webster because so many of Dickinson's poems are about possession. Such possession goes beyond what can be bought and sold, but it is often spoken through a discourse of buying and selling. The speaker of poem 223 – "I Came to buy a smile – today" – resembles that of "I asked no other thing," except that here the emphasis is on the seller's power to withhold:

> I'm pleading at the "counter" –
> Could you afford to sell –
> I've *Diamonds* – on my fingers –
> You know what *Diamonds* are?

There is the same mismatch between two orders of exchange, emotional and pecuniary, which is seen to correspond to the mismatch between the woman's desires and the man's. Again, and in more desperate form, the woman's powerlessness is conveyed with reference to the very sphere in which she was supposed to become powerful: the store. And yet, Dickinson seizes on shopping as a trope through which she can re-imagine her relation to money, to men, to love. As with Jo March and a succession of other fictional heroines, the scene of oppression may also become the scene for a series of acts of creative subversion.[7]

Dickinson's value for Webster seems to be that she offered oppositional possibilities, but without the programmatic blandness and rigidity that one finds in much of the Progressive writing of Webster's own day. Webster's use of Dickinson reminds us of the potential of residual forms. It was precisely Dickinson's "antiquity" and "strangeness" that made her both attractive and difficult. Webster's attraction to Dickinson seems to correspond with that of the early reviewers, in that they associated the poet's power with the fact that she provided a questioning and otherworldly outlook within the hustling, commercial culture of "this artificial generation." The irony is that posthumous publication put Dickinson's poetry in the stores, elegantly bound and boxed to appeal to the Christmas market. There was no escape; there never had been. But her poems suggest to Webster – and perhaps also to us – the circumscribed and misleading power of women in a culture of commodified display. Perhaps Webster's citation of Dickinson also suggests the value for women in locating themselves in relation to specifically female traditions and interests. But Dickinson did end up "nowhere" in that she and her work remained for the most part unknown in her own lifetime. Such "privacy" would have been of no use to Webster or to her character. Finally, though, Webster seems to be drawn to Dickinson precisely because Dickinson does not pose a simple question, or accept an easy answer. Amid the insistent throng, Dickinson seems to urge later generations of women, young and old, to adopt the persona that she considered most worthy – that of the awkward customer.

Notes

INTRODUCTION: "BUYING INTO WOMANKIND"

1 Complaints about the "artificiality" of the modern age were legion in nineteenth-century America. An interesting case in point, however, is the response to Dickinson's poetry: her verse was perceived to be all the more authentic in the context of "our alleged modern artificiality" and "this artificial generation." See Mabel Loomis Todd, preface to *Poems by Emily Dickinson, Second Series*, eds. Thomas Wentworth Higginson and Mabel Loomis Todd (Boston: Roberts Brothers, 1891), pp. [3]–8; reprinted in Willis J. Buckingham, ed., *Emily Dickinson's Reception in the 1890s: A Documentary History* (Pittsburgh: University of Pittsburgh Press, 1989), pp. 236–37; also "Poems by Emily Dickinson," *Boston Evening Transcript*, 15 December 1891, p. 6; reprinted in Buckingham, *Emily Dickinson's Reception*, pp. 273–74. The term, "weightless," was used by Nietzsche. He observed that with the decline of Christianity "it will seem for a time as though all things had become weightless." T. J. Jackson Lears notes this in *No Place of Grace: Antimodernism and the Transformation of American Culture, 1880–1920* (New York: Pantheon, 1981), pp. 32, 36, and traces the perception in late nineteenth-century American culture. The phrase, "breathless audacity," is from Emerson's "The Conduct of Life." Martha Banta draws attention to it in *Taylored Lives: Narrative Productions in the Age of Taylor, Veblen, and Ford* (Chicago: University of Chicago Press, 1993), pp. 29, 56. William Dean Howells's comment was made in his "Editor's Study" column in *Harper's Monthly* in 1899; he is quoted by Alan Trachtenberg in *The Incorporation of America: Culture and Society in the Gilded Age* (New York: Hill and Wang, 1982), p. 185. Other useful resources on consumerism, modernism, and anti-modernism include Lears and Richard Wightman Fox, eds., *The Culture of Consumption: Critical Essays in American History, 1880–1980* (New York: Pantheon, 1983); William Leach, *Land of Desire: Merchants, Power, and the Rise of a New American Culture* (New York: Pantheon, 1993); Gary Cross, *Time and Money: The Making of Consumer Culture* (London: Routledge, 1993); and Mark Seltzer, *Bodies and Machines* (New York: Routledge, 1992).

2 Henry James, *The American Scene* ([1907] London: Penguin, 1994), pp. 317–18.

3 Lynn Wardley, "Reassembling Daisy Miller," *American Literary History* 3.2 (1991), pp. 232–54 (250).

4 Agnew adopts Baudrillard here, to excellent effect. See Jean-Christophe Agnew, "The Consuming Vision of Henry James," in Lears and Fox, *Culture of Consumption*, pp. 65–100, and "A House of Fiction: Domestic Interiors and the Commodity Aesthetic," in Simon J. Bronner, ed., *Consuming Visions: Accumulation and Display of Goods in America, 1880–1920* (New York: Norton, 1989), pp. 73–97. On class, see especially Stuart Blumin, *The Emergence of the Middle Class: Social Experience in the American City, 1760–1900* (Cambridge: Cambridge University Press, 1989).

5 Karl Mannheim, *Ideology and Utopia* (London: Kegan Paul, 1936), p. 8. Mannheim is using the Sophists of the Greek Enlightenment for his example. That this is particularly relevant to my own period of study, however, is made clear by the statistics to do with industrialization and urbanization provided by Alexander Keyssar in *Out of Work: The First Century of Unemployment in Massachusetts* (Cambridge: Cambridge University Press, 1986). I am grateful to my colleague, Michael Allen, for indicating Mannheim's usefulness for thinking about locale.

6 Richard Brodhead, *Cultures of Letters: Scenes of Reading and Writing in Nineteenth-Century America* (Chicago: Chicago University Press, 1993).

7 Mary P. Ryan, *Cradle of the Middle Class: The Family in Oneida County, New York, 1790–1865* (Cambridge: Cambridge University Press, 1981).

8 Gilman is quoted by Nancy Bentley; see *The Ethnography of Manners: Hawthorne, James, Wharton* (Cambridge: Cambridge University Press, 1995), p. 122. The phrase "consuming angel" I take from Lori Ann Loeb, *Consuming Angels: Advertising and Victorian Women* (New York: Oxford University Press, 1994).

9 Raymond Williams, *Marxism and Literature* (Oxford: Oxford University Press, 1977), p. 121.

10 Jean Baudrillard, *The Mirror of Production* (St. Louis: Telos, 1975), p. 144. See also Richard Ohmann, *Selling Culture: Magazines, Markets, and Class at the Turn of the Century* (London: Verso, 1996), and Rachel Bowlby, *Just Looking: Consumer Culture in Dreiser, Gissing, and Zola* (New York: Methuen, 1985).

11 I am drawing heavily here on Ross Posnock's "Henry James, Veblen and Adorno: The Crisis of the Modern Self," *Journal of American Studies* 21.1 (1987), pp. 31–54. Posnock does not acquiesce in an older perception of Jamesian aestheticism as a retreat before the consumerist vulgarities of capitalism – Posnock uses the phrase, "ideological blinding" – but draws attention to what he sees as James's dialectical view, which "sees a positive moment in commodity fetishism and conspicuous consumption as inevitably tangled with human expressiveness, creativity, and happiness" (p. 34).

12 G. Stanley Hall, *Adolescence: Its Psychology and its Relations to Physiology, Anthropology, Sociology, Sex, Crime, Religion and Education*, 2 vols., ([1904] New York: D. Appleton and Co., 1914), vol. 1, p. 28.

13 Hall is referring to Helen Thompson Woolley, author of *The Mental Traits of Sex: An Experimental Investigation of the Normal Mind in Men and Women* (Chicago: Chicago University Press, 1903).

14 Hall cites Allen's "Plain Words About the Woman Question," *Popular Science Monthly* (December 1889), and Cyrus Edson's "American Life and Physical Deterioration," *North American Review* (October 1893). He does not always explicitly endorse the point of view, but nor does he critique it.

15 Hall cites Vostrovsky's "A Study of Children's Reading Tastes," *Ped. Sem.* vi (December 1899), pp. 523–35.

16 I take the phrase, "directed invention," from Sartre, who comments in *Saint Genet*: "Lire, c'est faire une invention dirigée." Edmund White quotes and translates the phrase ("To read is to perform an act of directed invention") in *Genet* (London: Picador, 1994), pp. 436, 771. Richard Brodhead, *Cultures of Letters*, discusses "disciplinary intimacy." For discussion of the way in which children's fiction interpellates the adult as child, see Glenn Hendler, "Tom Sawyer's Masculinity," *Arizona Quarterly* 49.4 (1993), pp. 33–59.

17 Jeanette Porter Meehan, *The Life and Letters of Gene Stratton-Porter* (London: Hutchinson, 1925), p. 127.

I THE FATE OF MODESTY

1 Walter Benn Michaels, *The Gold Standard and the Logic of Naturalism: American Literature at the Turn of the Century* (Berkeley: University of California Press, 1987). See especially chapter 1, on "*Sister Carrie*'s Popular Economy."

2 Louisa May Alcott, *Eight Cousins, or, The Aunt-Hill* (1875; Boston: Little, Brown, 1996), pp. 155, 159–60.

3 See Richard L. Darling, *The Rise of Children's Book Reviewing in America, 1865–1881* (New York: R. R. Bowker, 1968), pp. 35–38.

4 Alcott to Louise Chandler Moulton, 18 January, 1883; see *The Selected Letters of Louisa May Alcott*, eds. Joel Myerson and Daniel Shealy (Athens: University of Georgia Press, 1995), p. 267.

5 *The Journals of Louisa May Alcott*, eds. Joel Myerson and Daniel Shealy (Athens, Georgia: University of Georgia Press, 1997), p. 45.

6 Anne Scott MacLeod, *A Moral Tale: Children's Fiction and American Culture, 1820–1860* (New Camden, Conn.: Archon Books, 1975), p. 17.

7 Alcott has been particularly well served by her biographers, though there have been quite strong elements of controversy. See Madeleine B. Stern, *Louisa May Alcott: A Biography* ([1950] New York: Random House, 1996), and Sarah Elbert, *A Hunger for Home: Louisa May Alcott's Place in American Culture* (New Brunswick: Rutgers University Press, 1987). Madelon Bedell gives a particularly full and interesting account of the Fruitlands episode in *The Alcotts: The Biography of a Family* (New York: Clarkson N. Potter, 1980). See also Claudia Nelson's essay, "Care in Feeding: Vegetarianism and Social Reform in Alcott's America," in eds. Claudia Nelson and Lynne Vallone, *The Girl's Own: Cultural Histories of the Anglo-American Girl, 1830–1915* (Athens: University of Georgia Press, 1994). A yet more radical dress code was also in evidence at Fruitlands, in that the community attracted a follower who wished to practice nudism, and who went out in a loose-fitting shift, which he would then remove in the woods.

8 He lifted many of his "Pictures" directly from his collection of emblem books, which were also available to Alcott in the library at Fruitlands. "Pride" is represented by the Peacock:

> Behold the silly bird; how proudly vain
> Of the bright colours of his gaudy train!

But the argument against prideful display does not amount to an egalitarian social vision. Sometimes hierarchy is reinforced, and in a way that relates specifically to gender. The emblem of "Retirement" is a drooping lily which, "proud of outward show," has been transplanted from her natural place in the shade. The explanation asserts:

> Thus do we often find a female, who might remain happy in peaceful retirement, running a thousand hazards for the sake of showing, and the idea of improving her accomplishments.

The implication is clear: that female modesty and female virtue are one and the same. The Fruitlands copies of "Pictures of Thought" and other emblem books (including a Fruitlands catalogue), are to be found in the Houghton Library. Richard Brodhead, in *Cultures of Letters*, offers a fascinating investigation into Bronson's educative principles in relation to broader patterns of self-control and to "disciplinary intimacy."

9 Owen's satire draws attention to the vices, worldliness, superficiality and theatricality of the fashionable classes. He notes that in fashionable society a "woman may expose her bosom, paint her face, assume a forward air, gaze without emotion, and laugh without restraint at the loosest scenes of theatrical licentiousness, and yet be after all – a *modest* woman" (p. 49). Elegant dress is deplored as a foolish competition, and the pamphlet ends with the call to make "the PEOPLE OF FASHION become the PEOPLE OF GOD" (p. 93). See John Owen, *The Fashionable World Displayed* (New York: J. Osborn, 1806); this is the edition that Abba Alcott revised, and page references refer to it. The copy containing her revisions and introductory material is in the Houghton Library.

10 The poem subsequently takes a much more serious turn, urging such as Flora to visit the poor, the starving, and the ill:

> As you sicken and shudder and fly from the door;
> Then home to your wardrobes, and say, if you dare –
> Spoiled children of Fashion – you've nothing to wear! (p. 67).

[William Allen Butler], *Nothing to Wear: An Episode of City Life* (reprinted from *Harper's Weekly*; New York: Rudd and Carlton, 1857), pp. 9–10. The copy in the Houghton is inscribed by Abba, and subsequently by Abby, and then "For Frederick Wolsey Pratt / Keep this book!"

11 See Michael Barton, "The Victorian Jeremiad: Critics of Accumulation and Display," in Bronner, ed., *Consuming Visions*, pp. 55–71.

12 Abigail May Alcott to Joseph May, 6 October, 1834; quoted by Elbert (p. 50). Bronson too was from successful Revolutionary stock, but his family's fortunes

had declined considerably before he was born. For historical context, see Richard N. Weintraub, "Stratification and Social Mobility in Concord, 1750–1850: A Sociological History," in *Chronos* 2 (Fall 1983), pp. 199–259, and Robert A. Gross, "Transcendentalism and Urbanism: Concord, Boston, and the Wider World," *Journal of American Studies* 18.3 (1984), pp. 361–81. More generally, Stuart Blumin notes the large body of scholarship which testifies to "striking increases in inequality in the antebellum era and to maintenance of high levels of inequality throughout the nineteenth century" (*The Emergence of the Middle Class* pp. 3, 312). In spite of her veiled threat to her father to take in washing, Abba showed enormous energy and ingenuity in trying to work and preserve caste. This was especially evident in her development of a city mission. Alcott described her mother's activities in her sketch, "How I Went Out to Service." Her mother "not only served the clamorous poor, but often found it in her power to help decayed gentlefolk by quietly placing them where they could earn their bread without the entire sacrifice of taste and talent which makes poverty so hard for such to bear." What Alcott fails to mention is that one of the "decayed gentlefolk" Abba seemed to be helping was Abba herself, and her mission broke up amidst the suspicion and bad feeling that this caused.

13 These comments are taken from reviews in, respectively, *Southern Review* 5 (April 1868), p. 474; *The Galaxy* 7 (January 1869), p. 137; *Southern Review* 8 (July 1870), pp. 228–29 (228); and *Atlantic Monthly* 25 (June 1870), pp. 752–53 (752).

14 Louisa May Alcott, *Little Women and Good Wives* ([1868–69] London: Everyman, 1992), p. 86.

15 For an extended and finely nuanced study of Alcott's fiction, and one that pays attention to gothic resonances, see Elisabeth Keyser's *Whispers in the Dark: The Fiction of Louisa May Alcott* (Knoxville: University of Tennessee Press, 1993).

16 Brodhead, *Cultures of Letters*, p. 96. Brodhead is not interested in girls' fiction *per se* (though he has many fascinating insights to offer), and nor does he show how the work of Alcott and others serves as a part of a process of "buying into." But his work is particularly useful to me in that it looks at the class-ing of literary output; in his own words, Brodhead places Alcott in the context of "the rearticulation of the American literary field" (p. 80), especially as it relates to emergent ideas of "high" and "low" and the moral burden attached to each. He assesses the "circuit of social relations" implied by different genres with "the segmentation of American literary cultures in the decades after 1850," and Alcott "affords a glimpse . . . of [this] larger process of cultural discrimination" (p. 109).

There is a strong biographical resonance in Amy's trip to Europe, in that Abby Alcott got to go. Louisa May half-rejoiced in Abby's opportunity, and half-bemoaned her own exclusion. Eventually, she would be able to pay for her own tour.

17 *An Old-Fashioned Girl* was serialized in *Merry's Museum* from July to December of 1869, and was published in book form in March 1870, with an initial American print run of 27, 500. As Alcott noted in her journal, the novel "sold well" (p. 174). A fascinating study which is not directly relevant here, but

which does look at *An Old-Fashioned Girl*, is Glenn Hendler's "The Limits of Sympathy: Louisa May Alcott and the Sentimental Novel," *American Literary History* 3.4 (1991), pp. 685–706.

18 Louisa May Alcott, *An Old-Fashioned Girl* (1870; New York: Penguin, 1996), p. 8. Boston and Concord are never mentioned by name, but Alcott makes no attempt to obscure the obvious circumstantial points of identification.

19 Eliza Lynn Linton, "The Girl of the Period," *Saturday Review* 25 (14 March 1868), p. 340; quoted by Christina Boufis in "'Of Home Birth and Breeding': Eliza Lynn Linton and the Girl of the Period," in Nelson and Vallone, eds., *The Girl's Own*, pp. 98–123. Boufis discusses the "Girl" in relation to English sensation fiction, and it is interesting to note that Alcott too represents sensation fiction as part of the consumerist and sexualised enervation of "Girl" culture. Fanny's depravity is suggested by her reading of *Lady Audley's Secret*. There is a masculine counterpoint here, in that her brother reads fiction in which "the young heroes have thrilling adventures, kill impossible beasts, and, when the author's invention gives out, suddenly find their way home laden with tiger skins, tame buffaloes, and other pleasing trophies of their prowess" (p. 82). Of course Alcott is a double agent here, having herself written numerous sensational romances.

The progress from country to city as implying a journey toward a premature and improper sexual awakening is also discussed by Lynne Vallone in *Disciplines of Virtue: Girls' Culture in the Eighteenth and Nineteenth Centuries* (New Haven: Yale University Press, 1995). Vallone provides a broad cultural–historical context for this motif in her chapter on "The Pleasure of the Act: Charity, Penitence, and Narrative."

20 Chintz, with its glazed finish, is cheap but not likely to be have been "homespun." It is perhaps worth noting that homespun was part of the Revolutionary ethos in that it became fashionable as an anti-English gesture, as part of a boycott of fancy imported English goods.

21 Diane Price Herndl explores the ambiguities of this phrase in *Invalid Women: Figuring Feminine Illness in American Fiction and Culture, 1840–1940* (Chapel Hill: University of North Carolina Press, 1993).

22 This theme of the antique as both resistance to consumerism and as a superior form of consumerism, has been interestingly discussed in relation to the American novel from Cooper to Wharton, in a doctoral thesis. See Sara Elisabeth Quay, "Objects of Affection: Counter Cultures of Consumerism in American Fiction" (Brandeis, 1996).

23 Christine Stansell, *City of Women: Sex and Class in New York, 1789–1860* (New York: Alfred A. Knopf, 1986), pp. 128–29. For a study of the actualities of the dressmaking trade at this time, see Wendy Gamber, *The Female Economy: The Millinery and Dressmaking Trades, 1860–1930* (Urbana: University of Illinois Press, 1997).

24 Elizabeth Langland gives a more uniformly positive reading of Alcott's "feminist romance" in her discussion of *Work* (1873). See "Female Stories of Experience: *Little Women* in Light of *Work*," in Elizabeth Abel, Marianne Hirsch, and

Elizabeth Langland, eds. *The Voyage In: Fictions of Female Development* (Hanover: University Press of New England, 1983), pp. 112–27.

25 Henry James, *The Bostonians* (1886; London: Penguin, 2000), p. 56. If James is referring to an Alcott here, it would be Abba and not Louisa May; certainly Abba's snobbish paranoia was marked enough to be embarrassing in her later years, and there are strong echoes of the Alcotts and Fruitlands in the Tarrant marriage.

26 In 1875, her dress-making bills came to $210–10; in the same year, she was paying her cook, Mary McGrath, $3–50 per week. These accounts are to be found in the Houghton Library.

27 In December 1881, for instance, she spent $150 on "Dress & making."

28 She also selected her locales in a way that betrays a desire for exclusivity. She rented a fine house on Beacon Hill, and bought a holiday home at Nonquitt in Buzzards Bay, the more or less closed gate community where "the elegant summer residences of some of Boston's most exclusive set" were to be found. She rented the house in Louisberg Square, in 1885, for two years. The holiday home in Nonquitt was bought in 1884. Buzzards Bay, close to Newport, was where ex-President Cleveland spent his summers, along with General Sheridan, Standard Oil magnate Henry Huttleston Rogers, *Century* editor Richard Watson Gilder, and other assorted millionaires. See Edwin Fiske Kimball, "On the Shores of Buzzards Bay," *The New England Magazine* VII.i (new series; September 1892), pp. [2]–25 (18). Another aspect of her identification with the "leisure class" was her attendance at the ball for the Grand Duke Alexis in December, 1871, which was as clear an example of Eurocentric extravagance as Boston could offer. The *Boston Evening Transcript* for 9 December 1871, gave long lists of the "toilettes of the ladies," noting "garnet satin and magnificent ermine," "superb amethysts," "handsome diamonds," and so on. But Alcott was still something of a rebel in this context, in that she observed with pleasure that these distinctions of wealth had little influence on the Duke: "Went to the ball for the Grand Duke Alexis. A fine sight, and the big blonde boy the best of all. Would dance with the pretty girls, and leave the Boston dowagers and their diamonds in the lurch" (*Journal*, p. 180).

29 James, *The American Scene*, p. 12. By "constituted privacy," I take James to mean privacy that has been decided upon, rather than the privacy that is granted by public indifference. For an exploration of "nouveau luxe," see Edith Wharton's *The Custom of the Country* (1913).

2 MAGAZINES AND MONEY

1 Scholars with an interest in the magazines are heavily indebted to the work of R. Gordon Kelly. See especially *Mother Was a Lady: Self and Society in Selected American Children's Periodicals, 1865–1900* (Westport, Conn.: Greenwood Press, 1974), and *Children's Periodicals of the United States* (Westport, Conn.: Greenwood Press, 1984). Critical discussion has been greatly facilitated by the re-publication of a selection of this periodical fiction in eds. Jane Bernardete

and Phyllis Moe, *Companions of Our Youth. Stories by Women for Young People's Magazines, 1865–1900* (New York: Frederick Ungar, 1980); my discussion focuses on stories to be found in this volume. Kelly borrows his overall periodical estimates from Frank Luther Mott (Kelly, p. 8); he gives the "subscription" of *Youth's Companion* as 385,000 (Kelly, p. 8), but the "circulation" as 500,000 (*Children's Periodicals* xxv).

2 Kelly, *Mother Was a Lady*, p. 9.

3 Kelly, *Children's Periodicals*, pp. 161–63.

4 Ibid., pp. 379–80.

5 See Bernardete and Moe, eds., *Companions of Our Youth*, pp. 8–9. For discussion of Annie Fields's relationship with Sarah Orne Jewett, see Paula Blanchard, *Sarah Orne Jewett: Her World and Her Work* (Reading, Massachusetts: Addison Wesley, 1994). For the social–professional operations of Annie and James Fields, see also W. S. Tryon, *Parnassus Corner: A Life of James T. Fields* (Boston: Houghton Mifflin, 1963).

6 For details of Alcott's transactions, see Alcott, *Letters*, pp. 172–75, and *Journals*, pp. 182–85. For Hamilton's growing dissatisfaction with Fields, and the subsequent "battle of the books," see Tryon, *Parnassus Corner*, pp. 339–46.

7 Kelly, *Children's Periodicals*, pp. 377–78.

8 Ohmann, *Selling Culture*, develops this argument in relation to magazines for adults. Scholars who look at nineteenth-century children's magazines expecting to find advertizing material are likely to be disappointed, in that most library stock has been bound into annual volumes, and most often the advertizing pages have not been bound in. It is often only from the occasional unbound, individual issues that one can see the extent of advertizing in the children's periodicals.

9 See *Riverside Magazine* 1.12 (December 1867), p. 576, and *Our Young Folks* 1.12 (December 1865), p. 771, 3.12 (December 1867), p. 765–76, 5.1 (January 1869), p. 72, and 8.1 (January 1871). It is significant that, as Kelly notes, most of the responses on the characteristics of the gentleman came from girls (*Mother Was a Lady*, p. 84).

10 Kelly makes the point that "[i]n the very act of affirming their faith in childhood innocence, the gentry were driven by their anguished sense of moral purpose and by their sense of the intrusive future to expose the child who read their stories to the fever of the adult world" (*Mother Was a Lady*, pp. 115–16).

11 Laurie Shannon, "'The Country of Our Friendship': Jewett's Intimist Art," *American Literature* 71.2 (1999), pp. 227–62.

12 Elizabeth Ammons offers an interesting variant here, in that she looks at the matrifocal aspects of Jewett's pairings, and especially in relation to the myth of Demeter and Persephone. See *Conflicting Stories: American Women Writers at the Turn into the Twentieth Century* (New York: Oxford University Press, 1992), pp. 47–48.

13 Jewett criticism has been much preoccupied with argument as to whether indeed her work is that of an "empathetic artist of local life" or that of a "literary tourist." For further discussion, see Brodhead, *Cultures of Letters*, and

Sandra Zagarell, "Troubling Regionalism: Rural Life and the Cosmopolitan Eye in Jewett's *Deephaven*," *American Literary History* 10.4 (1998), pp. 639–63. Also, Jewett's alleged class bias and her "nordicism" have drawn unfavourable comment. A recent essay that surveys the debate, and offers a more positive reading than my own, is Marjorie Pryse's "Sex, Class, and 'Category Crisis': Reading Jewett's Transitivity," *American Literature* 70.3 (1998), pp. 517–49.

3 DRAMAS OF EXCLUSION

1 The success of the novel must surely have assuaged such fears, in that it was the bestselling book of its year. Susan Schwartz notes in her introductory material that only *Our Mutual Friend* sold as well, and *Hans Brinker* would go through one hundred editions in five languages in its first thirty years. See *Hans Brinker, or The Silver Skates* (1865; New York: Tor, 1993), p. vii. It is unlikely, though, that Dodge would have been able to collect royalties on more than a few of the many editions.

2 *Atlantic Monthly* 17 (July 1866), pp. 779–80 (779).

3 I find myself somewhat at odds with one of the few other scholars to have discussed this novel, Jerry Griswold. Yet I think my own reading is an alternative without being a contradiction. His argument is that Dodge was writing against the melancholy that caused her husband to commit suicide. In this reading, Dodge becomes a "literary version of Teddy Roosevelt," guarding against the broken dikes of oceanic madness: "the message of Dodge's *Hans Brinker* is control your feelings." See *Audacious Kids: Coming of Age in American Children's Classics* (New York: Oxford University Press, 1992), p. 192.

4 *The Galaxy* 17 (February 1874), pp. 284–85.

5 Margaret Sidney [Harriet D. Lothrop], *Five Little Peppers and How They Grew* (1881; Boston: Lothrop, Lee and Shepard, 1909), p. 12.

4 ROMANTIC SPECULATIONS

1 Published in Kate Douglas Wiggin, *My Garden of Memory: An Autobiography* (1923; London: Hodder and Stoughton, n.d.[1924]), p. 402. Although I go on to discuss Wiggin's Romantic antecedents, she borrows the phrase, "native woodnotes wild," from Milton's "L'Allegro."

2 Taliaferro's date of birth is given as 1893 in *The Oxford Companion to American Theatre*, ed. Gerald Bordman (New York: Oxford University Press, 1984). She played the role for three years, beginning with the opening night, 3 October 1910.

3 Ralph Waldo Emerson, *Nature*, in *The Works of Ralph Waldo Emerson*, vol. IV (New York: Harper, n.d.), p. 7; Kate Douglas Wiggin, *Rebecca of Sunnybrook Farm* (1903; London: Puffin, 1994), p. 18.

4 Colin Campbell makes this argument in *The Romantic Ethic and the Spirit of Modern Consumerism* (Oxford: Basil Blackwell, 1987). See especially pp. 200–08, in which Campbell records the Romantic loathing of the

hedonistic commercialism to which, he argues, it unwittingly contributed. The phrase about "high-flown speculations" is taken up by Michaels from *Sister Carrie*. Michaels is not discussing Romanticism, but his material is suggestive in this context: "The economy runs on desire, which is to say, money, or the impossibility of ever having enough money . . . Fancy or imagination is the very agent of excessive desire for Carrie, enabling her to get 'beyond, in her desires, twice the purchasing power of her bills'" (Michaels, *The Gold Standard*, p. 44).

5 For Wiggin's Romantic, Froebelian pedagogy, see the book that she wrote with her sister, Nora Archibald Smith, *Children's Rights: A Book of Nursery Logic* (Boston: Houghton Mifflin, 1892).

6 Again, Carrie is the archetypal figure here. For commentary, see Bowlby, *Just Looking*. Blanche Gelfant draws attention to the gaze that "takes things in"; see "What More Can Carrie Want? Naturalistic Ways of Consuming Women," in Donald Pizer, ed., *The Cambridge Companion to American Realism and Naturalism* (Cambridge: Cambridge University Press, 1995), pp. 178–210.

7 For more on the older, patriarchal model that is to be found in sensational domestic fiction, see G. M. Goshgarian's *To Kiss the Chastening Rod: Domestic Fiction and Sexual Ideology in the American Renaissance* (Ithaca: Cornell University Press, 1992).

8 Nora Archibald Smith, *Kate Douglas Wiggin As Her Sister Knew Her* (London: Gay and Hancock, 1925), p. 316.

9 F. G., *Atlantic Monthly* 92 (December 1903), pp. 858–60 (860).

10 This interview is reprinted by Smith; see *Kate Douglas Wiggin*, p. 78.

5 PREPARING FOR LEISURE

1 This article, "A New Women's College," was written in response to the plans to create Smith College. The author refers to Mount Holyoke and Vassar as examples of the problems he describes. He also notes that the same problems would prevail at men's colleges, but for the fact that young men can be "parcelled out in families" and are "able to be out in all kinds of weather." My source is a transcription in the Smith College archive.

2 This was part of a series of articles on the women's colleges, written by John Palmer Gavit and published in the *Boston Herald* and the *New York Post* in 1922 and 1923. They too form part of the Smith College archive, where they have been shorn of specific dates or pagination.

3 For a good historical survey, see Barbara Miller Solomon, *In the Company of Educated Women: A History of Women and Higher Education in America* (New Haven: Yale University Press, 1985). Jennifer Scanlon reproduces the Woodbury's advert, and draws attention to the growing importance of the college girl as symbol and target, in *Inarticulate Longings: The Ladies' Home Journal, Gender, and the Promises of Consumer Culture* (New York: Routledge, 1995).

4 For statistics on women and higher education, see Solomon, *In the Company*, p. 64.

5 Jennifer Wicke makes this point, and draws attention to this passage in *Advertising Fictions: Literature, Advertisement, and Social Reading* (New York: Columbia University Press, 1988), p. 117.

6 See, for instance, Rollin Lynde Hartt, "Girl Undergraduates," *Frank Leslie's Popular Monthly* (1900), n.p.; Charles Belmont Davis, "A Hatless Paradise: The Adventures of a Lone Man Who Went to Discuss the 'College Girl,'" *Collier's* (10 June, 1905), p. 24; Jennett Lee, "With a College Education," *Good Housekeeping* (June 1914), p. 796; "Life at a Girl's College," *Munsey's* (September 1897), p. 869; Alice Katharine Fallows, "Undergraduate Life at Smith College," *Scribner's* (July 1898), p. 7.

7 Helen Thomas Flexner, "Bryn Mawr: A Characterisation" (Bryn Mawr, 1905), pp. 14, 4, 11.

8 Solomon argues that new money was more interested in higher education for girls than the old élites; see *In the Company*, p. 63.

9 This article has been cut out and archived at Smith, sadly shorn of further publishing information.

10 Quoted by Trachtenberg; see *The Incorporation of America*, p. 184.

11 See also Thomas Peyser, *Utopia and Cosmopolis: Globalization in the Era of American Literary Realism* (Durham, NC: Duke University Press, 1998), in which he notes in a reading of James's *The Golden Bowl* the "assimilative labor" implied in the treatment of the world as museum: "The museum is in effect the modern department store raised to sublimity, an intense revision of the Bond Street shop windows that attest to the link between emporium and imperium, windows 'in which objects massive and lumpish . . . were as tumbled together as if, in the insolence of Empire, they had been the loot of far-off victories'" (pp. 141, 145).

12 This sense of exclusiveness and enclosure would diminish in later, twentieth-century fiction, as romance and money came into view. See Shirley Marchalonis, *College Girls: A Century in Fiction* (New Brunswick: Rutgers University Press, 1995). Marchalonis writes of the "green world," and argues that the female environment is different from the male (pp. 26–27).

13 And, as Marchalonis also observes, so gained a wide general readership. But there was some contemporary debate as to whether this novel was correctly classed as a "juvenile" or not. The best source for reviews of Webster, and my source in this instance, is Webster's own collection of scrapbooks, compiled with the aid of Burelle's press-clippings service, though unfortunately pagination is often not given and extremely hard to trace. These scrapbooks are now in the Special Collections at Vassar.

14 Jacob Riis, *How the Other Half Lives* (1890; New York: Penguin, 1997). As Robert Bremner has shown in *From the Depths: The Discovery of Poverty in America* (New York: New York University Press, 1956), from 1890 on there was a growing body of literature of various kinds on the lives of the poor. There was the naturalist fiction of London, Crane, Norris, Dreiser, and others, of which Wiggin was so disapproving. There were also settlement house stories, such as Jane Addams's *Twenty Years at Hull House* (1910), and various other "inside views," such as

Bessie and Marie Van Vorst's *The Woman Who Toils: Being the Experiences of Two Gentlewomen as Factory Girls* (1903), and *The Long Day* (1905) by "Rose Fortune." There were also more sociological surveys, many with a special focus on children, such as John Spargo's *The Bitter Cry of the Children* (1906), and Ruth S. True's *The Neglected Girl* (1914) and *Boyhood and Lawlessness* (1914). At a less serious, and rather more popular level, there were romantic slum novels such as Edward Townsend's *A Daughter of the Tenements* (1895) and the "Chimmie Fadden" stories that he wrote for the New York *Sun*. Poverty, and childhood poverty in particular, was both of concern, and in vogue. See also Luc Santé, *Low Life: Lures and Snares of Old New York* (London: Granta, 1998). For a particularly astute recent study of changing perspectives in representations of the poor, see Keith Gandal, *The Virtues of the Vicious: Jacob Riis, Stephen Crane, and the Spectacle of the Slum* (New York: Oxford University Press, 1997).

15 Bremner, *From the Depths*, p. 15. See also Benjamin J. Klebaner, "Poverty and its Relief in American Thought, 1815–1861," in Frank R. Breul and Steven J. Diner, eds. *Compassion and Reponsibility: Readings in the History of Social Welfare Policy in the United States* (Chicago: University of Chicago Press, 1980), pp. 114–31; Martha Banta, *Taylored Lives*; and Cindy Weinstein, *The Literature of Labor and the Labors of Literature: Allegory in Nineteenth-Century American Fiction* (New York: Cambridge University Press, 1995).

16 For a biographical study, see Alan Simpson with Ralph Connor, *Jean Webster: Storyteller* (n.p.: Tymor Associates, 1984). With regard to Webster's Progressive interests, while at Vassar she was a member of the Settlement Association, as noted in the *Vassarion* for 1899 (p. 99), 1900 (p. 13), and 1901 (p. 94). She wrote her senior dissertation on "The Socialism of William Morris." The dissertation, in the Jean Webster McKinney Papers at Vassar, attempts to mediate between privilege and poverty, with Morris as a useful bridging figure. Also, Webster's mother was actively pro-suffrage. The Standard Oil millionaire was Ralph McKinney, the alcoholic son of one of the most successful of Rockefeller's cohorts.

17 Jean Webster, *Just Patty* (1911; London: Hodder and Stoughton, 1918), p. 26.

18 New York *Independent* (4 December 1911); *Literary Digest* (11 November, and 2 December, 1911); my source is the Webster archive at Vassar (Box 32)

19 Jean Webster, *When Patty Went to College* (New York: Century, 1903), pp. 65–66. It is worth noting that this "sequel" actually predates the school stories, at least in collected form. It makes sense, then, that the later school stories show more impatience with the limitations of the genre than do the Vassar stories. Much of Webster's writing for the adult market occupies a similar range. She wrote of charming, worldly men and good-looking, leisured young women. She managed a stock-in-trade of elegant bemusement over mild, romantic escapades, featuring period characters such as lawyers and businessmen who suffer from "nervous prostration." These were politely reimagined versions of her father's frightening peculiarities, and her lover's alcoholism. Her later work, however, was more ambitious. Her own favourite among her novels was *The Wheat Princess* (1905), about a young woman who goes to Europe and

realizes that the poverty she sees around her is due to her rich father's efforts to corner the market in wheat.

20 Jean Webster, *Daddy-Long-Legs* (1912; New York: Puffin, 1995), pp. 25–26, 18.

21 Another financial resonance is perhaps to be found in the fact that the novel begins on the first Wednesday of a month, an awful day because it sees the visit of the trustees, and Judy must oversee the appearance of the other orphans. She thinks of these occasions as a "Blue Wednesday." This signifies their depressing nature, but also perhaps sounds a more particular contemporary note, in that the financial panic of 1901 was known as "Blue Thursday." "Blue" days were usually wash days, which tended to be a "Blue Monday."

22 Michael Moon, "'The Gentle Boy from the Dangerous Classes': Pederasty, Domesticity, and Capitalism in Horatio Alger," *Representations* 19 (summer 1987), pp. 87–110.

23 Interview in the Brooklyn *Eagle*, 28 November 1915; my source is the Webster archive at Vassar (Box 32).

24 Following her interview with the Brooklyn *Eagle*, which was widely copied in other papers, and in which she spoke of the need to "fatten" and "polish," asylum-managers complained that her comments, and indeed her novel, had caused subscriptions to fall. In a letter published in the *Eagle* for 12 December 1915, Siegfried Geismar, Superintendent of the Hebrew Orphan Asylum in Brooklyn, wrote of the damage he thought she had done to institutions that were doing their best with very little support from the public at large. This interview, copies and edited versions of it, and responses to it, are in the Webster scrapbooks at Vassar College (Box 32).

25 This formed part of the *Century*'s announcement that it was to serialize *Dear Enemy* in 1915. This promotional material is in the Webster archive at Vassar (Box 32). Webster had pushed the boundaries as far as was feasible. As it was, the novel drew praise for its ability to incorporate material that might not be thought to fall within its genre. Referring to both *Daddy-Long-Legs* and *Dear Enemy*, the New York *Times* declared: "The real achievement in [*Dear Enemy*], as in [*Daddy-Long-Legs*] is her combination of serious social modernity with the other modernity of gaiety and humor, so that both are alive and convincing, and neither loses a jot." *Publishers' Weekly* for 11 December 1915, was equally clear about what it took to be Webster's particular talent: "'Dear Enemy' has a solid sociological basis – much as one hates to say a thing of such drab connotation about so sprightly and altogether adorable a tale." The sequel represents a reversal of its precursor, in that Sallie McBride, a middle class college friend of Judy, is put in charge of the John Grier Home by Judy and Jervis. So while the poor girl goes off to be benevolent and wealthy, the rich girl must adjust to harder circumstances. She is aided in her efforts by a well-bred banker, Percy Witherspoon, who takes the boys on an "Indian camp" to help him forget his broken engagement. That Sallie takes a personal servant with her, and her chow, Singapore, indicates that the novel does not carry the same drama of class endangerment as does *Daddy-Long-Legs*. For Percy and Sallie, the Home represents a rejuvenating excursion, and both can

buy the Home out of some of its problems. Nonetheless, Webster uses *Dear Enemy* even more obviously to make arguments on the correct way of treating orphans and the people who would adopt them. She had at least created a generic variant of girls' fiction that permitted her to satisfy her sense of social justice.

26 The promotional material, and the press coverage, is in the Webster archive at Vassar (Box 25).

27 New York *Sun*, 22 January 1915. The play was so successful that three companies were required to satisfy the demand. Chatterton starred in the first and most profitable production, which played New York and the East Coast theatres. There was also a Western and a Southern touring company. The other Judys were Renée Kelly (West) and Frances Carson (South). After Chatterton, Kelly in particular enjoyed considerable publicity from her connection with the role, and the Western company did much more business than the Southern. The press estimated that the play made its author $30 000 within nine months of opening. Looking at the accounts in the Webster Papers, this would seem a conservative estimate. Most weeks, her share was over $1000, and in a good week, over $2000.

The play drew mixed critical responses. The *World* admired the "satirical thrusts it takes at these alleged charitable institutions and at the social worship of wealth." Others seemed to enjoy its more anodyne element, proclaiming it as part of the "Success of Clean Plays," alongside a stage version of *Little Women* that was doing the rounds at the same time. The only severe criticism came from George Jean Nathan, writing in the *North American Review*. He saw the play as trite and conventional, regardless of nods to contemporary issues. Framing his comments within a discourse of the nursery, he deplored it as a further contribution to the infantilizing complacency of American culture: "[W]hen the Cinderella of the piece is treated with conventional cruelty by the mean stepmother (in this case the head of an orphanage), the flow of tears dampens the very aisles, and when the persecuted baggage, at 11 o'clock, is folded to the bosom of her prince, the hearts beat gayly and the faces reveal expansive satisfaction . . . You cannot go on indefinitely giving children pie without ruining their digestion" (*North American Review*, 11 October 1914). See the Webster archive at Vassar (Box 32).

28 New York *Globe and Commercial Advertiser*, 6 October 1914; my source is the Webster archive at Vassar (Box 32).

29 Jean Webster to Glenn Ford McKinney, 26 August 1913; see Simpson, *Jean Webster*, p. 152.

6 SERIAL PLEASURES

1 Ohmann, *Selling Culture*, pp. 55–56.

2 Jennifer Scanlon notes the description of the *Journal* as a "handbook for the middle class"; see *Inarticulate Longings*, p. 14. Of the magazine fiction Ohmann writes that the goal of the genre was to establish "the affinities and relations within and between the two main higher classes, and especially the

rosy prospects of the professional-managerial class at this fluid moment in its history"; see *Selling Culture*, pp. 320–21.

3 Carol Billman, *The Secret of the Stratemeyer Syndicate: Nancy Drew, The Hardy Boys, and the Million Dollar Fiction Factory* (New York: Ungar, 1986), p. 20.

4 For discussion of the Stratemeyer system and the writers' backgrounds, I rely on Billman, *Secret*, and also on Deirdre Johnson, "From Paragraphs to Pages: The Writing and Development of the Stratemeyer Syndicate Series," in Carol Dyer Stewart and Nancy Tillman Romalov, eds., *Rediscovering Nancy Drew* (Iowa City: Iowa University Press, 1995), pp. 29–40, and on Romalov's "Modern, Mobile, and Marginal: American Girls' Series Fiction, 1905–1925" (PhD. Dissertation, University of Iowa, 1994). In many individual points my own argument has been pre-empted by these excellent studies, but my intention is to re-orient analysis of series fiction. Although the series is a phenomenon worthy of the separate study accorded by these writers, I want to relate my treatment to a more developed sense of the wider traditions and contingencies of the girl's ideological role in a consumerist society.

5 For a detailed account of Stratemeyer aliases, see Deirdre Johnson, *Stratemeyer Pseudonyms and Series Books: An Annotated Checklist of Stratemeyer Syndicate Publications* (Westport, Conn.: Greenwood Press, 1982).

6 This was quite rare, and usually women wrote the girls' stories, but on at least one occasion Laura Lee Hope was Walter Karig, later to become book-editor of the *Washington Post and Times-Herald*. See Billman, *Secret*, p. 23.

7 Ibid., p. 25.

8 Ibid., pp. 21, 94.

9 Ibid., pp. 32–33, Romalov, "Modern," pp. 64–65.

10 Alice Emerson, *Ruth Fielding at Cameron Hall*, quoted by Billman, *Secret*, p. 60.

11 MacLeod, in her discussion of Lucy Larcom's *A New England Girlhood* (1889), produces this observation in relation to nineteenth-century adolescents and pre-adolescents; see *A Moral Tale*, p. 10.

12 I do not dwell on boys' series, but it is as well to note that there are important differences. Boys can have more institutionalized and career-oriented adventures, as with stories of life at West Point or Annapolis. Also, boys' series often take a different and much less right-wing political angle, as with the Range and Grange Hustlers who do battle with a "packers' combine" and who uncover a conspiracy at the Chicago wheat-pit, and the Square Dollar Boys, who fight a "trolley franchise steal." Also, boys tend to win meaningfully large rewards, whereas girls, as we will see, are rewarded with tokens which symbolize social ascent. Although he is looking at earlier texts, a very interesting study of male labor and class identification in relation to popular fiction is Michael Denning's *Mechanic Accents: Dime Novels and Working-Class Culture in America* (New York: Verso, 1987).

13 Laura Dent Crane, *The Automobile Girls at Newport, or Watching the Summer Parade* (Philadelphia: Henry Altemus, 1910), pp. 102, 51.

14 Crane, *Newport*, p. 148.

15 Laura Dent Crane, *The Automobile Girls at Palm Beach, or Proving their Mettle under Southern Skies* (Philadelphia: Henry Altemus, 1913), p. 20.
16 Crane, *Newport*, pp. 201–02.
17 Crane, *Newport*, p. 10.
18 Margaret Penrose, *The Motor Girls Through New England, or Held by the Gypsies* (New York: Goldsmith, 1911), p. 109.
19 Crane, *Palm Beach*, pp. 47–48.
20 Crane, *Newport*, p. 125.
21 Penrose, *New England*, pp. 19, 26.
22 Nancy T. Romalov, "Lady and the Tramps: The Cultural Work of Gypsies in Nancy Drew and her Foremothers," *The Lion and the Unicorn* 18 (1994), pp. 25–39 (29).
23 Laura Lee Hope, *The Moving-Picture Girls at Rocky Ranch, or Great Days Among the Cowboys* (Cleveland: Goldsmith, 1914), p. 8.
24 Hope, *Rocky Ranch*, p. 16.
25 Laura Lee Hope, *The Moving-Picture Girls at Oak Farm, or Queer Happenings While Taking Rural Plays* (Cleveland: World Syndicate Publishing Company, 1914), p. 15.
26 Hope, *Oak Farm*, p. 15.
27 Hope, *Rocky Ranch*, pp. 1, 9; Hope, *Oak Farm*, pp. 24, 49, 117.

7 THE CLEAN AND THE DIRTY

1 C. L. P., *Lippincott's Magazine* 6 (August 1870), pp. 230–32 (230); "Books for Young People," *Riverside Magazine* 1 (September 1867), pp. 431–32 (432). The early spread of Darwinism is equally apparent from Philip Quilibet's "Darwinism in Literature," *Galaxy* 15 (1873), pp. 695–98: "Not only does all physical research take color from the new theory, but the doctrine sends its pervasive hues through poetry, novels, history." This essay is cited by Lou Budd in "The American Background"; see Pizer, ed., *The Cambridge Companion*, p. 28.
2 For a fuller and more nuanced account of the relation between evolutionary theory and naturalism, see Cynthia E. Russett, *Darwin in America: The Intellectual Response, 1865–1912* (San Francisco: W. H. Freeman, 1976), and Donald Pizer, *Realism and Naturalism in Nineteenth-Century American Literature* (Carbondale: Southern Illinois University Press, 1984).
3 Judith Reick Long, *Gene Stratton-Porter: Novelist and Naturalist* (Indianapolis: Indiana Historical Society, 1990), p. 223.
4 This commentary is to be found on Grosset and Dunlap's first edition of *Her Father's Daughter* (New York, 1921), and also on their reprints of her earlier novels.
5 This essay was written for *World's Work*, and was published in 1911. Jeanette Porter Meehan reprints it in *The Life and Letters of Gene Stratton-Porter* (London: Hutchinson, 1925), pp. 126–29 (127).
6 Meehan, *Life and Letters*, p. 127.

7 Gene Stratton-Porter, *A Girl of the Limberlost* (1909; London: Hodder and Stoughton, 1915), p. 15.

8 Gene Stratton-Porter, *Freckles* (1904; London: Hodder and Stoughton, 1915), p. 240.

9 Mark Seltzer, *Bodies and Machines* (New York: Routledge, 1992), pp. 21, 172.

10 The reference is to Lothrop Stoddard's *The Rising Tide of Color against White World-Supremacy* (New York: Scribner, 1920), which was one among many books warning white America of the dangers it was running.

11 See Matthew Frye Jacobson, *Whiteness of a Different Color: European Immigrants and the Alchemy of Race* (Cambridge: Harvard University Press, 1998). Analyzing lithographs from the 1850s, Jacobson draws attention to the way in which Celticism was given a black tint, and both African-Americans and Irish were simianized.

12 Carey McWilliams, *Prejudice: Japanese-Americans: Symbol of Racial Intolerance* ([1944] Hamden, Conn.: Archon 1971), pp. 18–19, 52–53; Roger Daniels, *Not Like Us: Immigrants and Minorities in America, 1890–1924* (Chicago: Ivan R. Dee-American Ways, 1998), pp. 61, 73–74, 104–42; John Modell, *The Economics and Politics of Racial Accommodation: The Japanese of Los Angeles, 1900–1942* (Urbana: University of Illinois Press, 1977), pp. 38–39, 144–45; Lewis L. Gould, *The Presidency of Theodore Roosevelt* (Lawrence: University Press of Kansas, 1991), pp. 89–91, 257–58; and Gina Marchetti, *Romance and the 'Yellow Peril': Race, Sex, and Discursive Strategies in Hollywood Fiction* (Berkeley: University of California Press, 1993).

13 Thomas Peyser's recent study proves useful here, in that, in a discussion of Gilman, he observes that the search for utopia can move through cosmopolitanism and back towards a racist self-enclosure. The "territorial integrity" of Herland can become a force for ghettoization. See Peyser, *Utopia and Cosmopolis*, pp. 90–91.

14 Meehan, *Life and Letters*, p. 177.

15 See Christopher Lane, *The Ruling Passion: British Colonial Allegory and the Paradox of Homosexual Desire* (Durham: Duke University Press, 1995). This argument appears in various forms in many studies of the intersections of race and national-imperial identity. For a much earlier example, see George Santayana, *Soliloquies in England* (1922; Ann Arbor: University of Michigan Press, 1967). Similarly, Toni Morrison argues that white America depends on the dark, illicit other in order to define its own licensed, controlling identity, in *Playing in the Dark: Whiteness and the Literary Imagination* (Cambridge, MA: Harvard University Press, 1992).

8 "BLACK TUESDAY"

1 Carolyn Keene, *The Sign of the Twisted Candles* (1933; New York: Grosset and Dunlap, n.d.), p. 4.

2 For Mildred Wirt Benson's account, and for a question and answer session with a recent Carolyn Keene, see Carol Stewart Dyer and Nancy Tillman Romalov,

eds., *Rediscovering Nancy Drew* (Iowa City: Iowa University Press, 1995). For accounts of the production of the Nancy Drew Mysteries, see Carol Billman, *The Secret of the Stratemeyer Syndicate*, and Deirdre Johnson's "From Paragraphs to Pages: The Writing and Development of Stratemeyer Syndicate Series," in *Rediscovering Nancy Drew*, pp. 29–40.

3 Johnson, "From Paragraphs to Pages," in Dyer and Romalov, eds., *Rediscovering Nancy Drew*, p. 36.

4 Carolyn Heilbrun, "Nancy Drew: A Moment in Feminist History," in Dyer and Romalov, eds., *Rediscovering Nancy Drew*, pp. 11–22 (16).

5 Dyer and Romalov record these responses from an open forum section of their conference in *Rediscovering Nancy Drew*.

6 Carol Stewart Dyer, "The Nancy Drew Phenomenon: Rediscovering Nancy Drew," in Dyer and Romalov, eds., *Rediscovering Nancy Drew*, pp. 1–10 (6).

7 Nancy Tillman Romalov, "Lady and the Tramps: The Cultural Work of Gypsies in Nancy Drew and Her Foremothers," *The Lion and the Unicorn* 18 (1994), pp. 25–36 (34).

8 Bobbie Ann Mason, *The Girl Sleuth: A Feminist Guide* (Old Westbury, New York: The Feminist Press, 1975), p. 22.

9 Keene, *Twisted Candles*, p. 4.

10 Carolyn Keene, *The Mystery of the Ivory Charm* (1936; New York: Grosset and Dunlap, n.d.), p. 163.

11 Billman observes this distinction in *Secret*, pp. 86–87.

12 Keene, *Ivory Charm*, p. 190.

13 Keene, *Twisted Candles*, p. 68; Keene, *Ivory Charm*, p. 137.

14 Keene, *Twisted Candles*, p. 67; Keene, *Ivory Charm*, p. 155.

15 Carolyn Keene, *The Message in the Hollow Oak* (1935; New York: Grosset and Dunlap, n.d.), p. 217.

16 Carolyn Keene, *The Haunted Bridge* (1937; New York: Grosset and Dunlap, n.d.), p. 76.

17 Keene, *Twisted Candles*, pp. 11–12, 23.

18 Keene, *Ivory Charm*, p. 182.

19 Keene, *Twisted Candles*, pp. 162–63.

20 Keene, *Ivory Charm*, p. 20.

21 Keene, *Twisted Candles*, p. 63.

22 Anne Scott MacLeod, *American Childhood*, p. 168.

23 Billman, *Secret*, and Linda S. Lestvik, "I am no lady!: the tomboy in children's fiction," *Children's Literature in Education* 14.1 (1983), pp. 14–20.

24 The text of Wilder's speech is in the Rose Wilder Lane Papers at the Herbert Hoover Memorial Library, West Branch, Iowa. My source is Janet Spaeth, who quotes from it in *Laura Ingalls Wilder* (Boston: Twayne, 1987), p. 1. The best resource on Wilder, and especially on her important creative relationship with her daughter, is the work of William T. Anderson. See his two lengthy essays, "The Literary Apprenticeship of Laura Ingalls Wilder," *South Dakota History* 13.4 (1983), p. 285–331, and "Laura Ingalls Wilder and Rose Wilder Lane: The Continuing Collaboration," *South Dakota History* 16.2 (1986), pp. 89–143. A

fascinating essay that teases out the political values and revisions, and that I return to later, is Anita Clair Fellman's "Laura Ingalls Wilder and Rose Wilder Lane: The Politics of a Mother–Daughter Relationship," *Signs* 15.3 (1990), pp. 535–61.

25 Laura Ingalls Wilder, *Little House in the Big Woods* (New York: Harper and Brothers, 1932), p. 21.

26 Laura Ingalls Wilder, *On the Banks of Plum Creek* (1937; London: Mammoth, 1998), p. 84.

27 Laura Ingalls Wilder, *By the Shores of Silver Lake* (1939; London: Puffin, 1967), pp. 138, 147. Although I discovered it too late to take full account of it here, I want to acknowledge Ann Romines' *Constructing the Little House* (Amherst: University of Massachusetts Press, 1997). Romines observes that although the series is "often touted for its 'antimaterialistic' values," it "acknowledges and scrutinizes the enormous importance... of choosing and buying *things*" (p. 9).

28 This scene is perhaps either an allusion to or borrowing from Susan Warner's *The Wide Wide World* (1850), which begins with the heroine's shopping expedition to buy writing materials.

29 Laura Ingalls Wilder, *Little House in the Big Woods* 129, and *The Long Winter* (1940; London: Puffin, 1968), p. 147.

30 Wilder, *The Long Winter*, p. 233.

31 Laura Ingalls Wilder, *Little House on the Prairie* (1935; London: Mammoth, 1998), p. 26.

32 Fellman, "Laura Ingalls Wilder," pp. 552–53.

CONCLUSION

1 Henry James, *The Awkward Age*, ed. Ronald Blythe (1899; London: Penguin, 1987), pp. 135, 204–05. Longdon is also a classic instance of the Jamesian observer who is never as detached as he may wish, but who is unable to resolve the crisis to which he stands witness. This "participant–observer" is both impotent and complicit. See Carolyn Porter, *Seeing and Being: The Plight of the Participant Observer in Emerson, James, Adams, and Faulkner* (Middletown, Connecticut: Wesleyan University Press, 1981).

2 Susan L. Mizruchi, "Reproducing Women in *The Awkward Age*," *Representations* 38 (spring 1992), pp. 101–30 (123).

3 In Thomas H. Johnson's *Emily Dickinson: The Complete Poems* (London: Faber and Faber, 1991), it is given as:

> I asked no other thing –
> No other – was denied –
> I offered Being – for it –
> The Mighty Merchant sneered –
>
> Brazil? He twirled a Button –
> Without a glance my way –
> "But – Madam – is there nothing else –
> That We can show – Today?"

Webster's version may well have been taken from one of the early editions, in which some of Dickinson's idiosyncrasies were removed, although it may have been copied from a Vassar blackboard. In the "Appeals to Readers" column of the *New York Times* for 15 June 1913, the following query from "A. W." was printed: "I am informed that the verses actually appeared on the blackboard of the English class at Vassar and that the students were asked to explain and comment on the text." I do not know if "A.W." had been reliably informed; Webster put the clipping in her scrapbook without annotation (Webster archive at Vassar, Box 30).

4 As George Monteiro observes in "Emily Dickinson's Merchant God", *Notes and Queries* (December 1959) pp. 455–56: "Like *Potosi, Tunis, Eden* and *Apennine* of other poems, [*Brazil*] is one of the poet's proliferating terms. In her idiosyncratic usage it denotes the exotic, the distant, the timeless, the spiritually valuable, the eternal, the immortal" (456). Judith Farr explains the currency of South America as an image in the form of Frederic Church's massively influential paintings, especially *The Heart of the Andes* (1859); see *The Passion of Emily Dickinson* (Cambridge, Mass.: Harvard University Press, 1992), pp. 231–36.

5 Ann Douglas, *The Feminization of American Culture* (New York: Alfred A. Knopf, 1977).

6 Similar testimony is to be found from another writer for girls, Louise Chandler Moulton, who reviewed Dickinson in "A Very Remarkable Book," Boston *Sunday Herald*, 23 November 1890, p. 24: "Madder rhymes one has seldom seen – scornful disregard of poetic technique could hardly go farther – and yet there is about the book a fascination, a power, a vision that enthralls you, and draws you back to it again and again . . . It enthralls me and will not let me go." This review is reprinted by Willis J. Buckingham in *Emily Dickinson's Reception in the 1890s* (Pittsburgh: University of Pittsburgh Press, 1989) pp. 33–37.

7 Mizruchi is again instructive, in that she finds James to offer a pessimistic form of dialectical irony, in that in "women's supposed liberation from reproductive roles" there come "new opportunities for exploitation" (p. 123).

Index